D0523304

Microsoft® Excel® 2010

FOR

DUMMIES®

eLEARNING KIT

by Faithe Wempen

WILEY

John Wiley & Sons, Inc.

Microsoft® Excel® 2010 eLearning Kit For Dummies®

Published by
John Wiley & Sons, Inc.
111 River Street
Hoboken, NJ 07030-5774

www.wiley.com

Copyright © 2012 by John Wiley & Sons, Inc., Hoboken, New Jersey

Published by John Wiley & Sons, Inc., Hoboken, New Jersey

Published simultaneously in Canada

No part of this publication may be reproduced, stored in a retrieval system or transmitted in any form or by any means, electronic, mechanical, photocopying, recording, scanning or otherwise, except as permitted under Sections 107 or 108 of the 1976 United States Copyright Act, without either the prior written permission of the Publisher, or authorization through payment of the appropriate per-copy fee to the Copyright Clearance Center, 222 Rosewood Drive, Danvers, MA 01923, (978) 750-8400, fax (978) 646-8600. Requests to the Publisher for permission should be addressed to the Permissions Department, John Wiley & Sons, Inc., 111 River Street, Hoboken, NJ 07030, (201) 748-6011, fax (201) 748-6008, or online at http://www.wiley.com/go/permissions.

Trademarks: Wiley, the Wiley logo, For Dummies, the Dummies Man logo, A Reference for the Rest of Us!, The Dummies Way, Dummies Daily, The Fun and Easy Way, Dummies.com, Making Everything Easier, and related trade dress are trademarks or registered trademarks of John Wiley & Sons, Inc. and/or its affiliates in the United States and other countries, and may not be used without written permission. Microsoft and Excel are registered trademarks of Microsoft Corporation. All other trademarks are the property of their respective owners. John Wiley & Sons, Inc. is not associated with any product or vendor mentioned in this book.

LIMIT OF LIABILITY/DISCLAIMER OF WARRANTY: THE PUBLISHER AND THE AUTHOR MAKE NO REPRESENTATIONS OR WARRANTIES WITH RESPECT TO THE ACCURACY OR COMPLETENESS OF THE CONTENTS OF THIS WORK AND SPECIFICALLY DISCLAIM ALL WARRANTIES, INCLUDING WITHOUT LIMITATION WARRANTIES OF FITNESS FOR A PARTICULAR PURPOSE. NO WARRANTY MAY BE CREATED OR EXTENDED BY SALES OR PROMOTIONAL MATERIALS. THE ADVICE AND STRATEGIES CONTAINED HEREIN MAY NOT BE SUITABLE FOR EVERY SITUATION. THIS WORK IS SOLD WITH THE UNDERSTANDING THAT THE PUBLISHER IS NOT ENGAGED IN RENDERING LEGAL, ACCOUNTING, OR OTHER PROFESSIONAL SERVICES. IF PROFESSIONAL ASSISTANCE IS REQUIRED, THE SERVICES OF A COMPETENT PROFESSIONAL PERSON SHOULD BE SOUGHT. NEITHER THE PUBLISHER NOR THE AUTHOR SHALL BE LIABLE FOR DAMAGES ARISING HEREFROM. THE FACT THAT AN ORGANIZATION OR WEBSITE IS REFERRED TO IN THIS WORK AS A CITATION AND/OR A POTENTIAL SOURCE OF FURTHER INFORMATION DOES NOT MEAN THAT THE AUTHOR OR THE PUBLISHER ENDORSES THE INFORMATION THE ORGANIZATION OR WEBSITE MAY PROVIDE OR RECOMMENDATIONS IT MAY MAKE. FURTHER, READERS SHOULD BE AWARE THAT INTERNET WEBSITES LISTED IN THIS WORK MAY HAVE CHANGED OR DISAPPEARED BETWEEN WHEN THIS WORK WAS WRITTEN AND WHEN IT IS READ.

For general information on our other products and services, please contact our Customer Care Department within the U.S. at 877-762-2974, outside the U.S. at 317-572-3993, or fax 317-572-4002.

For technical support, please visit www.wiley.com/techsupport.

Wiley also publishes its books in a variety of electronic formats and by print-on-demand. Not all content that is available in standard print versions of this book may appear or be packaged in all book formats. If you have purchased a version of this book that did not include media that is referenced by or accompanies a standard print version, you may request this media by visiting http://booksupport.wiley.com. For more information about Wiley products, visit us at www.wiley.com.

Library of Congress Control Number: 2011943935

ISBN 978-1-118-11079-9 (pbk); ISBN 978-1-118-22413-7 (ebk); ISBN 978-1-118-23240-8 (ebk); ISBN 978-1-118-24450-0 (ebk)

Manufactured in the United States of America

10 9 8 7 6 5 4 3 2 1

WILEY

About the Author

Faithe Wempen, MA, is a Microsoft Office Master Instructor and the author of more than 100 books on computer hardware and software, including the *PowerPoint 2007 Bible* and *A+ Certification Workbook For Dummies.* She is an adjunct instructor of Computer Information Technology at Purdue University, and her corporate training courses online have reached more than one-quarter of a million students for clients such as Hewlett-Packard, Sony, and CNET.

Dedication

To Margaret

Author's Acknowledgments

Thanks to the wonderful editorial staff at John Wiley & Sons, Inc. for another job well done. You guys are top notch!

Publisher's Acknowledgments

We're proud of this book; please send us your comments at http://dummies.custhelp.com. For other comments, please contact our Customer Care Department within the U.S. at 877-762-2974, outside the U.S. at 317-572-3993, or fax 317-572-4002.

Some of the people who helped bring this book to market include the following:

Acquisitions, Editorial, and Vertical Websites

Senior Editorial Manager: Leah Cameron

Acquisitions Editor: Katie Mohr

Copy Editor: Jennifer Riggs

Technical Editor: Michael Talley

Vertical Websites: Richard Graves, Jenny Swisher

Editorial Assistant: Amanda Graham

Sr. Editorial Assistant: Cherie Case

Cover Photo: © istockphoto.com/Henrik Jonsson

Cartoons: Rich Tennant (www.the5thwave.com)

Composition Services

Project Coordinator: Sheree Montgomery

Layout and Graphics: Andrea Hornberger, Jennifer Mayberry

Proofreaders: Jessica Kramer, Linda Seifert

Indexer: Potomac Indexing, LLC

Special Help: Paul Levesque

Publishing and Editorial for Technology Dummies

    Richard Swadley, Vice President and Executive Group Publisher

    Andy Cummings, Vice President and Publisher

    Mary Bednarek, Executive Acquisitions Director

    Mary C. Corder, Editorial Director

Publishing for Consumer Dummies

    Kathleen Nebenhaus, Vice President and Executive Publisher

Composition Services

    Debbie Stailey, Director of Composition Services

Contents at a Glance

Table of Contents

Introduction

If you've been thinking about taking a class on the Internet (it is all the rage these days), but you're concerned about getting lost in the electronic fray, worry no longer. *Microsoft Excel 2010 eLearning Kit For Dummies* is here to help you, providing you with an integrated learning experience that includes not only the book and CD you hold in your hands but also an online version of the course at www.dummieselearning.com. Consider this introduction your primer.

About This Kit

Each piece of this eLearning kit works in conjunction with the others although you don't need them all them to gain valuable understanding of the key concepts I cover here. Whether you pop the CD into your computer to start the lessons electronically, follow along with the book, or go online for the courses, *Microsoft Excel 2010 eLearning Kit For Dummies* teaches you how to

- ✔ Create basic worksheets and navigate the Excel interface — no previous experience required!

- ✔ Format and print attractive worksheets and easy-to-read graphical charts.

- ✔ Write formulas and functions that calculate and summarize data, including powerful specialized functions for financial, statistical, and logical operations.

✔ Manage tables and lists that store database data in Excel format, and use analysis tools, such as Goal Seek and Solver, to make sense of the data.

✔ Analyze and summarize data with PivotTables and PivotCharts.

✔ Find and fix common errors in formulas, and prevent future data entry errors with data validation tools.

✔ Protect, secure, and share Excel data, ensuring that authorized people can access it and unauthorized people can't.

This book is split into 11 lessons:

Lesson 1: Creating Basic Workbooks

Lesson 2: Creating Formulas and Functions

Lesson 3: Formatting and Printing Worksheets

Lesson 4: Formatting Data

Lesson 5: Storing and Managing Tables and Lists

Lesson 6: Exploring Financial Functions and Scenarios

Lesson 7: Working with Math, Statistical, and Text Functions

Lesson 8: Creating and Formatting Charts

Lesson 9: Working with PivotTables

Lesson 10: Correcting and Validating Data

Lesson 11: Protecting and Sharing Data

The appendix briefly outlines what the CD in the front of this book contains, and what you'll find in the online courses (available at www.dummieselearning.com). The appendix also contains a few technical details about using the CD and troubleshooting tips, should you need them.

How This Kit Works with the Electronic Lessons

Microsoft Excel 2010 eLearning Kit For Dummies merges a tutorial-based *For Dummies* book with eLearning instruction contained on the CD and in online courses. Each of the easy-to-access components feature foundational instruction, self-assessment questions, skill-building exercises, plentiful illustrations, resources, and examples. The CD contains interactive electronic lessons that correlate to the content of the book as well as sample files that you can use to practice with. You also find the practice files online at `www.dummies.com/go/excel2010elearningkit`. Used in conjunction with the tutorial text, the electronic components give learners the tools needed for a productive and self-guided eLearning experience. In this book, you find the following elements:

- ✔ **Lesson opener questions:** To get you warmed up and ready for class, the questions quiz you on particular points of interest. If you don't know the answer, a page number heads you in the right direction to find it.

- ✔ **Summing Up:** This section appears at the end of the lesson; it briefly reiterates the content you just learned.

- ✔ **Try-it-yourself lab:** Test your knowledge of the content just covered by performing an activity *from scratch* — that is, using general steps only and no sample files.

- ✔ **Know this tech talk:** Each lesson contains a brief glossary of related terms.

Conventions Used in This Book

A few style conventions help you navigate the book piece of this kit efficiently:

- ✔ Instructions and names of the files needed to follow along with the step lists are *italicized.*

- ✔ Website addresses, or URLs, are shown in a special monofont typeface `like this`.

- ✔ Numbered steps that you need to follow and characters you need to type are set in **bold.**

Foolish Assumptions

For starters, I assume you know what eLearning is, need to find out how to use Excel (and fast!), and want to get a piece of this academic action the fun and easy way with *Microsoft Excel 2010 eLearning Kit For Dummies.* I assume you have basic Windows and computer skills, such as starting the computer and using the mouse.

Icons Used in This Kit

The familiar and helpful *For Dummies* icons point you in the direction of really great information that's sure to help you as you work your way through assignments. Look for these icons throughout *Microsoft Excel 2010 eLearning Kit For Dummies,* in the book, and in the electronic lessons, too:

The Tip icon points out helpful information that's likely to make your job easier.

This icon marks an interesting and useful fact — something that you might want to remember for later.

The Warning icon highlights lurking danger. When you see this icon, you know to pay attention and proceed with caution.

Sometimes I might change things up by directing you to repeat a set of steps but with different parameters. If you're up for the challenge, look for the Practice icon.

In addition to the icons, you also find two friendly study aids that bring your attention to certain pieces of information:

- ✔ **Lingo:** When you see the Lingo box, look for a definition of a key term or concept.
- ✔ **Extra Info:** This box highlights something to pay close attention to in a figure or points out other useful information that's related to the discussion at hand.

Class Is In

Now that you're primed and ready, time to begin.

Lesson 1
Creating Basic Worksheets

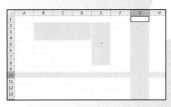

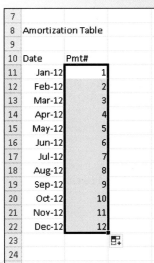

- ✔ Selecting ranges enables you to apply a single command to multiple cells at once.

- ✔ You can edit the content of a cell either in the cell itself or in the Formula bar.

- ✔ Moving and copying data between cells saves data entry time and effort.

- ✔ Dragging the fill handle copies cell content quickly into many cells at once.

- ✔ Inserting and deleting rows and columns in a worksheet changes its structure without moving content.

- ✔ Renaming a worksheet tab enables you to assign a more meaningful title to a sheet.

- ✔ Inserting new worksheets in a workbook enables you to expand a workbook's capacity.

Excel has many practical uses. You can use its orderly row-and-column worksheet structure to organize multi-column lists, create business forms, and much more. Excel provides more than just data organization, though; it enables you to write formulas that perform calculations on your data. This feature makes Excel an ideal tool for storing financial information, such as checkbook register and investment portfolio data.

In this lesson, I introduce you to the Excel interface and teach you some of the concepts you need to know. You learn how to move around in Excel, how to type and edit data, and how to manipulate rows, columns, cells, and sheets.

Understanding the Excel Interface

Excel is very much like Word and other Office applications. Excel has a File tab that opens a Backstage view, a Ribbon with multiple tabs that contain commands you can click to execute, a Quick Access toolbar, a status bar, scroll bars, and a Zoom slider. Figure 1-1 provides a quick overview.

The next several sections walk you through the Excel interface, including both the commands and the work area, and show you how to move around. After you get your bearings in Excel, you're ready to start creating worksheets.

Ribbon

Quick Access toolbar   Tabs

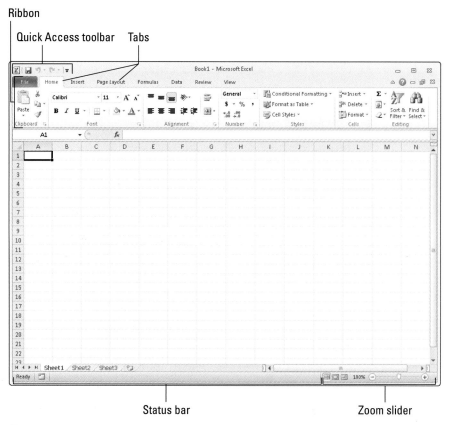

Status bar   Zoom slider

Figure 1-1

Take a tour of the Excel interface

The best way to learn about a new application is to jump in and start exploring. Work through this exercise to see how Excel is set up.

In the following exercise, you start Excel and explore its interface.

Files needed: None

LINGO

Starting out with some basic terminology is a good idea. A **spreadsheet** is a grid comprised of rows and columns. At the intersection of each row and column is a **cell.** You can type text, numbers, and formulas into cells to build your spreadsheet. In Excel, spreadsheets are dubbed **worksheets.** Worksheets are stored in data files, or **workbooks,** and each workbook can contain multiple worksheets. **Worksheet tabs** at the bottom of a workbook window enable you to quickly switch between worksheets.

1. **From Windows, choose Start⇨All Programs⇨Microsoft Office⇨ Microsoft Excel 2010 (see Figure 1-2).**

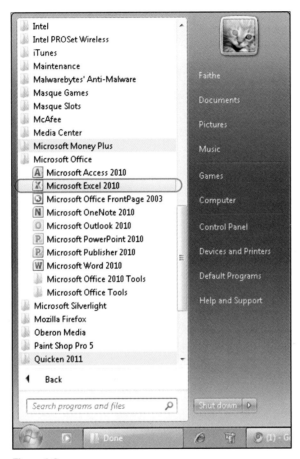

Figure 1-2

PRACTICE

If Excel has been used recently on your computer, it may appear on the top level of the Start menu; you can click it there if you see it. You can also click Start, type *Excel* in the search box, and then click Microsoft Excel 2010 when it appears in the search results. For more practice, close Excel and then reopen it using one of those methods.

2. **After Excel and a new workbook open, click the File tab to open Backstage view and then click Info.**

Information about the active document appears. See Figure 1-3.

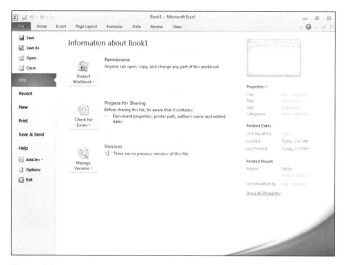

Figure 1-3

3. **Click the Home tab or press the Esc key to return to normal viewing (see Figure 1-4).**

Numbered row   Active cell address in Name box

Cell cursor on active cell   Lettered column

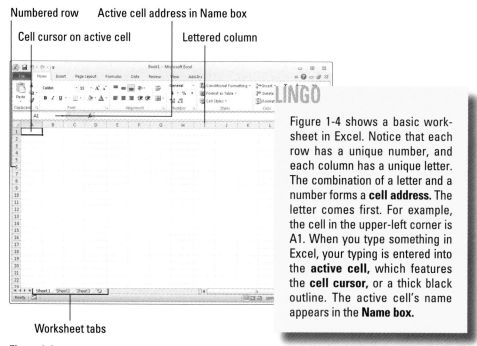

Figure 1-4 shows a basic worksheet in Excel. Notice that each row has a unique number, and each column has a unique letter. The combination of a letter and a number forms a **cell address.** The letter comes first. For example, the cell in the upper-left corner is A1. When you type something in Excel, your typing is entered into the **active cell,** which features the **cell cursor,** or a thick black outline. The active cell's name appears in the **Name box.**

Worksheet tabs

Figure 1-4

4. **Click the View tab on the Ribbon, and then click the Zoom button so that the Zoom dialog box opens (see Figure 1-5).**

5. **Select 200% and then click OK.**

   The dialog box closes, and the magnification changes to show each cell in a more close-up view.

6. **At the bottom-right corner of the Excel window, drag the Zoom slider left to 100%, changing zoom back to its original setting (see Figure 1-6).**

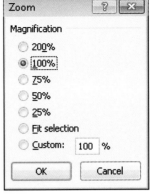

Figure 1-5

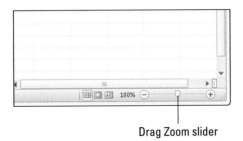

Drag Zoom slider

Figure 1-6

Leave the workbook open for the next exercise.

Move the cell cursor

To type in a cell, you must first make it active by moving the cell cursor there. As shown in Figure 1-4, the cell cursor is a thick black outline. You can move the cell cursor by pressing the arrow keys on the keyboard, by clicking the desired cell, or by using one of Excel's keyboard shortcuts. Table 1-1 provides some of the most common keyboard shortcuts for moving the cell cursor.

Table 1-1	Movement Shortcuts
Press This . . .	*To Move . . .*
Arrow keys	One cell in the direction of the arrow
Tab	One cell to the right
Shift+Tab	One cell to the left

continued

Table 1-1 *(continued)*

Press This . . .	To Move . . .
Ctrl+arrow key	To the edge of the current data region (the first or last cell that isn't empty) in the direction of the arrow
End	To the cell in the lower-right corner of the window*
Ctrl+End	To the last cell in the worksheet, in the lowest used row of the rightmost used column
Home	To the beginning of the row containing the active cell
Ctrl+Home	To the beginning of the worksheet (cell A1)
Page Down	One screen down
Alt+Page Down	One screen to the right
Ctrl+Page Down	To the next sheet in the workbook
Page Up	One screen up
Alt+Page Up	One screen to the left
Ctrl+Page Up	To the previous sheet in the workbook

* This works only when the Scroll Lock key has been pressed on your keyboard to turn on the Scroll Lock function.

In the following exercise, you move the cell cursor in a worksheet.

Files needed: None

1. **From any blank worksheet, such as the one from the preceding section, click cell C3 to move the cell cursor there.**

2. **Press the right-arrow key to move to cell D3, and then press the down-arrow key to moves to cell D4.**

3. **Press the Home key to move to cell A4.**

   Refer to Table 1-1; pressing Home moves to the beginning of the current row, which in this case, is row 4.

4. **Press the Page Down key.**

The cell cursor moves to a cell that is one screenful down from the preceding position. Depending on the window size and screen resolution, the exact cell varies, but you are still in column A.

5. **Use the vertical scroll bar to scroll the display up so that cell A1 is visible.**

Notice that the cell cursor does not move while you scroll. The Name box still displays the name of the cell you moved to previously.

6. Press Ctrl+Home to move to cell A1.

Leave the workbook open for the next exercise.

Select ranges

Range names are written with the upper-left cell address, a colon, and the lower-right cell address, such as A1:F3. A1:F3 means the range that begins in the upper-left corner with A1 and ends in the lower-right corner with F3. When a range contains noncontiguous cells, the pieces are separated by commas, like this: B8:C14,D8:G14. B8:C14,D8:G14 means the range from B8 through C14, plus the range from D8 through G14.

You can select a range by using either the keyboard or the mouse. Table 1-2 provides some of the most common range selection shortcuts.

LINGO

You might sometimes want to select a multi-cell **range** before you issue a command. For example, if you want to format all the text in a range a certain way, select that range and then issue the formatting command. Technically, a range can consist of a single cell; however, a range most commonly consists of multiple cells.

A range is usually **contiguous,** or all the cells are in a single rectangular block, but they don't have to be. You can also select **noncontiguous** cells in a range, by holding down the Ctrl key while you select additional cells.

Table 1-2	Range Selection Shortcuts
Press This . . .	*To Extend the Selection To . . .*
Ctrl+Shift+arrow key	The last nonblank cell in the same column or row as the active cell; or if the next cell is blank, to the next nonblank cell
Ctrl+Shift+End	The last used cell on the worksheet (lower-right corner of the range containing data)
Ctrl+Shift+Home	The beginning of the worksheet (cell A1)
Ctrl+Shift+Page Down	The current and next sheet in the workbook
Ctrl+Shift+Page Up	The current and previous sheet in the workbook
Ctrl+spacebar	The entire column where the active cell is located
Shift+spacebar	The entire row where the active cell is located
Ctrl+A	The entire worksheet

In the following exercise, you practice selecting ranges.

Files needed: None

1. **On any blank worksheet, such as the one from the preceding exercise, click cell B2 to move the cell cursor there.**

2. **While holding down the Shift key, press the right-arrow key twice and the down-arrow key twice, extending the selection to the range B2:D4 (see Figure 1-7).**

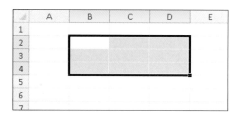

Figure 1-7

EXTRA INFO

The row and column headers turn yellow when cells within them are selected.

3. **Hold down the Ctrl key and click cell E2 to add only that cell to the selected range.**

4. **Holding down the left mouse button, drag from cell E2 to cell E8 so that the range is B2:D4,E2:E8, as shown in Figure 1-8.**

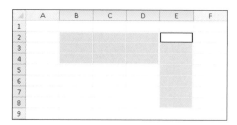

Figure 1-8

EXTRA INFO

Notice that the active cell is E2. Its name appears in the Name box, and it appears in white in Figure 1-8. That's because cell E2 is the cell you most recently clicked — the starting point of the most recent addition to the range. This points out the difference between the active cell and a multi-cell range. When you type text, it goes into the active cell only. When you apply formatting or some other command, it applies to all the cells in the selected range.

5. **Hold down the Ctrl key and click row 10's row header (the number 10 itself, at the left edge of the row) to add that entire row to the selected range.**

6. **Hold down Ctrl and click column G's column header (the letter G, at the top of the column) to add that entire column to the selected range.**

Your selection should look like Figure 1-9 at this point.

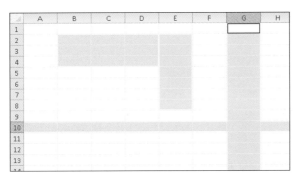

Figure 1-9

7. Click any cell to cancel the range selection; only that cell you clicked is selected.

8. Click in cell C4, and then press Ctrl+spacebar to select the entire column and then click any cell to cancel the range selection.

9. Click in cell C4 again, and press Shift+spacebar to select the entire row.

10. Click the Select All button (labeled in Figure 1-10) in the upper-left corner of the spreadsheet grid—where the row numbers and the column letters intersect—to select the entire worksheet, as shown in Figure 1-10.

 Instead of clicking the Select All button, you can press Ctrl+Shift+spacebar.

Select All button

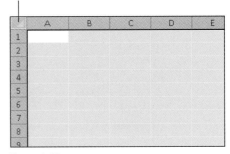

11. Click any cell to cancel the range selection.

Leave the workbook open for the next exercise.

Figure 1-10

Typing and Editing Cell Content

To this point in the lesson, I've introduced you to some spreadsheet basics. Now, it's time to actually do something: Enter some text and numbers into cells.

Type text or numbers into a cell

To type in a cell, simply select the cell and begin typing. When you finish typing, you can leave the cell in any of these ways:

- ✔ **Press Enter:** Moves you to the next cell down.
- ✔ **Press Tab:** Moves you to the next cell to the right.
- ✔ **Press Shift+Tab:** Moves you to the next cell to the left.
- ✔ **Press an arrow key:** Moves you in the direction of the arrow.
- ✔ **Click in another cell:** Moves you to that cell.

If you make a mistake when editing, you can press the Esc key to cancel the edit before you leave the cell. If you need to undo an edit after you leave the cell, press Ctrl+Z or click the Undo button on the Quick Access toolbar.

In the following exercise, you enter text into a worksheet.

Files needed: None

1. **On any blank worksheet, such as the one from the preceding exercise, click cell A1.**

2. **Type** Mortgage Calculator **and press Enter.**

3. **Click cell A1 again to reselect it and notice that the cell's content appears in the Formula bar (see Figure 1-11).**

Formula bar

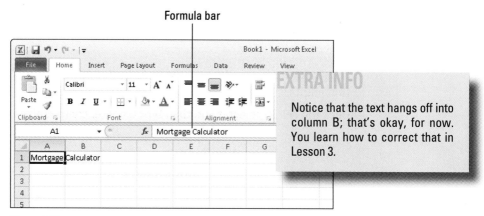

EXTRA INFO

Notice that the text hangs off into column B; that's okay, for now. You learn how to correct that in Lesson 3.

Figure 1-11

4. **Click cell A3, type** Loan Amount, **and press Tab so the cell cursor moves to cell B3.**

5. Type 250000 **and press Enter so the cell cursor moves to cell A4.**

6. **In cell A4, type** Interest, **and press Tab so the cell cursor moves to cell B4.**

7. Type .05 **and press Enter so the cell cursor moves to cell A5.**

8. Type Periods **and press Tab so the cell cursor moves to cell B5.**

9. Type 360 **and press Enter so the cell cursor moves to cell A6.**

10. Type Payment **and press Enter so the cell cursor moves to cell A7, and the worksheet looks like Figure 1-12 at this point.**

11. **To save the file as** *Mortgage.xlsx***:**

    a. *Choose File⇨Save.*

    b. *In the Save As dialog box that appears, navigate to the location where you want to save the file.*

    c. *In the File Name box, type* **Mortgage**.

    d. *Click Save.*

Leave the workbook open for the next exercise.

LINGO

The **Formula bar** is the text area immediately above the worksheet grid, to the right of the Name box. This bar shows the active cell's contents. When the content is text or a number, what appears in the cell and what appears in the Formula bar are identical. When the content is a formula or function, the Formula bar shows the actual formula/function and the cell itself shows the result of it.

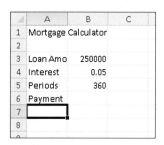

Figure 1-12

Edit cell content

If you need to edit what's in the cell, you can

- ✔ Click the cell to select it and then click the cell again to move the insertion point into it. Edit like you would in any text program.

- ✔ Click the cell to select it and then type a new entry to replace the old one.

If you decide you don't want the text you typed in a particular cell, you can get rid of it in several ways:

- ✔ Select the cell; then right-click the cell and choose Clear Contents from the menu that appears.

- ✔ Select the cell; then choose Home⇨Clear⇨Clear Contents.

- ✔ Select the cell, press the spacebar, and then press Enter. This technically doesn't clear the cell's content, but it replaces it with a space.

- ✔ Select the cell and press the Delete key.

EXTRA INFO

Don't confuse the Delete key on the keyboard (Clear) with the Delete command on the Ribbon. There is a Delete command on the Home tab, but using this doesn't *clear* the cell content; instead, it *removes* the entire cell. You find out more about deleting cells in the upcoming section, "Changing the Worksheet Structure."

And while I'm on the subject, don't confuse Clear with Cut, either. The Cut command works in conjunction with the Clipboard. Cut moves the content to the Clipboard, and you can then paste it somewhere else. In Excel though (unlike in other applications), using the Cut command doesn't immediately remove the content. Instead, it puts a flashing dotted box around the content and waits for you to reposition the cell cursor and issue the Paste command. If you do something else in the interim, the cut-and-paste operation is canceled, and the content that you cut remains in its original location. You learn more about cutting and pasting in the section "Copy and move data between cells" later in this lesson.

In the following exercise, you edit text in a worksheet.

Files needed: Mortgage.xlsx

1. **In the Mortgage file from the preceding exercise, click in cell A3.**

2. **Click in the Formula bar to move the insertion point there, double-click the word *Loan* to select it, press the Delete key, and then press the Delete key again to delete the space before the remaining word *Amount*.**

3. **Press Enter to finalize the edit.** The cell cursor moves to cell A4.

4. **Click in B3, type** 300000, **and press Enter.** The new value replaces the old one.

5. **Right-click cell B4 and choose Clear Contents. Then type 0.0635 and press Enter.**

6. **Click cell B5 to select it, and then double-click in B5 to move the insertion point there. Position the insertion point to the right of the 6, press the Backspace key twice, and type 18, changing the value in the cell to 180. Press Enter.**

   The worksheet looks like Figure 1-13.

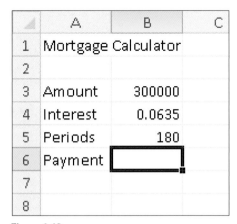

Figure 1-13

7. **Click the Save button on the Quick Access toolbar to save the changes to the workbook.**

Leave the workbook open for the next exercise.

Copy and move data between cells

When you're creating a spreadsheet, it's common to not get everything in exactly the right cells to begin with. Fortunately, moving content between cells is easy.

Here are the two methods you can use to move content:

- **Mouse method:** Point at the dark outline around the selected range and then drag to the new location. If you want to copy rather than move, hold down the Ctrl key while you drag.

- **Clipboard method:** Choose Home⇨Cut or press Ctrl+X. (If you want to copy rather than simply move, choose Home⇨Copy rather than Cut or press Ctrl+C.) Then click the destination cell and choose Home⇨Paste or press Ctrl+V.

TIP

If you're moving or copying a multi-cell range with the Clipboard method, you can either select the same size and shape of range for the destination, or you can select a single cell, in which case the paste occurs with the selected cell in the upper-left corner.

In the following exercise, you move and copy cell content using two methods.

Files needed: Mortgage.xlsx

1. **In the Mortgage file from the preceding exercise, select the range A1:B6.**

2. **Point at the border of the selection so the mouse pointer shows a four-headed arrow along with the arrow pointer.**

3. **Drag the selection to C1:D6. An outline shows the selection while you drag the selection, and a ScreenTip shows the cell address of the destination.** See Figure 1-14.

	A	B	C	D	E
1	Mortgage	Calculator			
2					
3	Amount	300000			
4	Interest	0.0635			
5	Periods	180			
6	Payment				
7				C1:D6	
8					
9					

Figure 1-14

4. **Click cell C1 and press Ctrl+X to cut.** A dotted outline appears around C1.

5. **Click cell B1 and press Ctrl+V to paste.** The text moves from C1 to B1.

6. **Select C3:D6 and then choose Home⇨Cut.**

7. **Click cell B3 and then choose Home⇨Paste.** The completed worksheet is shown in Figure 1-15.

8. **Save the changes to the workbook.**

◢	A	B	C	D
1		Mortgage Calculator		
2				
3		Amount	300000	
4		Interest	0.0635	
5		Periods	180	
6		Payment		
7				

Figure 1-15

Leave the workbook open for the next exercise.

Use AutoFill to fill cell content

When you have a lot of data to enter and that data consists of some type of repeatable pattern or sequence, you can save time by using AutoFill. To use AutoFill, you select the cell(s) that already contain an example of what you want to fill and then drag the fill handle.

LINGO

The **fill handle** is the little black square in the lower-right corner of the selected cell or range.

Depending on how you use it, AutoFill can either fill the same value into every cell in the target area, or it can fill in a sequence (such as days of the month, days of the week, or a numeric sequence like 2, 4, 6, 8). Here are the general rules for how it works:

✓ When AutoFill recognizes the selected text as a member of one of its preset lists, such as days of the week or months of the year, it automatically increments those. For example, if the selected cell contains August, AutoFill places September in the next adjacent cell.

✓ When AutoFill does not recognize the selected text, it fills with a duplicate of the selected text.

✓ When AutoFill is used on a single cell containing a number, it fills with a duplicate of the number.

✓ When Auto Fill is used on a range of two or more cells containing numbers, AutoFill attempts to determine the interval between them and continues filling using that same pattern. For example, if the two selected cells contain 2 and 4, the next adjacent cell would be filled with 6.

In the following exercise, you move and copy cell content using two methods.

Files needed: Mortgage.xlsx

1. **In the Mortgage file from the preceding exercise, select cell A8 and type** Amortization Table**.**
2. **Type the following:**
   a. In cell A10, type ***Date****.*
   b. In cell B10, type ***Pmt#****.*
   c. In cell A11, type ***January 2012****. (Note that Excel automatically changes it to Jan-12.)*
   d. In cell B11, type ***1****.*
3. **Click cell A11 and move the mouse pointer over the fill handle.**

   The mouse pointer becomes a black cross-hair (see Figure 1-16).

8 Amortization Table
9
10 Date Pmt#
11 Jan-12 1
12
13

Figure 1-16

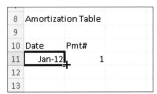

4. **Drag the fill handle down to cell A22.**

   The first year of dates fill in the cells. See Figure 1-17.

5. **Click cell B11 and drag the fill handle down to C22. The same number is filled into all cells. That's not what you want for this exercise so press Ctrl+Z to undo the fill.**
6. **Click cell B12, and type 2. Select B11:B12 and then drag the fill handle down to cell B22.**

   Figure 1-18 shows the completed series.

7. **Select A22:B22 and drag the fill handle down to B190.**

   Both series are filled in, down to row 190, where the date is December 2026 and the payment number is 180.

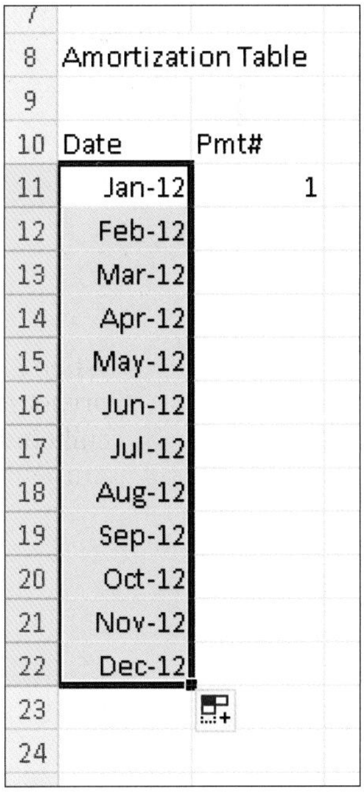

8 Amortization Table
9
10 Date Pmt#
11 Jan-12 1
12 Feb-12
13 Mar-12
14 Apr-12
15 May-12
16 Jun-12
17 Jul-12
18 Aug-12
19 Sep-12
20 Oct-12
21 Nov-12
22 Dec-12
23
24

Figure 1-17

7		
8	Amortization Table	
9		
10	Date	Pmt#
11	Jan-12	1
12	Feb-12	2
13	Mar-12	3
14	Apr-12	4
15	May-12	5
16	Jun-12	6
17	Jul-12	7
18	Aug-12	8
19	Sep-12	9
20	Oct-12	10
21	Nov-12	11
22	Dec-12	12
23		
24		

Figure 1-18

TIP Step 7 is performed because the number of periods for this loan is 180 (see cell C5), so the number of payments should be 180 in the amortization table.

8. **Press Ctrl+Home to return to the top of the worksheet.**

9. **Save the changes to the workbook.**

Leave the workbook open for the next exercise.

Changing the Worksheet Structure

Even if you're a careful planner, you'll likely decide that you want to change your worksheet's structure. Maybe you want data in a different column, or certain rows turn out to be unnecessary. Excel makes it easy to insert and delete rows and columns to deal with these kinds of changes.

Insert and delete rows and columns

When you insert a new row or column, the existing ones move to make room for it. You can insert multiple rows or columns at once by selecting multiple ones before issuing the Insert command. (There's no limit on the number you can insert at once!) Similarly, you can delete multiple rows or columns by selecting them before using the Delete command.

In the following exercise, you insert and delete rows and columns.

Files needed: Mortgage.xlsx

1. **In the Mortgage file from the preceding exercise, click anywhere in column A.**

2. **On the Home tab, click the down arrow on the Insert button and choose Insert Sheet Columns (see Figure 1-19).** A new column is placed to the left of the selected column.

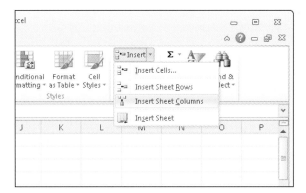

Figure 1-19

3. **Click the column header for column A to select the entire column and then choose Home⇨Delete.** The entire column is deleted.

4. **Select rows 7 and 8 by dragging across their row headers and then choose Home⇨Insert.** Two new rows are inserted.

5. **Right-click any cell in row 7; then from the Home tab, click the down arrow on the Delete button and choose Delete Sheet Rows.** Figure 1-20 shows the worksheet after the insertions and deletions.

◢	A	B	C	D	E
1		Mortgage Calculator			
2					
3		Amount	300000		
4		Interest	0.0635		
5		Periods	180		
6		Payment			
7					
8					
9	Amortization Table				
10					
11	Date	Pmt#			
12	Jan-12	1			
13	Feb-12	2			
14	Mar-12	3			
15	Apr-12	4			
16	May-12	5			

Figure 1-20

Save the changes, and leave the workbook open for the next exercise.

Insert and delete cells and ranges

You can also insert and delete individual cells, or ranges that do not neatly correspond to entire rows or columns. When you do so, the surrounding cells shift. In the case of an insertion, cells move down or to the right of the area where the new cells are being inserted. In the case of a deletion, cells move up or to the left to fill in the voided space.

Deleting a cell is different from clearing a cell's content, and this becomes apparent when you start working with individual cells and ranges. When you clear the content, the cell itself remains. When you delete the cell itself, the adjacent cells shift.

When shifting cells, Excel is smart enough that it tries to guess which direction you want existing content to move when you insert or delete cells. If you have content immediately to the right of a deleted cell, for example, it shifts it left. If you have content immediately below the deleted cell, it shifts it up. You can still override that, though, when needed.

In the following exercise, you insert and delete cells.

Files needed: Mortgage.xlsx

1. **In the Mortgage file from the preceding exercise, select A1:A6 and then choose Home⇨Delete.** Excel guesses that you want to move the existing content to the left, and it does so.

2. **Click cell A1, and choose Home⇨Insert.** Excel guesses that you want to move the existing content down, which is incorrect. The content in column B is off by one row (see Figure 1-21).

3. **Press Ctrl+Z to undo the insertion; then from the Home tab, click the down arrow to the right of the Insert button and choose Insert Cells.** The Insert dialog box opens (see Figure 1-22).

4. **Select Shift Cells Right and then click OK.** A new cell A1 is inserted, and the previous A1 content moves into B1.

5. **Save the changes to the workbook.**

Column B content shifted up

	A	B	C
1			
2	Mortgage	Calculator	
3		300000	
4	Amount	0.0635	
5	Interest	180	
6	Periods		
7	Payment		
8			
9			
10	Amortization Table		
11		Pmt#	
12	Date	1	
13	Jan-12	2	
14	Feb-12	3	

Figure 1-21

Leave the workbook open for the next exercise.

Working with Worksheets

Each new workbook starts with three sheets — Sheet1, Sheet2, and Sheet3. (Not the most interesting names, but you can change them.) You can add or delete worksheets, rearrange the worksheet tabs, and apply different colors to the tabs to help differentiate them from one another, or to create logical groups of tabs.

Figure 1-22

In the following exercise, you insert, rename, and delete worksheets, and change a tab color.

Files needed: Mortgage.xlsx

1. **In the Mortgage file from the preceding exercise, double-click the Sheet1 worksheet tab to move the insertion point into it.**

2. **Type** Calculator **and press Enter.**

   The new name replaces the old one.

3. **Right-click the worksheet tab, choose Tab Color, and click the Red standard color.**

   See Figure 1-23.

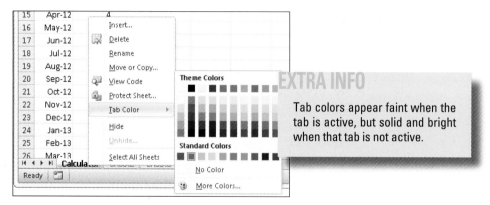

Figure 1-23

4. **Right-click the Sheet2 tab and choose Delete.**

   The sheet is deleted.

5. **Double-click the Sheet3 tab, type** Amortization, **and press Enter.**

6. **Right-click the Amortization tab and choose Insert.**

   The Insert dialog box opens. See Figure 1-24.

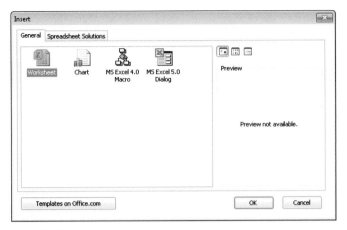

Figure 1-24

7. **Click Worksheet and then click OK.**

   A new sheet is inserted.

8. **Double-click the tab on the new sheet you inserted, type Chart, and press Enter.**

   The three tabs in the workbook are named and arranged, as shown in Figure 1-25.

Figure 1-25

9. **Save the changes to the workbook.**

Close the workbook and exit Excel.

Summing Up

Excel is an excellent choice for storing data in rows and columns. In this lesson, you learned how to navigate the Excel interface, including entering and editing content in cells, inserting and deleting cells, and selecting ranges. Here's a quick review:

- ✔ Excel data files are called workbooks. Each workbook can hold multiple worksheets. Each worksheet has a tab at the bottom of the Excel window for quick access to it.

- ✔ Each cell has a cell address consisting of the column letter and row number, such as A1.

- ✔ The active cell is indicated by the cell cursor, a thick black outline. You can move the cell cursor with the mouse or the keyboard arrow keys. When you type text, it is entered into the active cell.

- ✔ A range is a selection that consists of one or more cells. (It's usually more than one.) A contiguous range consists of a single rectangular block of cells.

- ✔ To clear cell contents, select the cell and press the Delete key or choose Home⇨Clear⇨Cell Contents.

- ✔ To move data between cells, drag them, or use the Cut and Paste commands. To copy data, hold down Ctrl and drag the cells, or use the Copy and Paste commands.

- ✔ To fill data from the selected range to adjacent cells, drag the fill handle, which is the black rectangle in the lower-right corner of the selected range.

- ✔ To insert a row or column, from the Home tab, open the Insert button's menu and choose either Insert Sheet Rows or Insert Sheet Columns, respectively.

- ✔ When you insert individual cells, the existing content moves over to make room. You can choose which direction it needs to move.

- ✔ To insert a new sheet, right-click an existing sheet and choose Insert. To delete a sheet, right-click its tab and choose Delete.

- ✔ To rename a sheet, double-click its tab name and type a new name.

Try-it-yourself lab

1. **Start Excel, and in cell A1, type Membership List.**

2. **In row 3, enter the column headings you would need to store information about the members of an organization you're part of.** For example, you might have First, Last, and Phone.

3. **Starting in row 4, enter the information about the members of the organization.** If the organization has many members, you do not have to enter every member in the list.

4. **Insert a new column between two of the existing columns.** For example, you could enter a MI column (for Middle Initial) between First and Last.

5. **Change the name of the worksheet tab to Membership.**

6. **Save your workbook as Lab1.xlsx.**

7. **Close your workbook and then close Excel.**

Know this tech talk

active cell: The cell in which new content that you type will be placed.

cell address: The column letter and row number of a cell, such as A1.

cell cursor: The thick black border surrounding the active cell.

cell: The intersection of a row and column in a spreadsheet.

contiguous: A range in which all the selected cells are adjacent to one another, in a rectangular block.

fill handle: The small square handle in the lower-right corner of a selected range.

Formula bar: The bar above the worksheet grid where the formula appears from the selected cell.

Name box: The box to the left of the Formula bar that lists the active cell's cell address.

range: One or more selected cells.

spreadsheet: A grid of rows and columns in which you can store data.

workbook: An Excel data file.

worksheet: The Excel term for a spreadsheet.

worksheet tabs: Tabs at the bottom of a workbook for each worksheet that it contains.

Lesson 2
Creating Formulas and Functions

- ✔ Formulas perform math calculations on fixed numbers or on cell contents.

- ✔ The order of precedence settles any uncertainties about which math operations execute first.

- ✔ Cell references that include sheet names can reference cells on other sheets.

- ✔ Relative cell referencing allows cell references to automatically update when copied.

- ✔ Absolute cell referencing keeps a cell reference fixed when copied to other locations.

- ✔ Functions perform complex math operations on cell content.

- ✔ The SUM function sums a range of cells.

- ✔ Insert Function helps you choose and construct a function.

- ✔ Named ranges substitute friendly, easy-to-understand words for plain cell and range addresses.

*M*ath. Excel is really good at it, and it's what makes Excel more than just data storage. Even if you hated math in school, you might still like Excel because it does the math for you.

In Excel, you can write math formulas that perform calculations on the values in various cells, and then if those values change later, the formula results update automatically. You can also use built-in functions to handle more complex math activities than you might be able to set up yourself with formulas. That capability makes it possible to build complex worksheets that calculate loan rates and payments, keep track of your bank accounts, and much more.

In this lesson, I show you how to construct formulas and functions in Excel, as well as how to move and copy formulas and functions (there's a trick to it) and how to use functions to create handy financial spreadsheets.

Introducing Formulas

In Excel, formulas are different from regular text in two ways:

- They begin with an equal sign, like this: =2+2.

- They don't contain text (except for function names and cell references). They contain only symbols that are allowed in math formulas, such as parentheses, commas, and decimal points.

LINGO

A **formula** is a math calculation, like 2+2 or 3(4+1), and in Excel, a formula can perform calculations with fixed numbers or cell contents.

Write formulas that calculate

Excel's formulas can do everything that a basic calculator can do, so if you're in a hurry and don't want to pull up the Windows Calculator application, you can enter a formula in Excel to get a quick result. Experimenting with this type of formula is a great way to get accustomed to formulas in general.

TIP

Excel also has an advantage over some basic calculators (including the one in Windows): It easily does exponentiation. For example, if you want to calculate 5 to the 8th power, you would write it in Excel as =5^8.

REMEMBER

Just like in basic math, formulas are calculated by an order of precedence. Table 2-1 lists the order.

Table 2-1	Order of Precedence in a Formula	
Order	*Item*	*Example*
1	Anything in parentheses	=2*(2+1)
2	Exponentiation	=2^3
3	Multiplication and division	=1+2*2
4	Addition and subtraction	=10-4

In the following exercise, you enter some formulas that perform simple math calculations.

Files needed: None

1. **Start Excel, if needed, so that a new blank workbook appears. If you already have another workbook open, press Ctrl+N to create a new one.**

2. **Click cell A1, type** =2+2, **and press Enter.** The result of the formula appears in cell A1.

3. **Click cell A1 again to move the cell cursor back to it, and then look in the Formula bar.** Notice that the formula you entered appears there. See Figure 2-1.

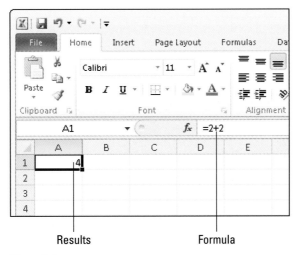

Results   Formula

Figure 2-1

4. Click cell A2, type =2+4*3, **and press Enter.** The result of the formula appears in cell A2.

In this case, because of the order of operations (see Table 2-1), the multiplication was done first (4 times 3 equals 12) and then 2 was added, for a total of 14. See Figure 2-2.

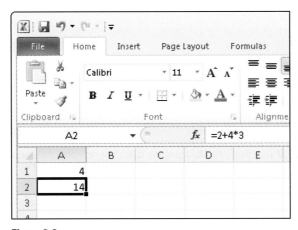

Figure 2-2

5. In cell A3, type =(2+4)*3 **and press Enter.**

In this case, the parentheses forced the addition to occur first (2 plus 4 equals 6) and then 3 was multiplied, for a total of 18. See Figure 2-3.

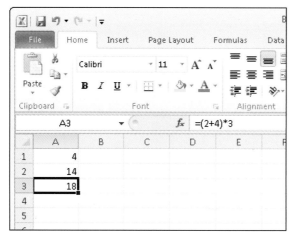

Figure 2-3

6. **Close the workbook without saving changes to it.**

Leave Excel open for the next exercise.

Write formulas that reference cells

One of Excel's best features is its ability to reference cells in formulas. When a cell is referenced in a formula, whatever value it contains is used in the formula. When the value changes, the result of the formula changes, too.

In the following exercise, you enter some formulas that contain cell references.

Files needed: Budget.xlsx

1. **Open Budget.xlsx from the data files for this lesson and save it as Budget Calculations.**

2. **In cell E6, type** =E4. **The value shown in E4 is repeated there.**

TIP

In cell E6, you could have just as easily retyped the value from E4, but this way if the value in E4 changes, the value in E6 also changes.

3. **In cell B7, type** =B4+B5+B6 **so that B7 shows $1,425; in cell B15, type** =B10+B11+B12+B13+B14 **so that B15 shows $975.**

TIP Typing each cell reference is a lot. Later in this lesson in the section "Introducing Functions," you see how to use the SUM function to dramatically cut down on the typing required to sum the values in many cells at once.

4. **In cell B17, type** =B7+B15 **so that B17 shows $2,400; in cell E9, type** =E6–B17 **so that E9 shows –$578 (see Figure 2-4).**

	A	B	C	D	E	F
1	**Budget**					
2						
3	**Fixed Expense**			**Income**		
4	Rent	$850		Paycheck	$1,822	
5	Car Payment	$325				
6	Student Loan	$250		**Total Income**	$1,822	
7	**Total Fixed**	$1,425				
8						
9	**Variable Expense**			**Overall**	-$578	
10	Utilities	$175				
11	Food	$450		Correction %	-24%	
12	Entertainment	$150				
13	Clothes	$100				
14	Miscellaneous	$100				
15	**Total Variable**	$975				
16						
17	**Total Expenses**	$2,400				
18						
19						

Figure 2-4

5. **In cell E11, type** =E9/B17. The value –24% appears in E11, and the completed worksheet appears in Figure 2-4.

6. **Save and close the workbook.**

Leave Excel open for the next exercise.

TIP This worksheet was set up to use the appropriate formatting for each cell so that the formulas make sense. You learn to do this in Lesson 3.

Reference a cell on another sheet

When referring to a cell on the same sheet, you can simply use its column and row: A1, B1, and so on. However, when referring to a cell on a different sheet, you have to include the sheet name in the formula.

The syntax for doing this is to list the sheet name, followed by an exclamation point, followed by the cell reference, like this:

```
=Sheet1!A2
```

In the following exercise, you practice using this notation by creating some multi-sheet formulas.

Files needed: Sheets.xlsx

1. **Open Sheets.xlsx from the data files for this lesson and save it as Budget Sheets.xlsx.**

TIP

This workbook has the same data that you worked with in the preceding exercise, but the data is split into multiple worksheets.

2. **Click the workbook's Expenses tab, and look at the data there. When calculating the overall budget amount, refer to cell B15 there.** See Figure 2-5.

	A	B	C
1	**Fixed Expense**		
2	Rent	$850	
3	Car Payment	$325	
4	Student Loan	$250	
5	**Total Fixed**	$1,425	
6			
7	**Variable Expense**		
8	Utilities	$175	
9	Food	$450	
10	Entertainment	$150	
11	Clothes	$100	
12	Miscellaneous	$100	
13	**Total Variable**	$975	
14			
15	**Total Expenses**	$2,400	
16			
17			

Figure 2-5

3. **Click the workbook's Income tab and look at the data there. On this sheet, refer to cell B4.** See Figure 2-6.

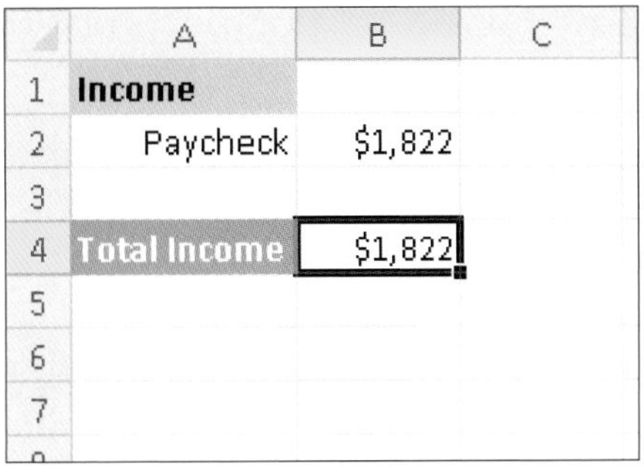

4. **Click the workbook's Overall tab, and in cell B3, type** =Income!B4-Expenses!B15. Cell B3 displays –$578.

If you had not looked beforehand at the cells to reference on the other tabs, you might have been at a loss as to what to type when constructing the formula in Step 4. There is another way to refer to cells when writing a formula. The next steps practice that method:

a. In cell B5, type =, and in cell B3, type /.

b. Click the Expenses tab, click cell B15, and press Enter. The display jumps back to the Overall tab, and completes the formula. See Figure 2-7.

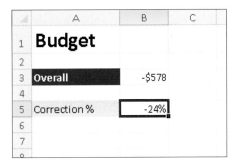

Figure 2-6

Figure 2-7

5. **Save the changes to the workbook and close it.**

Leave Excel open for the next exercise.

Moving and Copying Formulas

In Lesson 1, you learn how to move and copy text and numbers between cells, but when it comes to copying formulas, there are a few gotchas. The following sections explain relative and absolute referencing in formulas, and how you can use them to get the results you want when you copy.

Copy formulas with relative referencing

When you move or copy a formula, Excel automatically changes the cell references to work with the new location. That's because by default, cell references in formulas are *relative references*. For example, in Figure 2-8, suppose you wanted to copy the formula from B5 into C5. The new formula in C5 should refer to values in column C, not to column B; otherwise, the formula wouldn't make much sense. So, when B5's formula is copied to C5, it becomes =C3+C4 there.

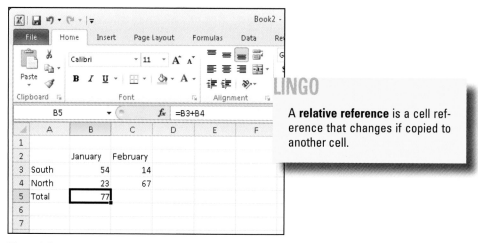

Figure 2-8

In this exercise, you copy formulas using relative referencing (the default) and examine the results.

Files needed: Appliance.xlsx

1. **Open Appliance.xlsx from the data files for this lesson and save it as Appliance Sales.xlsx.**

2. **On Sheet1, click cell B13 and examine the formula in the Formula bar, which contains references to values in column B.** See Figure 2-9.

3. **Press Ctrl+C to copy the formula to the Clipboard (a dotted outline appears around B13), and then select C13:E13 and press Ctrl+V to paste the formula into those cells.**

4. **Click cell C13 and examine the formula in the Formula bar, which contains references to values in column C.** See Figure 2-10.

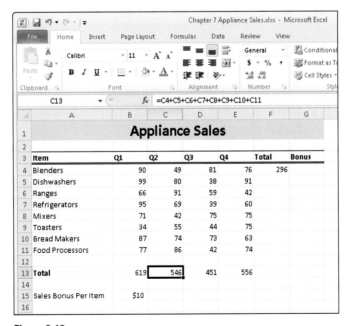

Figure 2-9

Figure 2-10

5. **Click cell F4 and then drag the fill handle down to F13.** The formula from F4 is copied into that range, with the row numbers changed to refer to the new positions. See Figure 2-11.

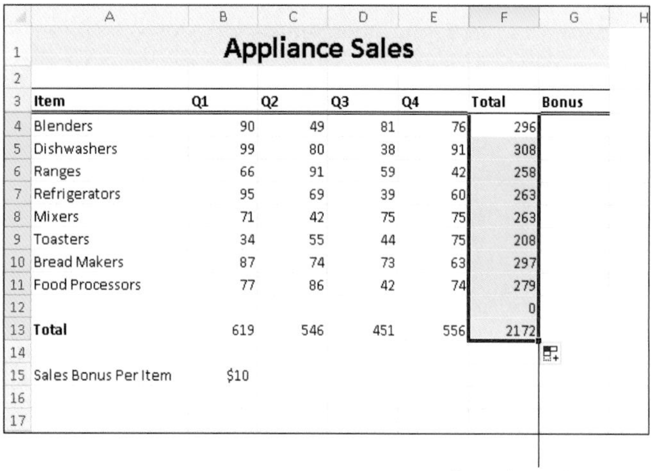

	A	B	C	D	E	F	G	H
1			**Appliance Sales**					
2								
3	**Item**	Q1	Q2	Q3	Q4	**Total**	**Bonus**	
4	Blenders	90	49	81	76	296		
5	Dishwashers	99	80	38	91	308		
6	Ranges	66	91	59	42	258		
7	Refrigerators	95	69	39	60	263		
8	Mixers	71	42	75	75	263		
9	Toasters	34	55	44	75	208		
10	Bread Makers	87	74	73	63	297		
11	Food Processors	77	86	42	74	279		
12						0		
13	**Total**	619	546	451	556	2172		
14								
15	Sales Bonus Per Item	$10						
16								
17								

Drag the fill handle

Figure 2-11

6. **Click each of the cells in the F column and examine their formulas in the Formula bar.** Note that each one uses the correct row number.

7. **Save the changes to the workbook.**

Leave the workbook open for the next exercise.

Copy formulas with absolute referencing

You might not always want the cell references in a formula to change when you move or copy it. In other words, you want an *absolute reference* to that cell. To make a reference absolute, you add dollar signs before the column letter and before the row number. So, for example, an absolute reference to cell C1 would be =$C$1.

LINGO

An **absolute reference** is a cell reference that doesn't change when copied to another cell. You can mix relative and absolute references in the same formula. When you do, the result is a **mixed reference**.

If you want to "lock down" only one dimension of the cell reference, you can place a dollar sign before only the column, or only the row. For example, =$C1 would make only the column letter fixed, and =C$1 would make only the row number fixed.

In this exercise, you create absolute references and copy formulas that contain them.

Files needed: Appliance Sales.xlsx from the preceding exercise

1. **In Appliance Sales.xlsx, click cell G4 and type** =F4*$B$15, **which multiplies cell F4 by cell B15, referring to F4 with a relative reference and referring to B15 with an absolute reference.**

2. **Click cell G4 again and then drag the fill handle down to G11, copying the formula to that range.**

3. **Click cell G11 and examine its formula in the Formula bar, as shown in Figure 2-12.** Notice that the reference to column F is updated to show cell F11, but the reference to cell B15 has remained fixed.

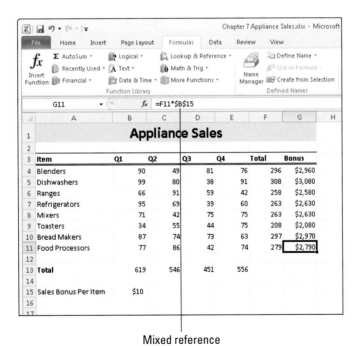

Mixed reference

Figure 2-12

4. **Select F11:G11 and then press Ctrl+C to copy; select F13:G13 and then press Ctrl+V to paste.**

5. **Click cell G13 and examine the formula in the Formula bar to confirm it is correct.**

You could have dragged the fill handle all the way down to cell G13 in Step 2, so you wouldn't have to copy and paste the formula into G13 in Step 4. However, there still would have been another step because you would have had an extraneous function in cell G12 that you would've had to delete.

6. **Save the changes to the workbook.**

Leave the workbook open for the next exercise.

Introducing Functions

Sometimes, as you've seen in earlier exercises in this lesson, it's awkward or lengthy to write a formula to perform a calculation. For example, suppose you want to sum the values in cells A1 through A10. To express that as a formula, you'd have to write each cell reference individually, like this:

$$=A1+A2+A3+A4+A5+A6+A7+A8+A9+A10$$

With a function, you can represent a range with the upper-left corner's cell reference, a colon, and the lower-right corner's cell reference. In the case of A1:A10, there is only one column, so the upper left is cell A1 and the lower right is cell A10.

LINGO

In Excel, a **function** refers to a certain math calculation. Functions can greatly shortcut the amount of typing you have to do to create a particular result. For example, instead of using the $=A1+A2+A3+A4+A5+A6+A7+A8+A9+A10$ formula, you could use the SUM function like this: $=SUM(A1:A10)$.

Range references cannot be used in simple formulas — only in functions. For example, the formula =A6:A9 is invalid because no math operation is specified in it. You can't insert math operators within a range. To use ranges in a calculation, you must use a function.

Each function has one or more arguments, along with its own rules about how many required and optional arguments there are, and what they represent. You don't have to memorize the sequence of arguments (the *syntax*) for each function; Excel asks you for them. Excel can even suggest a function to use for a certain situation if you aren't sure what you need.

Use the SUM function

The SUM function is by far the most popular function; it sums (that is, adds) a data range consisting of one or more cells, like this:

```
=SUM(D12:D15)
```

You don't *have* to use a range in a SUM function; you can specify the individual cell addresses if you want. Separate them by commas, like this:

```
=SUM(D12, D13, D14, D15)
```

LINGO

An **argument** is a placeholder for a number, text string, or cell reference. For example, the SUM function requires at least one argument: a range of cells. So in the preceding example, A1:A10 is the argument. The arguments for a function are enclosed in a set of parentheses.

LINGO

The **syntax** is the sequence of arguments for a function. When there are multiple arguments in the syntax, they are separated by commas.

If the data range is not a contiguous block, you need to specify the individual cells that are outside the block. The main block is one argument, and each individual other cell is an additional argument, like this:

```
=SUM(D12:D15, E22)
```

In this exercise, you replace some formulas with equivalent functions.

Files needed: Appliance Sales.xlsx from the preceding exercise

1. **In Appliance Sales.xlsx, click cell B13 and type** =SUM(B4:B11) **and press Enter.** This function replaces the formula that was previously there. The value in the cell is 619.

2. **Enter a function using another method:**

    a. *Click cell C13 and type* =**SUM(**.

    b. *Drag across the range C4:C11 to select it and then press Enter to enter that range into the function in cell C13. The value in the cell is 546.*

3. **Use the AutoSum button to enter a function:**

Figure 2-13

a. *Click cell D13, and then choose Formulas⇨AutoSum. See Figure 2-13.* A dotted outline appears around B13:C13. However, this is not the range you want to sum.

b. *Drag across D4:D11 to select that range and then press Enter.* The value in D13 is 451.

c. *Click cell C13 and drag the fill handle to cell F13, copying the function to the adjacent cells.* Figure 2-14 shows the sheet when finished.

Note that the sheet doesn't look any different than before; the functions perform the exact same calculations that the formulas did previously.

	A	B	C	D	E	F	G
1				Appliance Sales			
2							
3	Item	Q1	Q2	Q3	Q4	Total	Bonus
4	Blenders	90	49	81	76	296	$2,960
5	Dishwashers	99	80	38	91	308	$3,080
6	Ranges	66	91	59	42	258	$2,580
7	Refrigerators	95	69	39	60	263	$2,630
8	Mixers	71	42	75	75	263	$2,630
9	Toasters	34	55	44	75	208	$2,080
10	Bread Makers	87	74	73	63	297	$2,970
11	Food Processors	77	86	42	74	279	$2,790
12							
13	Total	619	546	451	556	2172	$21,720
14							
15	Sales Bonus Per Item	$10					

Figure 2-14

4. **Save the changes to the workbook.**

Leave the workbook open for the next exercise.

Insert a function

Typing a function and its arguments directly into a cell works fine if you happen to know the function you want and its arguments. Many times, though, you may not know these details. In those cases, you can use the Insert Function feature to help you.

Insert Function enables you to pick a function from a list based on descriptive keywords. After you make your selection, it provides fill-in-the-blank prompts for the arguments.

In this exercise, you find an appropriate function and use Insert Function to create it.

Files needed: Appliance Sales.xlsx from the preceding exercise

1. **In Appliance Sales.xlsx, click cell A16 and type** Average Per Item/Qtr.

2. **Click in cell B16 and then choose Formulas⇨Insert Function.** The Insert Function dialog box opens.

3. **In the Search for a Function box, delete the placeholder text, type** average, **and click the Go button.** A list of all the functions that has something to do with averages appears. See Figure 2-15.

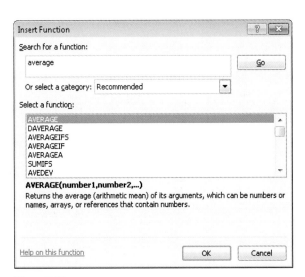

Figure 2-15

4. **From the Select a Function list, choose Average and click OK.** The Function Arguments dialog box opens.

5. **If there is already a cell reference in the Number1 box, delete it; then click the Collapse Dialog button next to the Number1 text box.** See Figure 2-16.

6. **Drag across B4:E11 to select that range, as shown in Figure 2-17.**

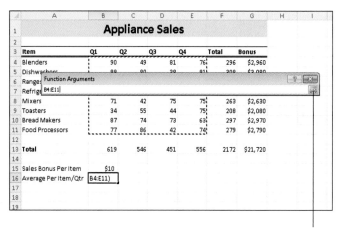

Figure 2-16

Expand Dialog button

Figure 2-17

7. **Press Enter or click the Expand Dialog button to return to the Function Arguments dialog box, and then click OK.** The function enters into cell B16 with the result of 67.875.

8. **Click cell B16 and examine the =AVERAGE(B4:E11) function in the Formula bar.**

9. **Save the changes to the workbook.**

Leave the workbook open for the next exercise.

Take a tour of some basic functions

Excel has hundreds of functions, but most of them are very specialized. The basic set that the average user works with is much more manageable.

Start with the simplest functions of them all — those without arguments. Two prime examples are

✔ **NOW:** Reports the current date and time.

✔ **TODAY:** Reports the current date.

Even though neither uses any arguments, you still have to include the parentheses, so they look like this:

```
=NOW( )
=TODAY( )
```

Another basic kind of function performs a single, simple math operation and has a single argument that specifies what cell or range it operates on. Table 2-2 summarizes some important functions that work this way.

Table 2-2	Simple One-Argument Functions	
Function	*What It Does*	*Example*
SUM	Sums the values in a range of cells.	=SUM(A1:A10)
AVERAGE	Averages the values in a range of cells.	=AVERAGE(A1:A10)
MIN	Provides the smallest number in a range of cells.	=MIN(A1:A10)
MAX	Provides the largest number in a range of cells.	=MAX(A1:A10)
COUNT	Counts the number of cells that contain numeric values in the range.	=COUNT(A1:A10)
COUNTA	Counts the number of non-empty cells in the range.	=COUNTA(A1:A10)
COUNTBLANK	Counts the number of empty cells in the range.	=COUNTBLANK(A1:A10)

In this exercise, you add some basic functions to a worksheet.

Files needed: Appliance Sales.xlsx from the preceding exercise

1. **In Appliance Sales.xlsx, in cell A17, type** Lowest **and in cell A18, type** Highest.

2. **In cell B17, type** =MIN(, **drag across B4:E11 to select the range, and press Enter to complete the function.** You do not need to type the closing parenthesis; Excel fills it in for you. The result is 34.

3. **In cell B18, type** =MAX(B4:E11). The result is 99.

4. **In cell H1, type** As of, **and in cell I1, type** =TODAY( ). Today's date appears there. Figure 2-18 shows the completed worksheet.

	A	B	C	D	E	F	G	H	I	J
1			**Appliance Sales**					As of	1/19/2011	
2										
3	**Item**	**Q1**	**Q2**	**Q3**	**Q4**	**Total**	**Bonus**			
4	Blenders	90	49	81	76	296	$2,960			
5	Dishwashers	99	80	38	91	308	$3,080			
6	Ranges	66	91	59	42	258	$2,580			
7	Refrigerators	95	69	39	60	263	$2,630			
8	Mixers	71	42	75	75	263	$2,630			
9	Toasters	34	55	44	75	208	$2,080			
10	Bread Makers	87	74	73	63	297	$2,970			
11	Food Processors	77	86	42	74	279	$2,790			
12										
13	**Total**	619	546	451	556	2172	$21,720			
14										
15	Sales Bonus Per Item	$10								
16	Average Per Item/Qtr	67.875								
17	Lowest	34								
18	Highest	99								
19										
20										

Figure 2-18

5. **Save the changes to the workbook and then close it.**

Leave Excel open for the next exercise.

Working with Named Ranges

Naming a range can be helpful because when constructing formulas and functions, you can refer to that name rather than the cell addresses. Therefore, you don't have to remember the exact cell addresses, and you can construct formulas based on meaning.

For example, instead of remembering that the number of employees is stored in cell B3, you could name cell B3 *Employees.* Then in a formula that used B3's value, such as =B3*2, you could use the name instead: =Employees*2.

Naming a range

You can name a range in three ways, and each has pros and cons:

- ✔ **If the default names are okay to use, you may find choosing Formulas⇨ Create from Selection useful.** With this method, Excel chooses the name for you based on text labels it finds in adjacent cells (above or to the left of the current cells). This method is very fast and easy, and works well when you have to create a lot of names at once and when the cells are well-labeled with adjacent text.

- ✔ **You can select the range and then type a name in the Name box (the area immediately above the column A heading, to the left of the Formula bar).** With this fast and easy method, you get to choose the name yourself. However, you have to do each range separately; you can't do a big batch at a time like you can with Formulas⇨Create from Selection.

- ✔ **If you want to more precisely control the options for the name, you can choose Formulas⇨Define Name.** This method opens a dialog box from which you can specify the name, the scope, and any comments you might want to include.

In this exercise, you name several ranges using three methods.

Files needed: Appliance Sales.xlsx from the preceding exercise

1. **Select cells B3:G11 and then choose Formulas⇨Create from Selection. The Create Names from Selection dialog box opens.**

2. **Select the Top Row check box (see Figure 2-19) and then click OK.**

    The ranges are assigned names based on the labels in row 3. For example, cells G4:G11 now form a Bonus range because that's the label in G3.

3. **Choose Formulas⇨Name Manager.**

    The Name Manager dialog box opens. The names appear on the list that you just created. See Figure 2-20.

Figure 2-19

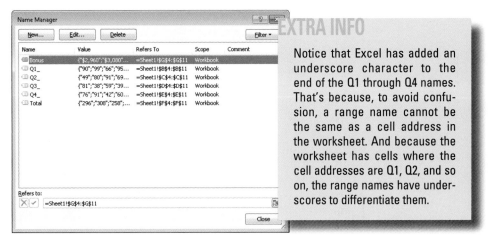

Figure 2-20

EXTRA INFO

Notice that Excel has added an underscore character to the end of the Q1 through Q4 names. That's because, to avoid confusion, a range name cannot be the same as a cell address in the worksheet. And because the worksheet has cells where the cell addresses are Q1, Q2, and so on, the range names have underscores to differentiate them.

4. **Click Close to close the Name Manager dialog box.**

5. **Click cell B15, and in the Name box above column A, type** BonusPer **and press Enter.** See Figure 2-21.

Name box

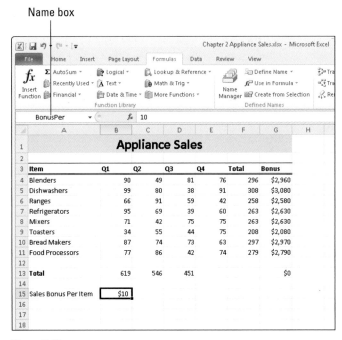

Figure 2-21

6. **Click cell B13 and then choose Formulas⇨Define Name.**

    The New Name dialog box opens.

7. **In the Name text box, type Q1Total, and from the Scope drop-down list, choose Sheet1.**

    Q1 Total applies only to this worksheet. See Figure 2-22.

8. **Click OK to create the name.** The dialog box closes.

9. **Choose Formulas⇨Name Manager.** The Name Manager dialog box reopens.

Figure 2-22

10. **Examine the list of all the named ranges you have created, and then click Close to close the dialog box.**

11. **Save the workbook.**

Leave the workbook open for the next exercise.

Using a named range in a formula

The main reason for naming a range is to refer to it in a formula. You can substitute the range name for the cell addresses in any situation where using a range would be appropriate.

When a range contains multiple cells and you use the name in a formula, Excel treats it as if you had specified the range with the starting and ending cell addresses.

In this exercise, you use range names in formulas.

Files needed: Appliance Sales.xlsx from the preceding exercise

1. **In cells B13, C13, D13, and E13 respectively, enter the following formulas that sum based on the range names (see Figure 2-23):**

    ```
    =SUM(Q1_)
    =SUM(Q2_)
    =SUM(Q3_)
    =SUM(Q4_)
    ```

Range name used in formula

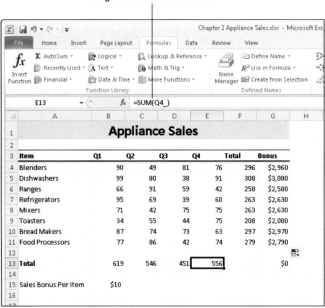

Figure 2-23

2. **In cell G4, edit the formula in the Formula bar as follows:**
   `=F4*BonusPer.`

3. **Select cell G4 and drag the fill handle down to G11, copying the revised formula there.**

TIP

The reference to BonusPer is an absolute reference (as are all named range references), so it copies correctly.

4. **Save the workbook, close it, and exit Excel.**

EXTRA INFO

Range names that refer to multiple cells may produce an error in a formula where a multi-celled range would not be an appropriate argument. For example, if a Sales range referred to B4:B8, the formula `=Sales` would result in an error because no math operation is specified. However, `=SUM(Sales)` would work just fine, as would `=SUM(B4:B8)`.

 *Summing Up*

Here are the key points you learned about in this lesson:

- A formula is a math calculation. Formulas begin with an equal sign.

- The order of precedence determines the order in which math is processed in a formula: first parentheses, then exponentiation, then multiplication and division, and finally, addition and subtraction.

- Formulas can contain cell references that substitute the cell's value for the reference when the formula is calculated.

- When you copy a formula, by default, the cell references in it are relative, so they change based on the new position.

- Placing dollar signs in a cell reference, such as $A$1, makes it an absolute reference so it does not change when the formula is copied.

- A function is a word or string of letters that refers to a certain math calculation. A function starts with an equal sign, followed by the function name and a set of parentheses. Arguments for the function go in the parentheses.

- In functions, you can refer to ranges of cells, such as =SUM(A1:A4).

- If you don't know which function you want, choose Formulas⇨Insert Function.

- The NOW function shows the current date and time; the TODAY function shows the current date.

- SUM sums a range of cells. AVERAGE averages a range of cells.

- MIN shows the smallest number in a range, and MAX shows the largest number in a range.

- COUNT counts the number of cells in a range that contains numeric values. Two related functions are COUNTA, which counts the number of non-empty cells, and COUNTBLANK, which counts the number of empty cells.

- Naming a range enables you to refer to it by a friendly name. Use the commands in the Defined Names group on the Formulas tab.

Try-it-yourself lab

1. **Start Excel and enter at least six numeric values, along with text labels that explain what each value represents.**

   For example, you might enter the calorie counts of the last six food items you ate, or the prices you paid for the last six books you purchased.

2. **Analyze the data you entered using at least four functions.**

   For example, you could sum, average, and count the data. You could find the minimum and maximum values. You could add text labels that clearly identify what each function's result represents.

3. **Save your work as Try It Formulas.xlsx.**

Know this tech talk

absolute reference: A cell reference that does not change if copied to another cell.

argument: A placeholder for a number, text string, or cell reference in a function.

AVERAGE: A function that averages a range of values.

COUNT: A function that counts the number of cells that contain numeric values in a range.

COUNTA: A function that counts the number of non-empty cells in the range.

COUNTBLANK: A function that counts the number of empty cells in the range.

formula: A math calculation performed in a cell.

function: A text name that represents a math calculation, such as SUM or AVERAGE.

MAX: A function that provides the largest number in a range of cells.

MIN: A function that provides the smallest number in a range of cells.

mixed reference: A cell reference in which either the row is absolute and the column is relative, or vice versa.

NOW: A function that reports the current date and time.

relative reference: A cell reference that changes if copied to another cell.

SUM: A function that sums a range of values.

syntax: The rules that govern how arguments are written in a function.

TODAY: A function that reports the current date.

Lesson 3
Formatting and Printing Worksheets

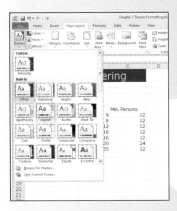

- Resizing rows and columns prevents content from being truncated when an entry is larger than the cell.

- A worksheet background allows a graphic to be used as a backdrop to the worksheet content.

- Headers and footers place repeated information on each page of a printout.

- Customizing a theme enables you to reuse custom font, color, and effect settings easily.

- Formatting a range as a table enables you to apply table styles for quick formatting.

- Creating a new table style enables you to reuse custom table formatting easily.

- Printing a worksheet enables you to share it with others who may not have computer access.

ace it: Plain worksheets aren't that much to look at. A worksheet packed full of rows and columns of numbers is enough to make anyone's eyes glaze over. However, formatting can dramatically improve a worksheet's readability, which, in turn, enables the reader to understand its meaning much more easily.

You can apply formatting at the whole-worksheet level, or on an individual cell level. This lesson focuses on formatting entire worksheets — or at least big chunks of them. You learn how to adjust rows and columns, apply worksheet backgrounds, create headers and footers, and format ranges as tables, complete with preset table formatting. You also learn how to print your work in Excel.

Adjusting Rows and Columns

Each column in a worksheet starts with the same width: 8.43 characters (based on the default font and font size), unless you've changed the default setting. That's approximately seven digits and either one large (such as $) or two small (such as decimal points and commas) symbols.

You can define what the default width setting will be for new worksheets: Choose Home⇨Format⇨Default Width and then fill in the desired default width.

As you enter the actual data into cells, those column widths may no longer be optimal. Data may overflow out of a cell if the width is too narrow, or there may be excess blank space in a column if it's too wide. (Blank space is not always a bad thing, but if you're trying to get all the data to fit on one page, for example, it can be a hindrance.)

In some cases, Excel will make an adjustment for you automatically, as follows:

- ✓ **For column widths:** When you enter numbers in a cell, Excel widens a column as needed to accommodate the longest number in that column, provided you have not manually set a column width for it.

- ✓ **For row heights:** Generally, rows adjust automatically to fit the largest font used in it. You don't have to adjust row heights manually to allow text to fit. You can change the row height if you want, though, to create special effects, such as extra blank space in the layout.

After you manually resize a row's height or a column's width, it won't change its size automatically for you anymore. That's because manual settings override automatic ones.

The units of measurement are different for rows versus columns, by the way. Column width is measured in characters of the default font size. Row height is measured in points. A point is 1/72 of an inch.

Change a row's height

You can resize rows and columns in several ways. You can auto-fit the cells' sizes to the content they contain, manually drag the widths and heights, or enter a precise value for the widths and heights.

In the following exercise, you adjust row heights in a variety of ways.

Files needed: Catering.xlsx

1. **Start Excel, if needed, open Catering.xlsx, and save it as Catering Format.xlsx.**

2. **Click the row header for row 4 to select the entire row and then choose Format⇨Row Height.** The Row Height dialog box opens. Note that the row height is currently set to around 18.75. (Yours may be slightly off from that.) See Figure 3-1.

   The largest font in this row is 14 point, and the additional 4.75 points of height are used for padding. What would happen if you didn't have that extra for padding? The next few steps show this.

3. **Type** 14 **in the Row Height box and click OK.** Notice how the top of the capital letters in row 4 is too close to the cell's upper border now.

4. **Position the mouse pointer between the 4 and 5 row headers, so the pointer turns into a double-headed arrow, and then click and hold the mouse pointer over the divider.** A ScreenTip appears showing the current height.

Figure 3-1

5. **Drag downward until the ScreenTip reads 20.25 points, as shown in Figure 3-2, and then release the mouse button.**

Drag here   See Height setting here

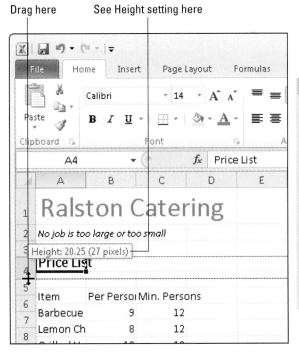

EXTRA INFO

You might not be able to drag to an exact amount because the amount has to match with a whole number of pixels. Depending on your screen resolution, the number of pixels that corresponds to a certain number of points may vary. In Figure 3-2, 27 pixels equal 20.25 points, but that might not be so for you. The same goes in Steps 5 and 7; the amounts may be slightly off depending on your screen resolution.

Figure 3-2

6. **Position the mouse pointer again over the divider between the row 4 and 5 headers, and double-click.** The row height auto-resizes to fit.

7. **Click the row 4 header to select the row, and then right-click anywhere in the row and choose Row Height.** The Row Height dialog box opens again. Notice that its setting is back to somewhere around 18.75.

8. **Click Cancel to close the dialog box.**

Leave the workbook open for the next exercise.

Change a column's width

When content overruns a cell's width, different results occur depending on the type of data it is and whether the cell's column width has been adjusted manually.

In the following exercise, you adjust row heights in a variety of ways.

Files needed: Catering Format.xlsx from the preceding exercise

1. **In Catering Format.xlsx, double-click the divider between columns A and B headers.**

   Column A widens enough that the title in cell A1 fits in the cell. See Figure 3-3. Although that looks okay, it's not optimal because column A appears too wide.

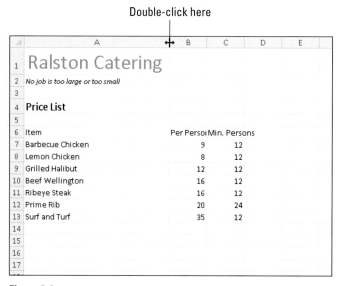

Figure 3-3

2. **Click and drag the divider between columns A and B headers to the left so that the content of cell A7 fits in the cell with a few characters of space to spare.** The content of cell A1 hangs off into cells B1 and C1, but that's okay because they're empty.

3. **Click the column header for column B to select that column, and then choose Home⇨Format⇨AutoFit Column Width.** Column B's width increases to accommodate the longest entry (in cell B6).

4. **Click the column header for column C to select it, and then choose Home⇨Format⇨Column Width.** The Column Width dialog box opens.

5. **Type** 12 **in the dialog box, as shown in Figure 3-4, and then click OK.** The column width changes to exactly 12 characters.

Figure 3-4 shows the worksheet after the column width adjustments.

Figure 3-4

Figure 3-5

6. **Save the changes to the workbook and close it.**

Leave Excel open for the next exercise.

Formatting an Entire Worksheet

In addition to formatting individual cells, you can also apply some types of formatting to the entire sheet. For example, you can apply a worksheet background that appears onscreen and can optionally be set to print, and you can control what text appears in a printout's header and footer areas.

Apply a worksheet background

TIP

You can't set a worksheet background to be a solid color with the Background command. However, you can select the entire worksheet by pressing Ctrl+A and then apply a solid color fill to every cell on that worksheet, creating essentially the same effect as applying a solid-color background.

In the following exercise, you apply a worksheet background.

Files needed: Sheet.xlsx

LINGO

A **worksheet background** is a picture that appears behind the cells. If a cell has no background fill assigned to it, the worksheet background image or color appears as its fill. If the cell already has its own fill, that fill obscures the worksheet background.

1. **Open Sheet.xlsx and then save it as Sheet Formatting.xlsx.**

2. **Choose Page Layout⇨Background.**

   The Sheet Background dialog box opens.

3. **Navigate to the folder containing the data files for this lesson and click Image.jpg.**

   See Figure 3-6.

4. **Click the Insert button.**

   The image appears as the worksheet background. See Figure 3-7.

5. **Choose Page Layout⇨Delete Background, and then choose Page Layout⇨Background.**

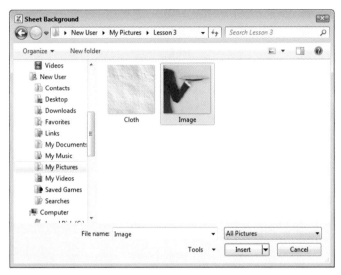

Figure 3-6

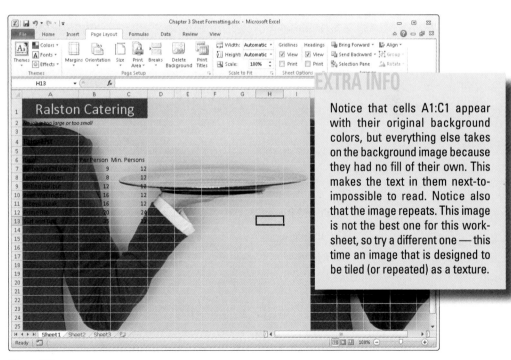

EXTRA INFO

Notice that cells A1:C1 appear with their original background colors, but everything else takes on the background image because they had no fill of their own. This makes the text in them next-to-impossible to read. Notice also that the image repeats. This image is not the best one for this worksheet, so try a different one — this time an image that is designed to be tiled (or repeated) as a texture.

Figure 3-7

6. **In the folder containing the data files for this lesson, click Cloth.jpg and then click the Insert button.**

This image is more suitable for a background because it tiles attractively. See Figure 3-8.

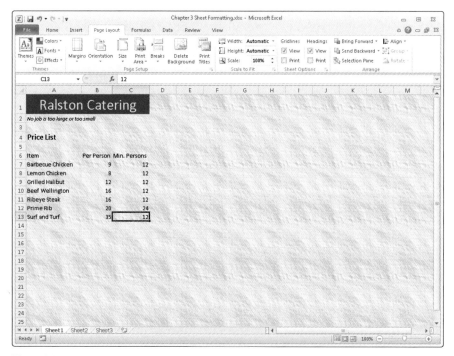

Figure 3-8

7. **Choose File⇨Print and examine the print preview.**

Notice that the background will not print.

8. **Press Esc to return to normal viewing and save the workbook.**

Leave the workbook open for the next exercise.

Create a header or footer

TIP

In Excel 2010, by default there is no header or footer text; you must enter any text or codes you want. This is a change from some earlier versions of Excel, which printed the sheet name and a page number by default in the footer.

In the following exercise, you create a header and footer that prints the company name and a page number.

Files needed: Sheet Formatting.xlsx from the preceding exercise

LINGO

If you plan to print your worksheet, you might want to set up a **header** and/or **footer**, which are lines of information that repeat at the top and bottom of each page. These lines can contain any text you want plus codes that print page numbers, the current date and time, or other information.

1. **In Sheet Formatting.xlsx, choose Insert⇨Header & Footer. Then view changes to Page Layout view, so you can see the Header and Footer sections.** The insertion point moves to the center section of the header.

2. **Type** Ralston Catering Price List **in the center section of the header, as shown in Figure 3-9.**

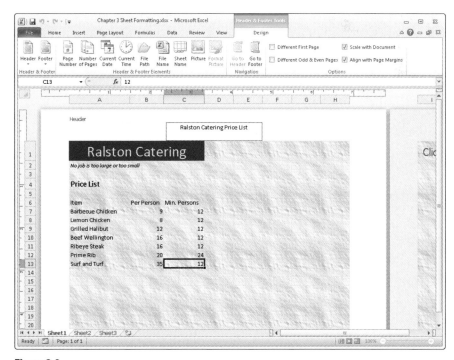

Figure 3-9

3. **Choose Header & Footer Tools Design⇨Go to Footer. The display jumps down to the footer, and you click in the right section of the footer to move the insertion point there.**

4. **Choose Header & Footer Tools Design⇨Page Number.** The &[Page] code appears.

5. **Press the spacebar, type of, and press the spacebar again.**

6. **Choose Header & Footer Tools Design⇨Number of Pages.** The &[Pages] code appears there. See Figure 3-10.

Figure 3-10

7. **Click in the middle section of the footer to move the insertion point away from the page number codes.** They change to appear as the actual page numbers: 1 of 1.

8. **Choose Header & Footer Tools Design⇨Go to Header to return to the top of the page and then click in the left section of the header to move the insertion point there.**

9. **Choose Header & Footer Tools Design⇨File Name.** The &[File] code appears. See Figure 3-11.

Figure 3-11

10. **Click in the right section of the header to move the insertion point away from the filename code.** The actual filename appears in the header.

For more practice, examine the rest of the tools on the Header & Footer Tools Design tab on the Ribbon, and see whether you can determine what each might be used for. Consult the Help system as needed.

11. **Choose File⇨Print and examine the print preview. Notice that the header and footer appear on the page. Press Esc to leave Backstage view without printing.**

12. **Save your changes and close the workbook.**

Leave Excel open for the next exercise.

Using Theme Formatting

Themes and table styles are two ways of applying formatting to an entire worksheet or data range at once. Each one can be used with preset settings or customized for an individual look. For each one, you can then save your custom formatting to reuse in other workbooks and tables.

Apply a workbook theme

Themes are standard across most of the Office applications (including Word, Excel, and PowerPoint), so you can standardize your formatting across all the documents you create in your office.

LINGO

Themes are formatting presets that you can apply to entire worksheets.

In the following exercise, you apply a theme and a color theme.

Files needed: Theme.xlsx

1. **Open Theme.xlsx and save it as Theme Formatting.xlsx.**

2. **Choose Page Layout⇨Themes.** A list of themes appears. See Figure 3-12.

3. **Choose the Aspect theme to apply it.** Notice that the color of the fill behind cells A1:C1 changes, as do the fonts. See Figure 3-13.

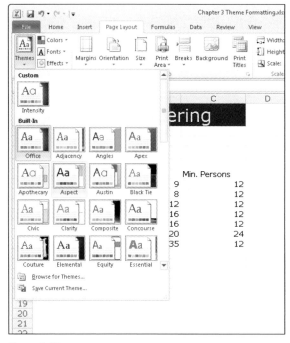

Figure 3-12

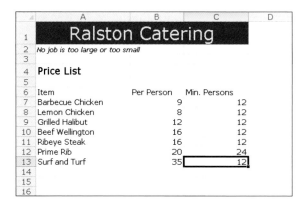

Figure 3-13

4. **Choose Page Layout⇨Colors.** A list of color themes appears. See Figure 3-14.

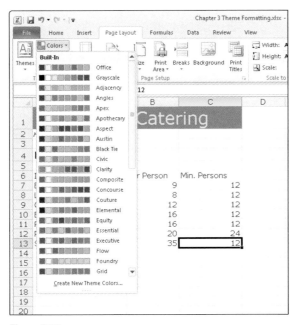

Figure 3-14

5. **Choose Clarity.** The colors change to a red background and yellow letters in cells A1:C1.

6. **Save the workbook.**

Leave the workbook open for the next exercise.

Customize a theme

If none of the themes suit your needs, you may want to create your own theme. You can do this by choosing the colors, fonts, and effects that you want (from the Page Layout tab) and then saving the unique combination you chose as a new theme.

In this exercise, you create a custom theme.

Files needed: Theme Formatting.xlsx from preceding exercise

1. **Choose Page Layout⇨Colors and then choose Austin from the list of color themes that appears.** See Figure 3-15.

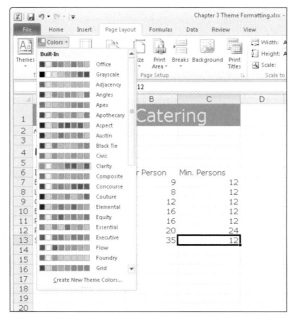

Figure 3-15

TIP

You can also create a custom theme by choosing one of the existing themes from the Theme button and then customizing it by selecting a different set of colors, fonts, or effects.

2. **Choose Page Layout⇨Fonts and then choose Apothecary from the list of font themes that appears.** See Figure 3-16.

3. **Choose Page Layout⇨Effects and then choose Elemental from the list of effect themes that appears.**

4. **Choose Page Layout⇨Themes⇨Save Current Theme.** The Save Current Theme dialog box opens.

5. **In the File Name box, type** Intensity, **as shown in Figure 3-17, and then click Save to save the new theme.**

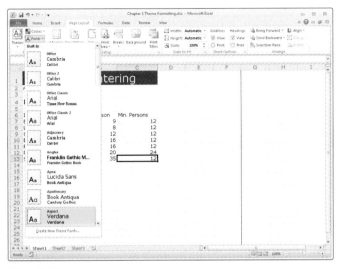

Figure 3-16

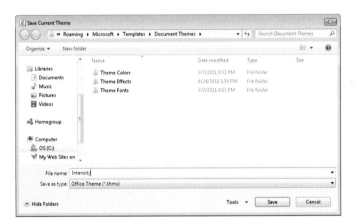

Figure 3-17

Themes are stored in a common location for all Office applications, so you can reuse your custom theme in Word and PowerPoint.

6. **Choose Page Layout➪Themes. Notice that your new theme appears at the top of the list.**

7. **Click away from the menu to close it without making a selection.**

8. **Save the workbook.**

Leave the workbook open for the next exercise.

Format a range as a table

You can format certain ranges as tables in Excel, which not only enables you to apply formatting presets more easily, but also gives the range special properties that make it easier to search and sort them. You learn more about working with tables in Lesson 5, but this lesson shows you how to convert a range to a table purely for formatting purposes.

LINGO

A **table,** in the context of an Excel worksheet, is a range that has been marked as a single logical unit for data storage and retrieval.

In this exercise, you convert a range to a table and apply table style formatting.

Files needed: Theme Formatting.xlsx from the preceding exercise

1. **In Theme Formatting.xlsx, select cells A6:C13 and then choose Home➪Format as Table.** A gallery of formatting styles appears. See Figure 3-18.

2. **Click the Table Style Medium 9 style.** The Format as Table dialog box opens, with the range already filled in from the selection you made in Step 1. See Figure 3-19.

3. **Click OK.** The range is converted to a table and the style is applied.

4. **Click the Table Tools Design tab.** On this tab are commands for formatting that can be used only on ranges that are defined as tables.

5. **Deselect the Banded Rows check box.** The alternate-row color banding is removed. Re-select the check box to restore the banding.

6. **Save the workbook.**

Leave the workbook open for the next exercise.

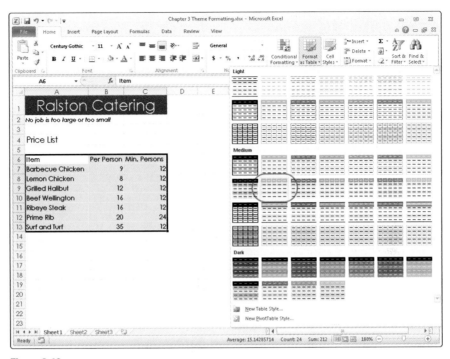

Figure 3-18

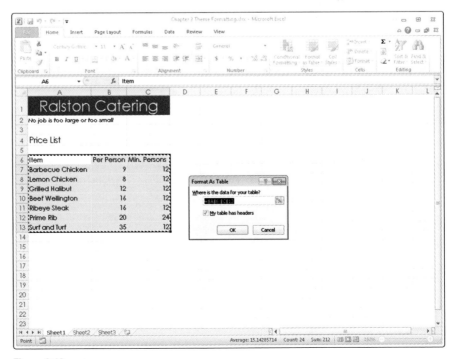

Figure 3-19

Create a custom table style

You can rely on the standard table styles that Excel provides, or you can customize a table style and then save it as a new style that you can then apply to other ranges.

In this exercise, you create a custom table style.

Files needed: Theme Formatting.xlsx from the preceding exercise

1. **Choose Home⇨Format as Table⇨New Table Style.** The New Table Quick Style dialog box opens.
2. **In the Name box, replace the default name with Custom Table 1.**
3. **In the Table Element list, select Header Row.** See Figure 3-20.

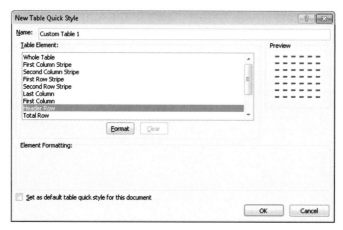

Figure 3-20

4. **Click the Format button.** The Format Cells dialog box opens.
5. **Click the Fill tab and then click the fifth square (dark green) in the next-to-the-last row of colors.** See Figure 3-21.
6. **Click the Font tab; then open the Color drop-down list and choose the white square in the Theme Colors section.** See Figure 3-22.
7. **Click OK to return to the new Table Quick Style dialog box and then click OK to create the new table style.**

TIP

Creating a new table style does not automatically apply it to the selected range, so you must apply the style.

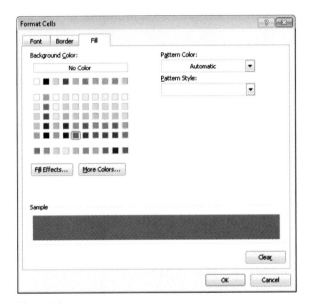

Figure 3-21

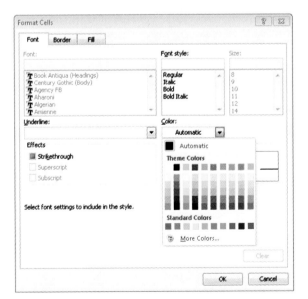

Figure 3-22

8. **Select cells A6:C13 and then choose Home⇨Format as Table; in the Custom section at the top of the menu, select the new style you just created.** See Figure 3-23.

Custom style

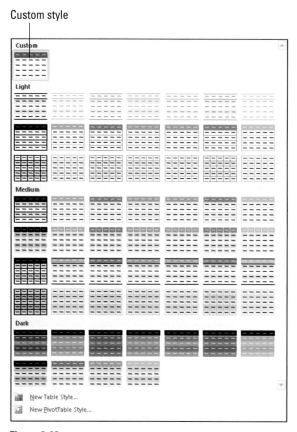

Figure 3-23

9. **Save the workbook.**

Leave the workbook open for the next exercise.

Printing Worksheets

You can print your work in Excel on paper, to share with people who may not have computer access, or to pass out as handouts at meetings and events. You can print quick-and-easy with the default settings or customize the settings to fit your needs.

Preview and print the active worksheet

By default, when you print, Excel prints the entire active worksheet — that is, whichever worksheet is displayed or selected at the moment. But Excel also gives you other printing options:

- **Print multiple worksheets:** If more than one worksheet is selected (for example, if you have more than one worksheet tab selected at the bottom of the Excel window), all selected worksheets are included in the printed version. As an alternative, you can print all the worksheets in the workbook.

- **Print selected cells or ranges:** You can choose to print only selected cells, or you can define a print range and print only that range (regardless of what cells happen to be selected).

In Excel 2010, Print Preview is built into Backstage view, so you see a preview of the printout at the same place where you change the print settings.

In this exercise, you preview and print a worksheet.

Files needed: Theme Formatting.xlsx from the preceding exercise

1. **Choose File⇨Print.**

   The Print settings appear, along with a preview of the printout. See Figure 3-24.

2. **In the Copies box, click the up-increment arrow to change the value to 2.**

3. **Click the Print button to send the job to the printer.**

Leave the workbook open for the next exercise.

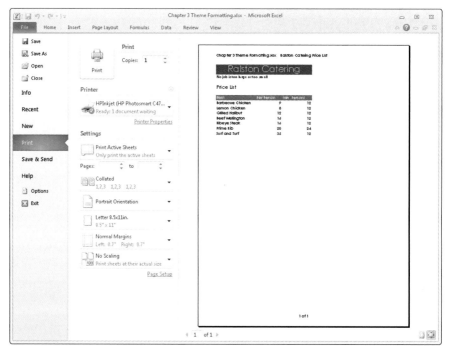

Figure 3-24

Set and use a print range

There are two ways to print only a certain range of cells on the active worksheet. If you want to select a certain range for a one-time print job, you can just select them and then choose to print only the selection. If you want the same cells (only) to print each time you print this worksheet in the future too, you can select them as a print range, and Excel remembers them.

In this exercise, you print only certain cells using two methods.

Files needed: Theme Formatting.xlsx from the preceding exercise

1. **Select the range A6:C13 and then choose File⇨Print.**

2. **Click the Print Active Sheets button, and then choose Print Selection from the menu that appears.** See Figure 3-25.

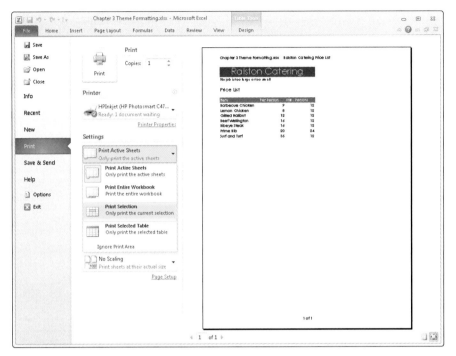

Figure 3-25

> 3. **Click Print.** A copy prints that contains only the range you specified.
>
> 4. **Choose Page Layout⇨Print Area ⇨Set Print Area.** See Figure 3-26.

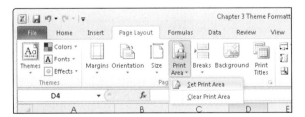

Figure 3-26

> 5. **Click away from the selected range to deselect it and then choose File⇨Print.**
>
> 6. **Examine the preview of the print job.** See Figure 3-27.

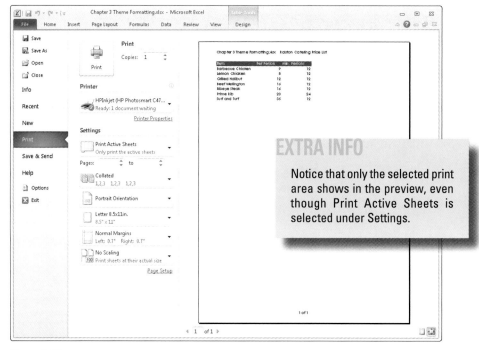

Figure 3-27

7. Click the Home tab to close Backstage view.

8. Choose Page Layout⇨Print Area⇨Clear Print Area.

9. Save the workbook.

Leave the workbook open for the next exercise.

Adjust the page size, orientation, and margins while printing

You can set the page size, orientation, and margins at any time from the Page Layout tab. Doing so permanently changes those settings. If you want to change any of those settings only for one particular print job, though, you can change them from Backstage view, as part of the printing options. When you change the settings there, they don't "stick." The next time you open and work with the workbook, the settings go back to what they were before.

In this exercise, you change the page size, orientation, and margins for a one-time print job.

Files needed: Theme Formatting.xlsx from the preceding exercise

1. **Choose File⇨Print.**

2. **Click the Portrait Orientation button to open a menu and choose Landscape Orientation.**

   See Figure 3-28. The print preview will change to show the new orientation.

Figure 3-28

3. **Click the Letter 8.5x11in. button to open a menu and choose 4x6in.**

   See Figure 3-29.

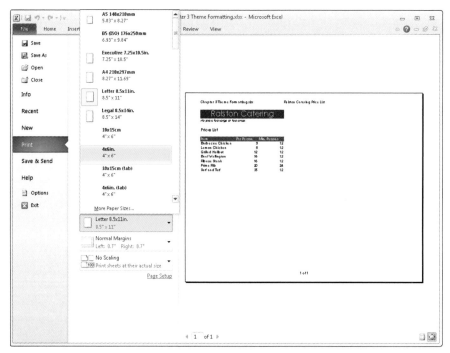

Figure 3-29

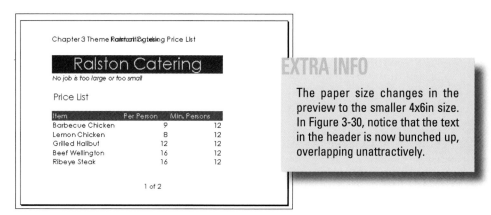

Figure 3-30

EXTRA INFO

The paper size changes in the preview to the smaller 4x6in size. In Figure 3-30, notice that the text in the header is now bunched up, overlapping unattractively.

4. **Click the Page Setup hyperlink.**

   The Page Setup dialog box opens.

5. **Click the Header/Footer tab and then click the Custom Header button.**

   The Header dialog box opens. See Figure 3-31.

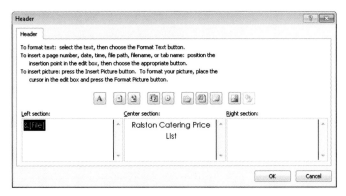

Figure 3-31

6. **Delete the code in the Left Section box, click OK to close the Header dialog box, and then click OK to close the Page Setup dialog box.**

   The entire spreadsheet does not fit on the page, so try two ways to make it fit.

7. **Click the Normal Margins button and choose Narrow Margins.**

   This helps fit more text on the first page, but it doesn't all fit.

8. **Click the No Scaling button, and choose Fit Sheet on One Page.**

   See Figure 3-32. Now it all fits.

9. **Click Print to print the worksheet.**

10. **Save the workbook and close it.**

Exit Excel.

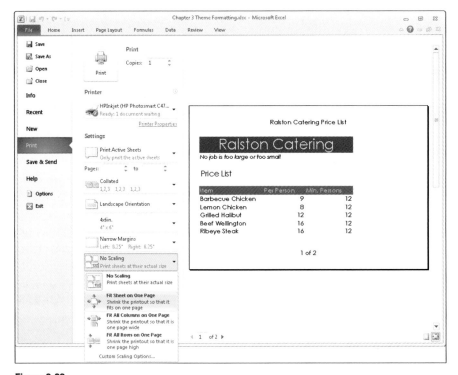

Figure 3-32

 # Summing Up

Here are the key points you learned about in this lesson:

- You can adjust the sizes of rows and columns by dragging the dividers between row or column headers, or by double-clicking the dividers to auto-size.

- To add a background to a worksheet, choose Page Layout⇨Background.

- Choose Insert⇨Header & Footer to create headers and footers that repeat on each page of a printout.

- Themes standardize the fonts, colors, and effects across multiple workbooks. To apply a theme, choose Page Layout⇨Theme.

- Formatting a range as a table enables you to apply the table formatting presets from the Home tab. It also has some other benefits, which you learn about in Lesson 5.

- You can format the text in a cell in much the same way as in Word: Use the controls in the Font group on the Home tab, or on the Mini Toolbar.

Try-it-yourself lab

1. Start Excel, open the file Try It Table.xlsx, and save it as Try It Table Final.xlsx.

2. Adjust the column widths so that no text is truncated.

3. Format cells A10:F12 as a table, using your choice of table styles.

4. In the footer of the worksheet, in the center, place the text Thank You for Your Business. Then return to Normal view.

5. Apply the Angles theme.

6. Print one copy of the worksheet in Landscape orientation.

7. Save the workbook and close Excel.

Know this tech talk

footer: Repeated text at the bottom of each page of a printout.

header: Repeated text at the top of each page of a printout.

print range: A defined range of cells that prints whenever the active worksheet is printed, rather than the entire worksheet printing.

table: In Excel, a range that has been marked as a single logical unit for data storage and retrieval.

theme: A formatting preset that you can apply to an entire worksheet, consisting of fonts, colors, and effects.

worksheet background: A picture that appears behind the cells of a worksheet.

Lesson 4
Formatting Data

- Applying a background fill and outline to a cell makes it stand out.

- Formatting the text in a cell makes it more attractive and readable.

- Wrapping text in a cell enables a cell's height to expand as needed to accommodate more content.

- Aligning text in a cell in ways different from the default allows flexibility in worksheet design.

- Applying number formats gives context to a number by presenting it as currency, a percentage, or some other type.

- Conditional formatting formats the text in a cell differently depending on its content.

In this lesson, you learn a variety of techniques for formatting the data in individual cells of a worksheet —— and for formatting the cells themselves. You can use these techniques to improve your own worksheets and to quickly make plain worksheets that you receive from someone else more readable. You learn how to change the row and column sizes, how to format the text in cells, and how to apply fill formatting to the cells themselves. You also learn how to create conditional formatting rules that change the way the data is formatted depending on its value.

Formatting Cells

By modifying cell fill and border, you can make a worksheet much easier to read and interpret. For example, you could make the background of the cell that contains a grand total a different color from the rest, and place a thick border around it to draw attention to it. Borders can also be used to create dividing lines between certain rows and columns, and alternate-row shading within a dense list of data can help the eye follow a long row across the page.

LINGO

Cells can have formatting assigned to them, independently of the formatting assigned to their content. Each cell has two main formatting properties: its **fill** (that is, its inner color) and its **border** (that is, the outline around it). By default, cell borders are set to No Border.

Apply a fill to a cell or range

A background fill can be any solid color, or a gradient or pattern. You can choose from the theme colors or some fixed standard colors, or open a Color dialog box in which you can select from many other colors or specify a color by number.

In this exercise, you fill cells with theme colors, standard colors, and custom colors.

Files needed: Catering.xlsx

1. **Open Catering.xlsx and save it as Catering Final.xlsx.**

2. **Select cells A6:C6; then from the Home tab, click the down arrow to the right of the Fill Color button, opening a color palette.**

3. **Click the bright red square under Standard Colors.** See Figure 4-1.

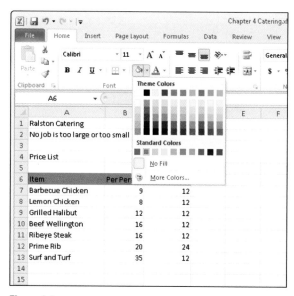

Figure 4-1

For more practice, before you click the red square in Step 3, point at several other colors to preview them on the selected range behind the open palette.

4. **Click the arrow to the right of the Fill Color button again, and in the Theme Colors section, choose Olive Green, Accent 3, Darker 25%. Point to a color to see a ScreenTip showing its name.**

> To determine a color's name, point the mouse at it and read the ScreenTip.

5. **Click the arrow to the right of the Fill Color button again, and choose More Colors.**

6. **Click the Custom tab if it's not already selected, and in the Color Model drop-down list, choose RGB if it's not already selected.**

7. **Enter the following values, as shown in Figure 4-2: Red 255, Green 204, and Blue 196.**

8. **Click OK to accept the new custom color and then save the changes to the workbook.**

Leave the workbook open for the next exercise.

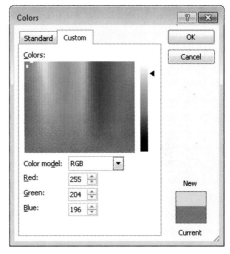

Figure 4-2

Format a cell's border

Borders are a bit more complex than fills because not only can they have a color, but also a style (such as dotted or dashed) and a weight (or thickness). You can also place a border around individual sides of a cell or range of cells.

In this exercise, you apply several types of borders to cells, using several methods.

Files needed: Catering Final.xlsx from the preceding exercise

LINGO

Do not confuse borders with gridlines. The **gridlines** are the edges of the cells that you see by default onscreen in gray. They don't print. A **border** is an outline that you specifically apply to a cell; it does print. You can turn off the onscreen display of gridlines on the View tab.

1. In Catering Final.xlsx, select cells A1:C1.

2. From the Home tab, click the down arrow to the right of the Border button and choose Thick Bottom Border, which is one of several presets in the middle of the menu, as shown in Figure 4-3.

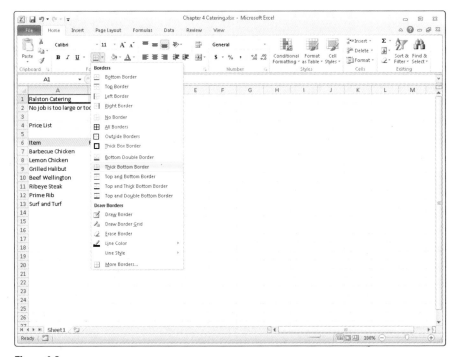

Figure 4-3

3. Click away from the selection so you can see the new line.

4. From the Home tab, click the down arrow to the right of the Border button and choose Line Color to open a color palette.

5. Click Dark Red from the Standard Colors section.

   See Figure 4-4. The menu closes, and the mouse pointer turns into a pencil symbol.

6. Click the down arrow to the right of the Border button again, choose Line Style, and choose a dashed line style.

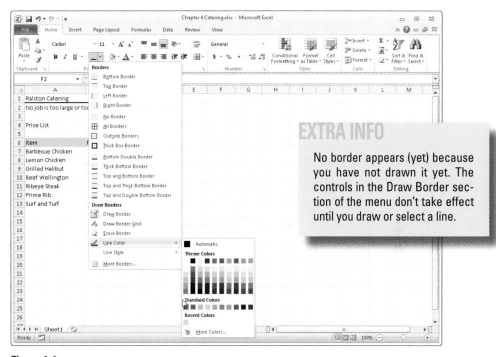

Figure 4-4

7. **Drag to draw a line under cell A4, and another one above cell A4. Then press the Esc key to turn off the pencil symbol.**

   See Figure 4-5.

8. **Select the range A6:C13, click the down arrow to the right of the Border button, and choose All Borders.**

   The same dashed dark red border is applied to all borders of all cells in the selected range.

9. **Press Ctrl+Z to undo the last action.**

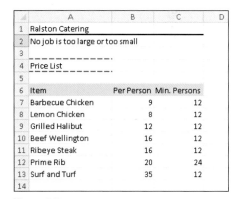

	A	B	C	D
1	Ralston Catering			
2	No job is too large or too small			
3				
4	Price List			
5				
6	Item	Per Person	Min. Persons	
7	Barbecue Chicken	9	12	
8	Lemon Chicken	8	12	
9	Grilled Halibut	12	12	
10	Beef Wellington	16	12	
11	Ribeye Steak	16	12	
12	Prime Rib	20	24	
13	Surf and Turf	35	12	
14				

Figure 4-5

EXTRA INFO

No border appears (yet) because you have not drawn it yet. The controls in the Draw Border section of the menu don't take effect until you draw or select a line.

10. **Click the down arrow to the right of the Border button and choose More Borders.**

The Format Cells dialog box opens with the Border tab displayed.

11. **In the Style section, click the thinnest solid line (the bottom line in the left column).**

12. **Open the Color drop-down list and click the bright red square under Standard Colors.**

13. **Click the Outline button and borders appear in the preview area around the outside of the selection.**

14. **Click the Inside button and borders appear in the preview area around the inner borders of the selection.**

Figure 4-6 shows the completed dialog box.

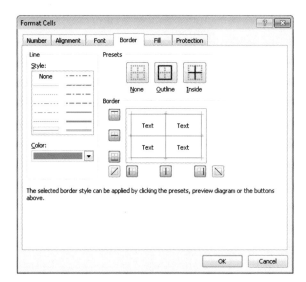

Figure 4-6

15. **Click OK to apply the border to the cells.**

16. **Click the down arrow to the right of the Border button and choose Erase Border.**

The mouse pointer turns into an eraser symbol.

17. **Click the borders above and below cell A4 to erase them.**

18. **Press the Esc key to turn off the eraser cursor on the mouse pointer.**

Figure 4-7 shows the completed worksheet.

19. **Save the changes to the workbook.**

Leave the workbook open for the next exercise.

	A	B	C	D
1	Ralston Catering			
2	No job is too large or too small			
3				
4	Price List			
5				
6	Item	Per Person	Min. Persons	
7	Barbecue Chicken	9	12	
8	Lemon Chicken	8	12	
9	Grilled Halibut	12	12	
10	Beef Wellington	16	12	
11	Ribeye Steak	16	12	
12	Prime Rib	20	24	
13	Surf and Turf	35	12	
14				
15				

Figure 4-7

Formatting Cell Content

In addition to formatting the cell itself, you can also format its content. This can include applying text formatting (such as font, size, color, and effect) much as you do in Word. You can also wrap text in the cell to multiple lines when it's too long to fit on one row, set the vertical and horizontal alignment within a cell, format numbers in different ways (such as currency or percentage), and apply cell styles that provide different preset combinations of the previously mentioned types of formatting.

When formatting cell contents, in addition to the Ribbon-based methods that the following exercises use, you can also use the Mini Toolbar. Right-click the selected cell(s) to make it appear, and then select commands from the Mini Toolbar rather than from the Home tab on the Ribbon, if you prefer.

Change font and font size

Font and font size are controlled with their respective drop-down lists on the Home tab, or from the Mini Toolbar.

If you want to format a worksheet using themes (on the Page Layout tab), as you learn in Lesson 3, the fonts in the theme will not be applied if you have manually changed to different fonts. To get back to using the defaults so the theme font changes will apply, choose a font from the Theme Fonts section of the Font drop-down list.

In the following exercise, you improve a worksheet's appearance by changing some fonts and sizes.

Files needed: Catering Final.xlsx from the preceding exercise

1. **In Catering Final.xlsx, select cell A1. Then from the Home tab, choose Aharoni from the Font drop-down list.**

   See Figure 4-8. The font is applied to the text in cell A1.

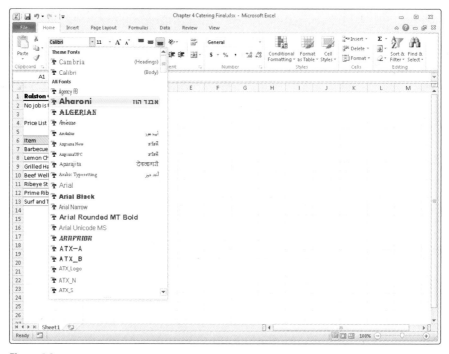

Figure 4-8

For more practice, change the font several more times, each time choosing a different font. You can also try changing it with the Mini Toolbar: Right-click cell A1 and then open the Font drop-down list from the Mini Toolbar that appears.

2. **With A1 still selected, from the Home tab, choose 24 from the Font Size drop-down list.**

   See Figure 4-9. The font size changes to 24-point.

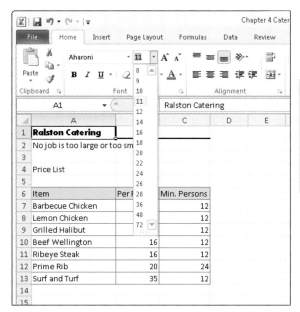

Figure 4-9

EXTRA INFO

Notice that the Font Size drop-down list does not increment by 1 point at the larger sizes. There are some fairly large gaps, such as the one between 28 and 36 points.

3. **Choose Home⇨Increase Font Size and the font goes up one size (2 points).**

   The new size reported in the Font Size box on the Home tab is 26 point.

4. **Click in the Font Size box on the Home tab, moving the insertion point into it, and type** 30, **replacing the current entry. Press Enter to apply the new font size to cell A1.**

   See Figure 4-10.

TIP

When you manually type in the font size, as in Step 4, you can use any size you want, with increments as small as 1/10th of a point.

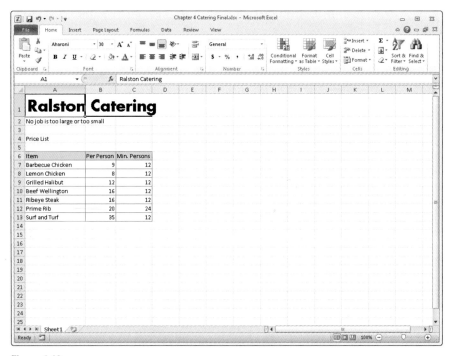

Figure 4-10

5. Save the changes to the workbook.

Leave the workbook open for the next exercise.

Change font color and attributes

Text color and attributes can impact the readability and attractiveness of a worksheet. As with font and size changes, you can apply color and attributes either from the Home tab, or from the Mini Toolbar that appears when you right-click the selected cell(s). You can also set text formatting from the Font tab of the Format Cells dialog box.

LINGO

Attributes include a variety of text effects, including bold and italic (which when together are sometimes referred to as a **font style**), underlining, strikethrough, superscript, and subscript.

In the following exercise, you improve the look of a worksheet by applying font colors and attributes.

Files needed: Catering Final.xlsx from the preceding exercise

1. **In Catering Final.xlsx, select cell A1. Then from the Home tab, click the down arrow to the right of the Font Color button to open its palette.**

2. **In the Theme Colors section of the palette, click Orange, Accent 6, changing to a theme color.**

   See Figure 4-11. You can point to a color on the palette to see a ScreenTip telling its name.

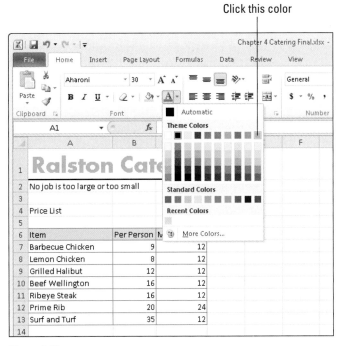

Figure 4-11

3. **Right-click cell A4, opening the Mini Toolbar, as shown in Figure 4-12. On the toolbar, click the down arrow to the right of the Font Color button, and click Orange, Accent 6, Darker 50%.**

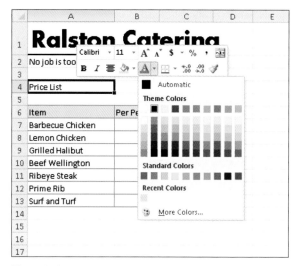

Figure 4-12

4. Choose Home⇨Bold. The text in cell A4 bolds. Choose Home⇨Italic.

The text in cell A4 italicizes.

You can also use keyboard shortcuts for Bold (Ctrl+B), Italic (Ctrl+I), and Underline (Ctrl+U).

5. Click the dialog box launcher in the Font group, opening the Font tab of the Format Cells dialog box (see Figure 4-13).

6. Choose Double from the Underline drop-down list and click OK.

The text in cell A4 is double-underlined.

The Underline button on the Home tab has a drop-down list with different underline styles, so you don't always have to open the Format Cells dialog box when you want a non-standard underline. However, the Underline drop-down list has only two choices: Underline and Double Underline. The drop-down list in the dialog box has some other choices too, such as Single Accounting and Double Accounting.

7. Save the workbook.

Leave the workbook open for the next exercise.

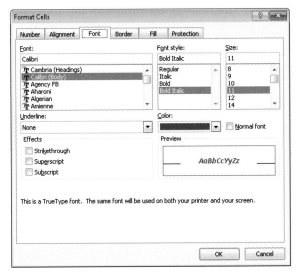

Figure 4-13

Wrap text in a cell

When a cell's entry is too wide for the cell, you can widen the cell, as you learn in Lesson 3. Or you can allow the cell's content to wrap to additional lines in the cell. The cell gets taller (automatically), but retains its width.

In the following exercise, you wrap text in cells so you can decrease column widths without truncating any entries.

Files needed: Catering Final.xlsx from the preceding exercise

EXTRA INFO

You can manually break the text to the next line in a cell by pressing Alt+Enter where you want the break to occur, but it's easier to use the automatic method shown in the following exercise.

1. **In Catering Final.xlsx, select the range B6:C6 and then choose Home⇨ Wrap Text (see Figure 4-14).**

    Nothing changes in the worksheet because the columns are wide enough that the text in those cells doesn't need to wrap to the next line.

Wrap Text button

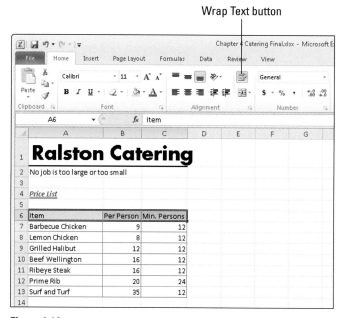

Figure 4-14

2. **With B6:C6 still selected, choose Home⇨ Format⇨Column Width. The Column Width dialog box opens (see Figure 4-15).**

3. **Type** 8 **and click OK. The column width changes for columns B and C to 8 characters.**

    Because the row height for row 6 has previously been adjusted manually, it no longer automatically adjusts to the new content, so the additional wrapped lines may be truncated. That makes it necessary to readjust the row height in the next step. You might not have to do that on your own worksheets.

Figure 4-15

4. **Point to the divider between the headers for rows 6 and 7 and double-click, auto-fitting the row height for row 6 to the wrapped content.**

    See Figure 4-16 for the final result.

	A	B	C	D	E
1	**Ralston Catering**				
2	No job is too large or too small				
3					
4	*Price List*				
5					
6	Item	Per Person	Min. Persons		
7	Barbecue Chicken	9	12		
8	Lemon Chicken	8	12		
9	Grilled Halibut	12	12		
10	Beef Wellington	16	12		
11	Ribeye Steak	16	12		
12	Prime Rib	20	24		
13	Surf and Turf	35	12		
14					
15					

Figure 4-16

PRACTICE

For more practice, select cell A2 and click the Wrap Text button to see an example of a cell where the height adjusts automatically when you wrap the text. That's because no previous manual row height adjustment was made to row 2. Click Wrap Text again to toggle the text wrapping off when finished experimenting with row 2.

5. Save the workbook.

Leave the workbook open for the next exercise.

Align text in a cell

By default, text in a cell lines horizontally to the left and vertically to the bottom. You can see this if you look at Figure 4-16, where the word *Item* is in the bottom-left corner of cell A6. Numbers align horizontally to the right, as you can see in cells B7:C13.

Each cell can have any of the following horizontal alignments. Some of them are available only via the Format Cells dialog box:

- ✔ **General:** The default setting. Left-aligns text, and right-aligns numbers.

- ✔ **Left (Indent):** Aligns the content to the left, regardless of its type. You can optionally specify an amount of indentation from the left side.

- ✔ **Center:** Centers the entry evenly between the left and right sides of the cell.

- ✔ **Right (Indent):** Aligns the content to the right, regardless of its type. You can optionally specify an amount of indentation from the right side.

- ✔ **Fill:** Repeats the value in the cell so that the cell is completely filled. For example, if you enter X, the cell is filled with as many Xs as it takes to stretch the width of the column.

- ✔ **Justify:** Applicable only in a cell that uses Text Wrap. On every line except the last one, adds space between words as needed so the entry stretches across the entire width of the column. The last line is left-aligned.

- ✔ **Center Across Selection:** Applicable only when you select multiple cells before you apply it, this setting centers the content of the top-left cell in the selected range across the selection.

- ✔ **Distributed (Indent):** Adds space between words as needed so the entry stretches across the entire width of the column. This is different from Justify in that it applies to all lines, so its effect can be seen on cells that are not word-wrapped. You can optionally specify an amount of indent.

Vertical alignment is simpler; it can only be set to Top, Middle, Bottom, Justify, or Distributed. Justify and Distributed both spread out a multi-line entry to align at both the bottom and top of a cell. The difference between them is that when applied to a single-line entry, Justify top-aligns the content, whereas Distributed center-aligns the content.

In the following exercise, you set the vertical and horizontal alignment for content in cells.

Files needed: Catering Final.xlsx from the preceding exercise

1. **In Catering Final.xlsx, select cell A6.**

2. **Choose Home⇨Center. The text is horizontally centered. Choose Home⇨Middle Align. The text is vertically centered.** See Figure 4-17.

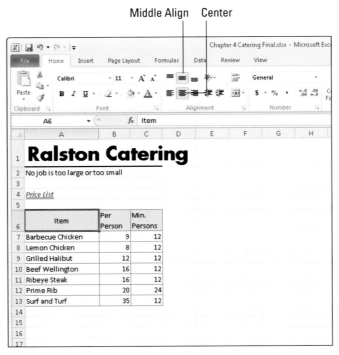

Figure 4-17

3. **Select the range A7:A13 and from the Home tab, click the Alignment group's dialog box launcher.**

    The Format Cells dialog box opens with the Alignment tab displayed.

4. **Choose Left (Indent) from the Horizontal drop-down list.**

5. **In the Indent box, click the up-increment arrow once to add a one-character indentation.**

6. **Choose Center from the Vertical drop-down list.**

    Figure 4-18 shows the completed dialog box.

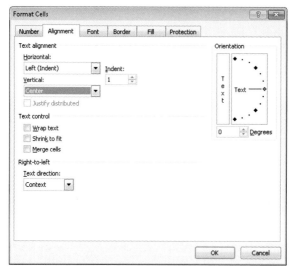

Figure 4-18

7. Click OK.

The alignments are applied, but you don't really notice a difference in the vertical alignments because the cell heights are auto-fitted. Vertical alignment becomes apparent only in cells with extra vertical space, such as cell A6.

For even more practice, set cell A2 to Wrap Text, and then apply the various horizontal and vertical Justify and Distribute settings to it to experiment with their differences.

8. Select the range A1:D1, and choose Home⇨Merge & Center.

This command simultaneously merges the selected cells into one unit, places the text from the leftmost cell in the range (cell A1) in that unit, and sets the horizontal alignment to Center Across Selection. See Figure 4-19.

Merge and Center button

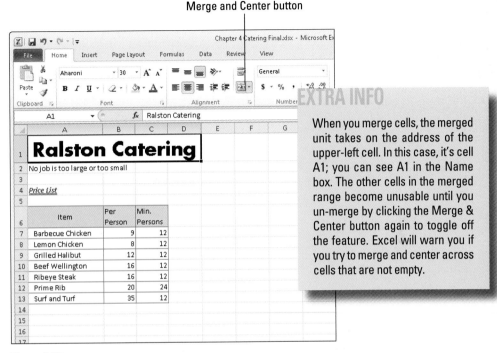

Figure 4-19

EXTRA INFO

When you merge cells, the merged unit takes on the address of the upper-left cell. In this case, it's cell A1; you can see A1 in the Name box. The other cells in the merged range become unusable until you un-merge by clicking the Merge & Center button again to toggle off the feature. Excel will warn you if you try to merge and center across cells that are not empty.

9. **Save the workbook.**

Leave the workbook open for the next exercise.

Apply cell styles

In the following exercise, you apply cell styles, and you create and apply your own custom cell style.

Files needed: Catering Final.xlsx from the preceding exercise

LINGO

Cell styles are formatting presets you can apply to cells. You can use any of the default presets that Excel provides, or you can create your own. Creating your own cell styles can help you format a worksheet more quickly when there is a lot of repetitive formatting to be done.

1. **In Catering Final.xlsx, click cell A4, choose Home⇨Cell Styles to open the gallery of cell style presets, and click Heading 1, as shown in Figure 4-20.**

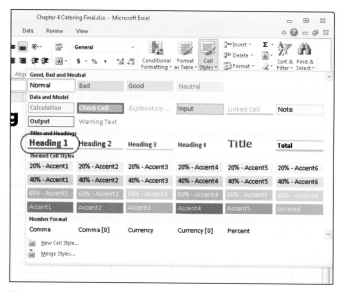

Figure 4-20

2. **Click the Undo button on the Quick Access Toolbar, or press Ctrl+Z, to undo the style application.**

3. **Choose Home⇨Cell Styles⇨New Cell Style to open the Style dialog box.**

When you create a new cell style, you base it on an example, so you must select a cell that already contains the formatting you want before issuing the command.

4. **In the Name box, type** Major Heading. **Clear all the check boxes in the dialog box except Font, as shown in Figure 4-21. Then click OK.**

5. **Click in cell A15 and type**
Setup Costs, **and then choose**
Home➪Cell Styles➪Major
Heading.

You find the Major Heading style
at the top of the gallery, in the
Custom section. The custom
style is applied to cell A15.

6. **Save the workbook.**

Leave the workbook open for the next
exercise.

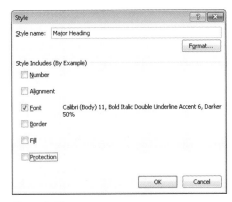

Figure 4-21

Formatting Numbers

You can apply number formats to cells to
specify how numeric data will display. The
major formatting types that number formats
apply are

✔ The helper characters (if any) such
as currency symbols, commas, and
percentage symbols that a number will
have in a cell

✔ The number of decimal places that will
show

✔ The manner in which a cell displays
negative numbers, such as parentheses,
minus signs, and/or red font.

LINGO

Number formats control how
numeric data displays, but they
do more than just make a worksheet attractive. They also help
the user understand what the data
represents. For example, when
presenting data that includes both
quantities and dollar amounts,
applying a Currency number format
to the dollar amounts can help dis-
tinguish them from the quantities.

Apply number formats

Basic number formatting is easy to apply from the Home tab. You can choose
from a variety of number formats from the buttons and drop-down lists in the
Number group.

In the following exercise, you apply number formats to cells.

Files needed: Catering Final.xlsx from the preceding exercise

1. **In Catering Final.xlsx, select the range B7:B13.**

2. **Choose Home⇨Accounting Number Format.**

   The numbers in the selected range are formatted with a dollar sign (left-aligned) and two decimal places. See Figure 4-22.

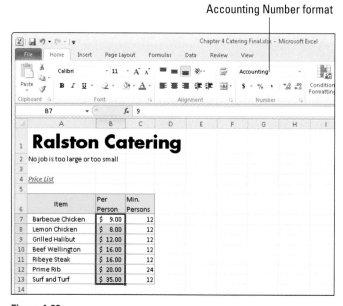

Figure 4-22

3. **Click the arrow to the right of the Accounting Number Format button and choose English (U.K.).**

   See Figure 4-23. The currency symbol changes to British pounds.

4. **From the Number Format drop-down list (which currently shows Accounting), choose Currency.**

   The currency changes back to U.S. dollars, and the dollar sign right-aligns. See Figure 4-24.

Figure 4-23

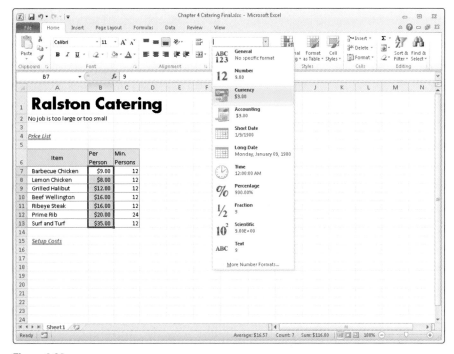

Figure 4-24

5. **From the Home tab, click the Decrease Decimal button twice to set the amounts to no decimal places, as shown in Figure 4-25.**

Decrease Decimal button

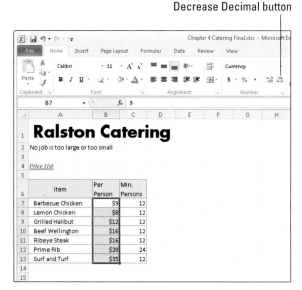

Figure 4-25

6. **From the Number Format drop-down list, choose More Number Formats.**

   The Format Cells dialog box opens with the Number tab displayed. Currency is already selected as the category, with 0 decimal places.

7. **In the Negative Numbers section, select the ($1,234) entry that appears in red, as shown in Figure 4-26, and click OK.**

   No change is apparent in the worksheet because all the numbers are positive.

8. **Change the value in cell B13 to –35 to see the effect of the negative number formatting and then change B13 back to 35.**

TIP

Pressing Ctrl+Z or clicking Undo on the Quick Access Toolbar reverses your last action, which is an easy way to change –35 to 35.

9. **Save the workbook and close it.**

Leave Excel open for the next exercise.

Figure 4-26

Format dates and times

Dates and times are stored in Excel as numbers, but you don't usually see them that way because they have a Date or Time number format applied. A date's raw number is the number of days between January 1, 1900 and the date being represented. For example, January 2, 1900 would be stored as 2, January 3, 1900 would be stored as 3, and so on.

Times are stored as values following the decimal place in the number. For example, the number 2.5 would be 12:00 noon (halfway through the day) on January 2, 1900.

In this exercise, you apply several date and time formats, and look behind the scenes to see how dates and times appear as raw numbers.

Files needed: Production.xlsx

1. **Open Production.xlsx and save it as Production Formatting.xlsx.**

2. **In the Sheet1 worksheet, click in cell E1, type** 1/30/2012, **and press Enter. Then click E1 to re-select it.**

3. **On the Home tab, in the Number group, open the Number Format drop-down list and choose General (see Figure 4-27).**

   The number in E1 changes to 40938. That's the number of days between January 1, 1900 and January 30, 2012.

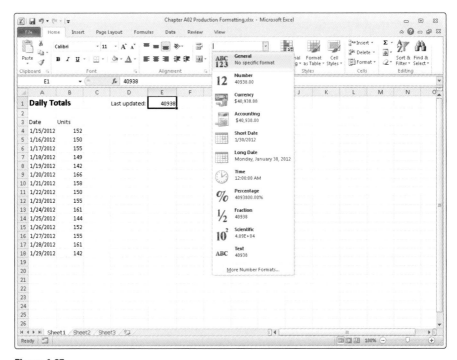

Figure 4-27

4. **With E1 still selected, click the Number group's dialog box launcher.**

   The Format Cells dialog box opens with the Number tab displayed.

5. **Select the Date category on the left, and in the Type list, scroll down and select 3/14/01 13:30 (that's just a sample date, not the actual date in the cell).**

   See Figure 4-28.

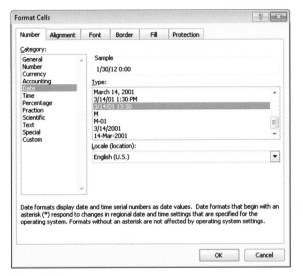

Figure 4-28

6. **Click OK. The format is applied to the number in the cell, and it appears as 1/30/12 00:00.**

7. **Select the range A4:A18.**

8. **In the Number group on the Home tab, open the Number Format drop-down list and choose More Number Formats.**

(This is an alternate method to using the dialog box launcher.)

The Format Cells dialog box reopens with the Number tab displayed.

9. **Select Date in the Category list (if not already selected). In the Type list, select 14-Mar and click OK.**

The dates in cells A4:A18 change to 15-Jan through 29-Jan. See Figure 4-29.

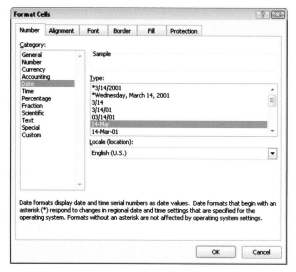

Figure 4-29

For more practice, try some other date formats, including a format with a time.

10. **Save the workbook.**

Leave the workbook open for the next exercise.

Create custom number formats

If none of the number format types listed in the Format Cells dialog box are exactly what you want, you can create your own type.

A custom number format may have up to four sections. If there are multiple sections, they are separated by a semicolon, in this order:

- Positive numbers
- Negative numbers
- Zero numbers
- Text

If a particular section is left out, no special formatting is applied. For example

```
0.00
```

contains only one section, and it's assumed that it's for positive numbers.

The code

```
0.00;[Red]0.00
```

contains two sections, and it's assumed that they're for positive and negative numbers.

If you want to omit a section but then use one that's later in the sequence, add an extra semicolon for the blank section. For example, to specify formatting for positive and zero numbers but not negative, use

```
0.00;;[Green]0.00
```

Table 4-1 lists some of the codes used for creating custom number formats.

Table 4-1	Common Custom Number Format Codes	
Code	*Represents*	*Example*
0	Any digit (required)	`0.00`
#	Any significant digit	`#,###`
A color name, such as black, green, white, blue, magenta, yellow, cyan, or red, in square brackets	The text in the named color	`[Green]#,##0`

Many other codes can be used for specific number formats. For example, various combinations of m, d, and y are used to build date formats. For more information, see the Help system.

Certain characters can be included in a custom number format simply by including them in the code string. These are listed in Table 4-2.

Table 4-2   Literal Symbols for Custom Number Format Code

Symbol	Name
$	Dollar sign
+	Plus sign
(	Left parenthesis
:	Colon
^	Circumflex accent (caret)
'	Apostrophe
{	Left curly bracket
<	Less-than sign
=	Equal sign
-	Minus sign
/	Slash mark
)	Right parenthesis
!	Exclamation point
&	Ampersand
~	Tilde
}	Right curly bracket
>	Greater-than sign
	Space character

If you want to include any other symbols or text as literal values in a code, you must either put the text characters in double quotation marks, or precede the single character with a backslash (\).

In this exercise, you create a custom number format.

Files needed: Production Formatting.xlsx from the preceding exercise

1. **Select the range B4:B18, and from the Home tab, click the Number group's dialog box launcher.**

   The Format Cells dialog box opens with the Number tab displayed.

2. **In the Category list, select Custom; in the Type box, delete the entry that is already there and type #,##0" Units". Make sure you type a space between the opening quotation mark and the word *Units*.**

   See Figure 4-30.

3. **Click OK.**

   Units appears after each number in B4:B18. See Figure 4-31.

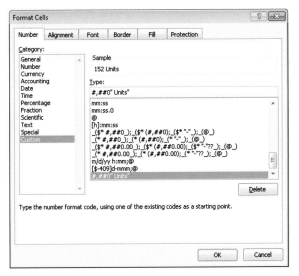

Figure 4-30

	A	B	C	D	E	F
1	**Daily Totals**			Last updated:	1/30/12 0:00	
2						
3	Date	Units				
4	15-Jan	152 Units				
5	16-Jan	150 Units				
6	17-Jan	155 Units				
7	18-Jan	149 Units				
8	19-Jan	142 Units				
9	20-Jan	166 Units				
10	21-Jan	158 Units				
11	22-Jan	150 Units				
12	23-Jan	155 Units				
13	24-Jan	161 Units				
14	25-Jan	144 Units				
15	26-Jan	152 Units				
16	27-Jan	155 Units				
17	28-Jan	161 Units				
18	29-Jan	142 Units				

Figure 4-31

4. **Click the Sheet2 tab, select the range B4:B7, and from the Home tab, click the Number group's dialog box launcher.**

The Format Cells dialog box opens with the Number tab displayed.

5. **In the Category list, select Custom; in the Type box, delete the current entry and type #,##0;[Red]#,##0;[Green]0.**

This code formats positive numbers with the #,##0 format in the default color (black), negative numbers the same way but in red, and zero values in green. See Figure 4-32.

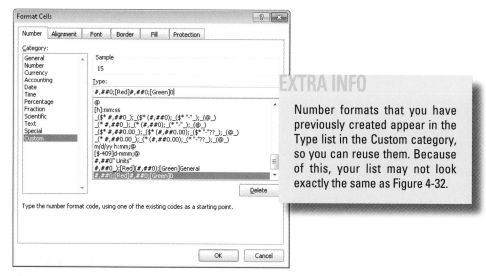

Figure 4-32

6. **Click OK. Cells B4 and B5 appear in red, cell B6 in green, and cell B7 in black.**

7. **In cell B4, type** 12, **and press Enter. Now that the value is positive, it appears in black.**

8. **Save the workbook.**

Leave the workbook open for the next exercise.

Using Conditional Formatting

Custom number formatting, as in the preceding section, can provide a rudimentary level of conditional formatting by formatting negative numbers differently. However, you can do much more with conditional formatting, such as specifying multiple formatting conditions and applying icon sets.

LINGO

Conditional formatting is formatting that is applied only when the content of the cell meets specified criteria.

Within the Extra Info box:

EXTRA INFO

Number formats that you have previously created appear in the Type list in the Custom category, so you can reuse them. Because of this, your list may not look exactly the same as Figure 4-32.

Conditionally format data

Excel provides many conditional formatting presets. For example, you can find the top and bottom values in a list, highlight cells that are greater-than or less-than certain values, or apply data bars that show gradient fills in proportion to the amounts in the cells.

Each of the conditional formatting presets has its own numeric or percentile settings that work well all by themselves in many situations. However, you can also change the settings in the Conditional Formatting Rules Manager to fine-tune what each formatting type represents. For example, you could choose to have formatting based on a specific number instead of a percentage or average value.

In this exercise, you apply conditional formatting.

Files needed: Production Formatting.xlsx from the preceding exercise

1. **On the Sheet1 worksheet, select the range B4:B18 and then choose Home⇨Conditional Formatting⇨Highlight Cells Rules⇨Greater Than.**

   See Figure 4-33. The Greater Than dialog box opens.

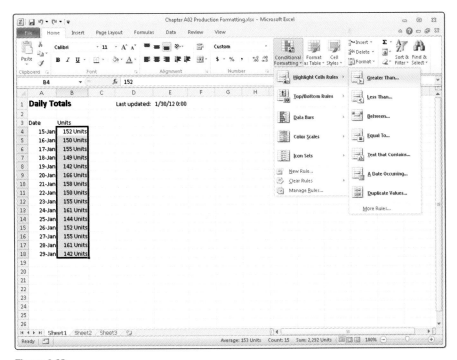

Figure 4-33

2. In the Format cells That Are GREATER THAN box, type 150 and in the With drop-down list, choose Green Fill with Dark Green Text (see Figure 4-34).

Figure 4-34

3. Click OK, and all values over 150 become green.

4. Click the Undo button on the Quick Access Toolbar or press Ctrl+Z to undo the conditional formatting you just applied.

Figure 4-35

5. Select the range B4:B18 again and choose Home⇨Conditional Formatting⇨Top/Bottom Rules⇨Below Average.

The Below Average dialog box opens. See Figure 4-35.

6. Click OK to accept the default formatting (red).

The values that are below the average of all values appear in red.

7. Click the Undo button on the Quick Access Toolbar or press Ctrl+Z to undo the conditional formatting you just applied.

8. Select B4:B18 again and choose Home⇨Conditional Formatting⇨Color Scales⇨Green-Yellow-Red Color Scale.

(That's the first one in the first row.)

Different colors are applied to the cells based on their values, with higher values in green and lower values in red.

9. Click away from the selection to deselect it so you can see the colors more clearly, as shown in Figure 4-36.

10. Select B4:B18 again and choose Home⇨Conditional Formatting⇨Manage Rules.

The Conditional Formatting Rules Manager dialog box opens. See Figure 4-37.

11. Click the Edit Rule button, and the Edit Formatting Rule dialog box opens.

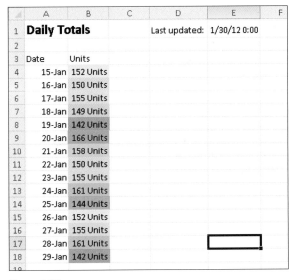

Figure 4-36

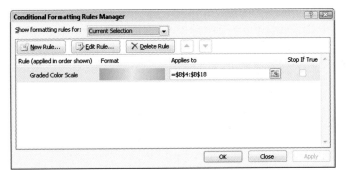

Figure 4-37

12. **In the Edit the Rule Description area below Midpoint, choose Number in the Type drop-down list.**

13. **In the Value box below Midpoint (which currently shows 0), type** 150.
See Figure 4-38.

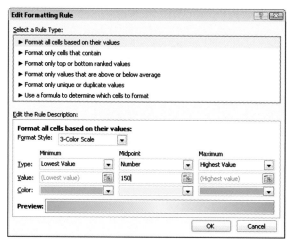

Figure 4-38

14. **Click OK to return to the Conditional Formatting Rules Manager dialog box, and click OK to apply the changes to the rule.**

15. **Click the Undo button on the Quick Access Toolbar twice or press Ctrl+Z twice to remove the conditional formatting you just applied.**

16. **Save the workbook.**

Leave the workbook open for the next exercise.

Create multiple formatting conditions

You can start with conditional formatting by selecting preset conditional formatting from Home⇨Conditional Formatting. You can then modify the presets as needed and create new conditions.

In this exercise, you apply a formatting condition preset and create a new condition.

Files needed: Production Formatting.xlsx from the preceding exercise

1. **On the Sheet1 worksheet, select the range B4:B18 and choose Home⇨ Conditional Formatting⇨Highlight Cell Rules⇨Greater Than.**

The Greater Than dialog box opens.

2. **In the Format Cells That Are GREATER THAN box, type** 150 **and in the With drop-down list, choose Green Fill with Dark Green Text.**

Figure 4-39

See Figure 4-39.

3. **Click OK and then choose Home⇨Conditional Formatting⇨Manage Rules.**

The Conditional Formatting Rules Manager dialog box opens. See Figure 4-40.

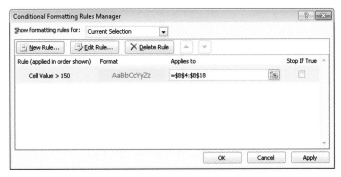

Figure 4-40

4. **Click the New Rule button.**

The New Formatting Rule dialog box opens.

5. **In the Select a Rule Type area, select Format Only Cells That Contain.**

6. **In the Format Only Cells With area, leave the first drop-down list set to its default of Cell Value. Leave the second drop-down list set to its default of Between. In the third box, type** 145. **In the fourth box, type** 149.

See Figure 4-41.

7. **Click the Format button, and the Format Cells dialog box opens.**

8. **Click the Fill tab and then click a pale blue color square (the fourth color in the second row).** See Figure 4-42.

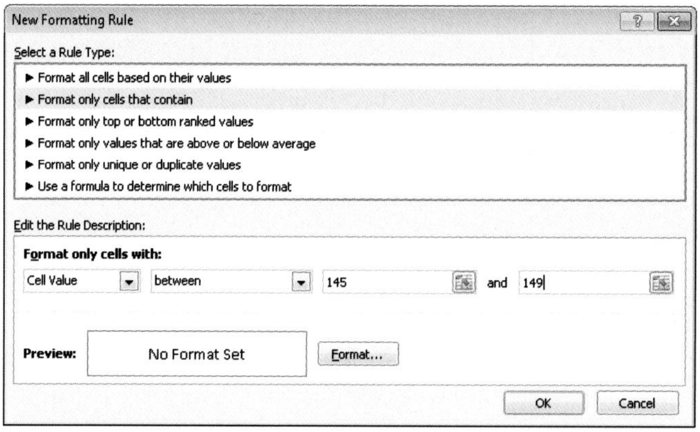

Figure 4-41

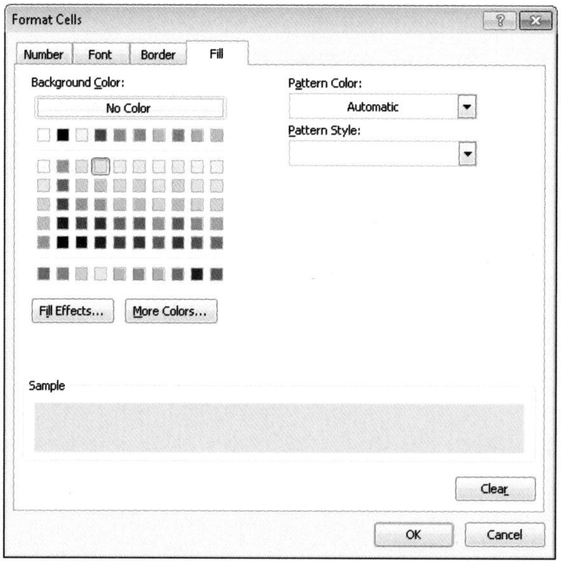

Figure 4-42

9. **Click the Font tab; from the Color drop-down list, choose a dark blue square (the fourth color in the first row), and click OK.**

10. **In the New Formatting Rule dialog box, click OK to finalize the rule. Both rules appear in the Conditional Formatting Rules Manager dialog box.** See Figure 4-43.

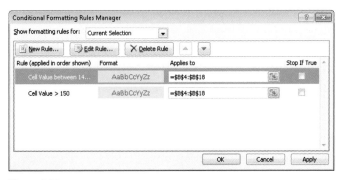

Figure 4-43

11. **Click OK. Then click away from the selection to deselect it. Cell B7 appears in blue because its value falls within the range specified by the new rule.**

12. **Click cell B17, type** 148, **and press Enter. The formatting changes in B17 to reflect the new conditional format.** See Figure 4-44.

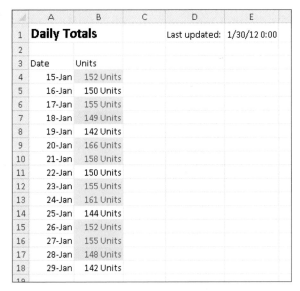

Figure 4-44

For more practice, set up an additional rule that colors values that are less than 145 with light red background and dark red text.

13. **Select the range B4:B18 again and choose Home⇨Conditional Formatting⇨Manage Rules.**

    The Conditional Formatting Rules Manager dialog box opens. See Figure 4-45.

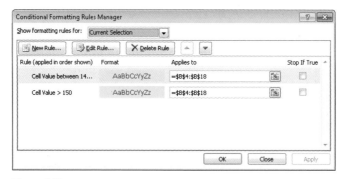

Figure 4-45

14. **Select the first rule and click the Delete Rule button; select the next rule and click the Delete Rule button again. (If there are any other rules, delete them also.)**

15. **Click OK.** The conditional formatting is removed.

16. **Save the workbook.**

Leave the workbook open for the next exercise.

Apply icon sets

In this exercise, you apply and customize an icon set.

Files needed: Production Formatting.xlsx from the preceding exercise

1. **On the Sheet1 tab, select the range B4:B18 and choose Home⇨Conditional Formatting⇨Icon Sets.**

LINGO

Icon sets are a form of conditional formatting that adds icons next to entries in cells depending on the cells' content. For example, you could place check marks next to values that are higher than a certain amount.

2. **In the Indicators section of the menu, click the set that contains a green check mark, yellow exclamation point, and red X.** See Figure 4-46.

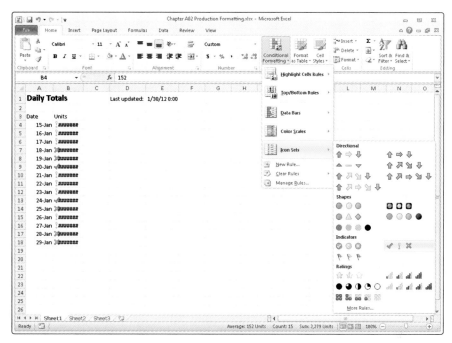

Figure 4-46

When you apply the icon set, the values in column B change to hash marks ####. This happens because the column is no longer wide enough to accommodate the content.

3. **Double-click between the B and C column headings to widen column B so the content is once again visible.**

Only two entries have green check marks. Next, you modify the criteria for the icon set so that more entries have green check marks.

4. Choose Home⇨Conditional Formatting⇨Manage Rules.

The Conditional Formatting Rules Manager dialog box opens, with the Icon Set rule in it. See Figure 4-47.

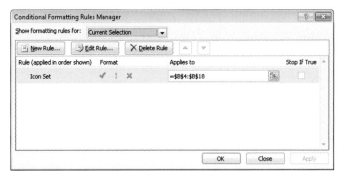

Figure 4-47

5. Click the Icon Set rule and then click the Edit Rule button.

The Edit Formatting Rule dialog box opens.

6. In the Type column at the bottom of the dialog box, open each of the drop-down lists (which currently show Percent) and choose Number.

When you switch between Percent and Number, as in Step 6, any previously entered values are erased. Make sure you choose the desired setting (Percent or Number) before you enter the values to be used, or you have to re-enter them.

7. In the Value column, on the first line (for the green check mark), enter 150 and on the second line (for the yellow exclamation point), enter 145, as shown in Figure 4-48.

8. Click OK to close the Edit Formatting Rule dialog box. Click OK to close the Conditional Formatting Rules Manager dialog box and apply the rule.

9. Click away from the selection to deselect it so you can see the icons more clearly, as shown in Figure 4-49.

10. Save the workbook and close Excel.

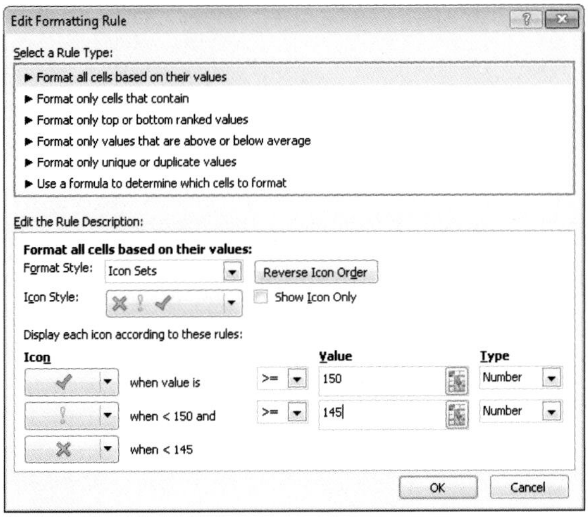

Figure 4-48

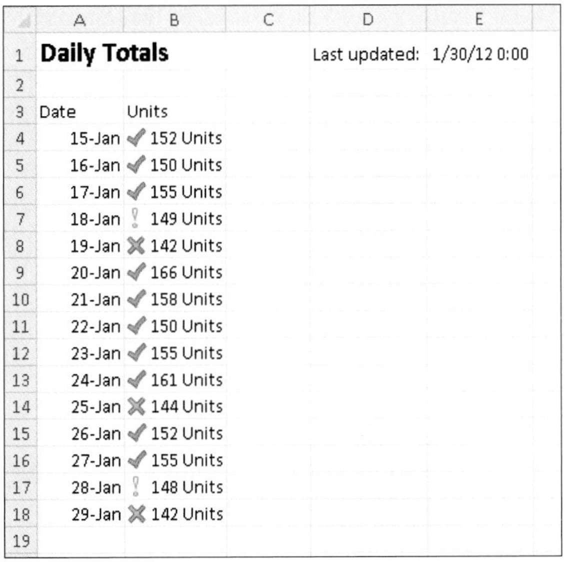

Figure 4-49

 *Summing Up*

Here are the key points you learned about in this lesson:

- Each cell has a fill (its inner color) and a border (its outline). By default, a cell is set for No Border. The faint gray outlines that define each cell onscreen are gridlines; they're not the same thing as borders.

- To apply a cell fill, use the Fill Color button on the Home tab.

- To apply a cell border, use the Border button on the Home tab. You can define the border of each side of a cell or range independently.

- You can format the text in a cell in much the same way as in Word: Use the controls in the Font group on the Home tab, or on the Mini Toolbar.

- Use the Wrap Text button on the Home tab to allow a cell's content to wrap to additional lines if needed.

- Cells have vertical and horizontal alignments that determine where the text will align in the cell when the cell is larger than it needs to be to accommodate that text.

- Cell styles are formatting presets you can apply to cells. You can create your own cell styles easily via the Cell Styles button on the Home tab.

- Number formats help put numbers in context and can be applied from the Number group on the Home tab. Examples include Currency and Percentage.

- To create your own custom number formats, choose Custom as the type and then enter the codes from Tables 4-1 and 4-2 to build your own format.

- To conditionally format cells, choose Home⇨Conditional Formatting.

Try-it-yourself lab

1. **Start Excel, open the file Try It Cells.xlsx, and save it as Try It Cells Final.xlsx.**

2. **Using the formatting skills you learn in this lesson, create a packing slip that as closely resembles Figure 4-50 as possible.**

   Skills you need include

   - Adjusting column widths and row heights
   - Changing horizontal and vertical alignments

• Changing fonts, sizes, colors, and attributes

• Applying cell borders and fills

• Applying number formats

• Merging and centering a heading across multiple cells

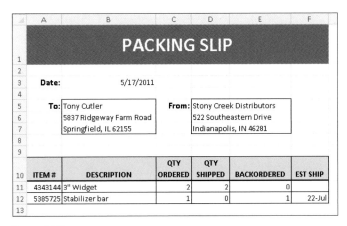

Figure 4-50

Know this tech talk

attributes: Text effects, including bold and italic, underlining, strike-through, superscript, and subscript.

border: The color and style of the outside of a cell.

cell style: A formatting preset that you can apply to a cell.

conditional formatting: Formatting that is applied only when the content of the cell meets specified criteria.

fill: The color of the inside of a cell.

gridlines: The edges of the cells that you see by default onscreen in gray.

horizontal alignment: The horizontal position of data in a cell, such as Left, Right, or Center.

icon sets: A form of conditional formatting that adds icons next to entries in cells depending on the cells' content.

number format: A format applied to a cell that makes numbers in it appear with certain characteristics, such as commas, dollar signs, or percentage symbols.

vertical alignment: The vertical position of data in a cell, such as Top, Middle, or Bottom.

Lesson 5
Storing and Managing Tables and Lists

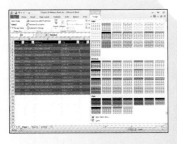

✔ Databases store information in a structured, consistent way.

✔ Tables in Excel provide extra sorting, filtering, and summarizing capabilities.

✔ Sorting data arranges records in a different order to more easily find the records you want.

✔ Filtering data hides records that don't match your specs.

✔ Table styles quickly apply professional-looking formatting to an entire table.

✔ A Total row provides an easy way to add summary statistics to a table.

✔ Merging data from two cells into one concatenates data.

✔ Splitting data from one column into two or more columns enables you to extract individual values from a combined entry.

✔ Converting a table to a range returns the data to a regular Excel range, without table features.

esides its calculation capabilities, Excel also has some great features for managing databases. You can store, search, sort, and filter large lists of information with ease in Excel. And by converting a range to a table in Excel, you can access certain sorting and filtering commands even more easily.

In this lesson, you learn some database concepts, and find out how to create and manage tables in a workbook. You also learn how to merge and split data, so you can combine values from two or more fields into a single one or split a single field into multiple pieces.

Understanding Databases

A two-dimensional grid of rows and columns is a table. Figure 5-1 points out the key elements in a simple database table. For most people, standalone database tables are all that's needed to store data. In this lesson, you learn how to create and manipulate a single-table database in Excel.

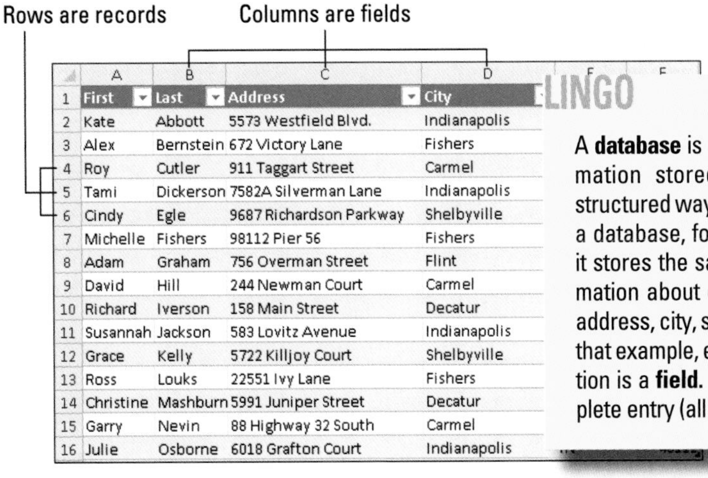

Rows are records   Columns are fields

	A	B	C	D	E
1	First	Last	Address	City	
2	Kate	Abbott	5573 Westfield Blvd.	Indianapolis	
3	Alex	Bernstein	672 Victory Lane	Fishers	
4	Roy	Cutler	911 Taggart Street	Carmel	
5	Tami	Dickerson	7582A Silverman Lane	Indianapolis	
6	Cindy	Egle	9687 Richardson Parkway	Shelbyville	
7	Michelle	Fishers	98112 Pier 56	Fishers	
8	Adam	Graham	756 Overman Street	Flint	
9	David	Hill	244 Newman Court	Carmel	
10	Richard	Iverson	158 Main Street	Decatur	
11	Susannah	Jackson	583 Lovitz Avenue	Indianapolis	
12	Grace	Kelly	5722 Killjoy Court	Shelbyville	
13	Ross	Louks	22551 Ivy Lane	Fishers	
14	Christine	Mashburn	5991 Juniper Street	Decatur	
15	Garry	Nevin	88 Highway 32 South	Carmel	
16	Julie	Osborne	6018 Grafton Court	Indianapolis	

LINGO A **database** is a collection of information stored in a consistent, structured way. An address book is a database, for example, because it stores the same pieces of information about each person: name, address, city, state, and zip code. In that example, each type of information is a **field**. Each person's complete entry (all fields) is a **record**.

Figure 5-1

Working with Tables in Excel

You can store database data in simple ranges in Excel, but for full access to Excel's data management features, it's often better to convert the range to a table. Tables have several advantages over ranges:

✔ You can filter by columns using an easy drop-down list.

✔ You can add a Total row that adds summary calculations without manually entering the formula for it.

✔ You can apply table formatting presets.

✔ You can publish a table to a SharePoint server.

EXTRA INFO

When most people think about databases, they think about complex, multi-table databases in which each table is related to another one in some way. Such databases are **relational databases**. You can use Microsoft Access to create such databases. (Access is included with some versions of Microsoft Office, but isn't covered in this book.)

Convert a data range to a table

Before you convert a range to a table, make sure you have properly prepared the range. Specifically, you need to do the following:

✔ Make sure that the first row contains the field names you want to use. The entries in the first row become column headings.

✔ Make sure that each row contains one record.

✔ Make sure that there are no blank rows between rows containing records.

When the data is cleaned up and ready to go, choose Insert⇨Table to convert the range to a table. Alternatively, you can choose Home⇨Format as Table, which applies a format of your choice and makes the range into a table in a single step. You see that method in Lesson 3.

In the following exercise, you convert a data range to a table.

Files needed: Addresses.xlsx.

1. **Start Excel, if needed, open Addresses.xlsx, and save it as Address Book.xlsx.**

2. **Select the range A1:F16 and then choose Insert⇨Table.**

   The Create Table dialog box opens with the selected range already filled in. See Figure 5-2.

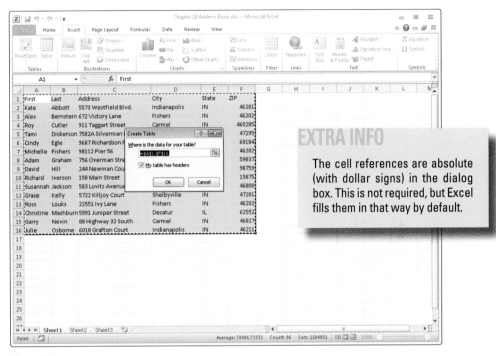

Figure 5-2

EXTRA INFO

The cell references are absolute (with dollar signs) in the dialog box. This is not required, but Excel fills them in that way by default.

3. Click OK.

The range is converted to a table, and default table formatting is applied to it. This formatting consists of banded blue and white rows and blue column headings, as well as a Filter arrow next to each field name at the top of each column, as shown in Figure 5-1.

4. Save the workbook.

Leave the workbook open for the next exercise.

Sort table data

You can sort a table's data by a single field or by multiple fields. When you sort by a single field, Excel rearranges the records in A to Z (ascending) or Z to A (descending) order based on the field you specify. When you sort by multiple fields, Excel does a single sort by the first field you specify, and then in the event of a tie for that field, it relies on the additional field(s) you specify to break it. For example, if you sort first by City and then by State, Decatur, GA comes before Decatur, IL.

In the following exercise, you sort table data.

Files needed: Address Book.xlsx from the preceding exercise

1. **In Address Book.xlsx, click in any cell in the State column and choose Data⇨Sort A to Z.**

   The records are reordered by state. A small arrow appears on the Filter arrow button (the up arrow to the right of the State field) to indicate that field is sorted. See Figure 5-3.

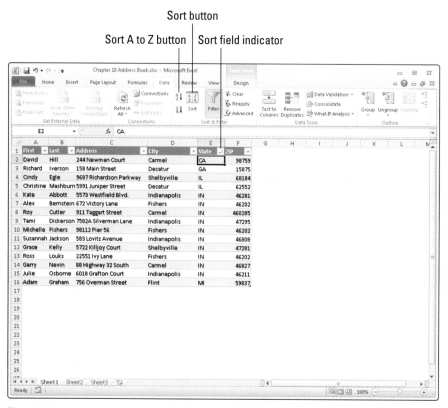

Figure 5-3

2. **Click the Filter arrow button to the right of the ZIP field to open a Filter menu, as shown in Figure 5-4, and then choose Sort Smallest to Largest.** The table is sorted by ZIP, and not State.

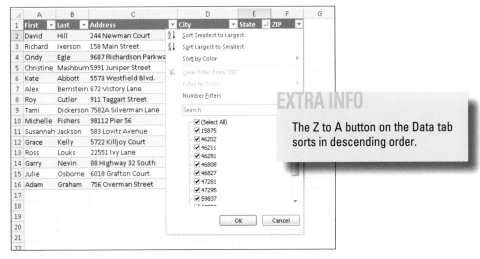

EXTRA INFO

The Z to A button on the Data tab sorts in descending order.

Figure 5-4

3. **Choose Data⇨Clear to remove the sort and then choose Data⇨Sort to open the Sort dialog box.**

4. **Choose State from the Sort By drop-down list.** This sets the primary sort as the State field.

5. **Click the Add Level button. Another line is added to the dialog box.**

6. **Choose City from the Then By drop-down list.** This sets the secondary sort as the City field, as shown in Figure 5-5.

Figure 5-5

7. **Click OK to apply the sort. Notice that both the City and State fields' Filter arrow buttons have a sort symbol on them.**

8. **Starting in cell A17, type a new record:** Brooke Sanner, 124 South
Street, Decatur, IL 62558.

Excel automatically extends the table to include the new record.

9. **Choose Data⟹Reapply, and the table is re-sorted to place the new
record in the appropriate order.**

10. **Save the workbook.**

Leave the workbook open for the next exercise.

Filter data in a table

Excel gives you several ways to specify filter
criteria so that you see only the database
records you want to see. You can use the
Filter menu for a particular field (from the
Filter down arrow to the right of each field
name) to choose certain values to include
and to omit others. Depending on the content of the field (text, date, number, and
so on), you can also use logical filter state-
ments for that type of data, such as Begins
With, Ends With, or Contains (for text) or
Greater Than, Less Than, or Between (for
numbers).

LINGO

Filtering data hides certain
records and displays only the
ones that match criteria you specify. Perhaps the easiest method is
to **filter by selection,** which hides
all records in which the specified
field does not contain a sample
value you select.

In the following exercise, you filter table data using a variety of methods.

Files needed: Address Book.xlsx from the preceding exercise

1. **In Address Book.xlsx, click the Filter arrow to the right of the State
field to open its Filter menu (see Figure 5-6). Notice that each check
box for the entries in that column is selected marked, indicating nothing is filtered.**

2. **Deselect the check boxes for all states except IL and IN, and then
click OK.**

The list is filtered to show only those two states.

3. **Choose Data⟹Clear to remove the filtering and any previously
applied sort.**

4. **Right-click in any cell in the State column that contains IL and choose
Filter⟹Filter by Selected Cell's Value, as shown in Figure 5-7.**

The table filters to show only Illinois (IL) records.

Figure 5-6

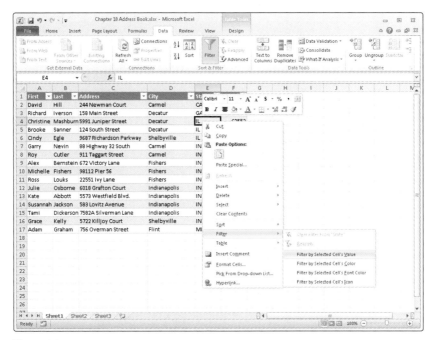

Figure 5-7

5. **Click the Filter arrow to the right of the State field's column heading and choose Clear Filter from "State," and the filter is removed.**

6. **Click the Filter arrow to the right of the ZIP field's column heading and choose Point to Number Filters⇨Between.**

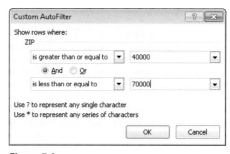

The Custom AutoFilter dialog box opens.

Figure 5-8

7. **In the first text box on the right, type** 40000. **In the second text box on the right, type** 70000, **as shown in Figure 5-8.**

For more practice, try some of the other number filters, such as Less Than or Greater Than. Still want more practice? Filter by last name using a Begins With filter to find only names that begin with a certain letter.

8. **Click OK.**

The list filters to show zip codes between the limits you specified. The list is not sorted by zip code; it is only filtered by it.

9. **Choose Data⇨Clear to clear the filter and then save the workbook.**

Leave the workbook open for the next exercise.

Format a table

In Lesson 3, you learn how to apply table formatting to a range, and the procedure is the same with an existing table. Excel offers a variety of table styles for quickly formatting a table; you can access these styles either from the Table Tools Design tab or by choosing Home⇨Format as Table. (The style choices are the same no matter which method you use.)

You can also specify which table style options will take effect by selecting or deselecting check boxes on the Table Tools Design tab in the Table Style Options group.

In the following exercise, you apply table formatting.

Files needed: Address Book.xlsx from the preceding exercise

1. **In Address Book.xlsx, click anywhere in the table, and then from the Table Tools Design tab, click the More button in the Table Styles group to open a palette of table styles, as shown in Figure 5-9.**

2. **In the Dark section, choose Table Style 3 Dark (the one with the black column headings and red striped rows).**

PRACTICE

For more practice, try some of the other table styles.

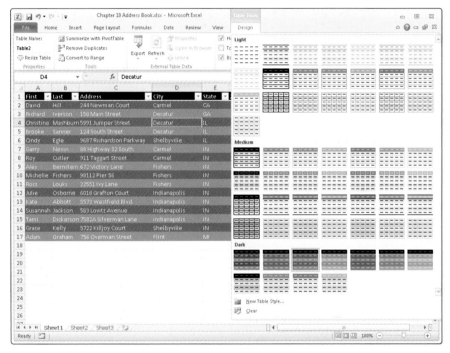

Figure 5-9

3. **In the Table Style Options group, deselect the Banded Rows check box and select the Banded Columns check box, as shown in Figure 5-10.**

PRACTICE

For more practice, select and deselect each of the check boxes in the Table Style Options group to see what they do. First Column and Last Column formatting would be useful if those columns contained something special; you learn about the Total Row option in the next exercise.

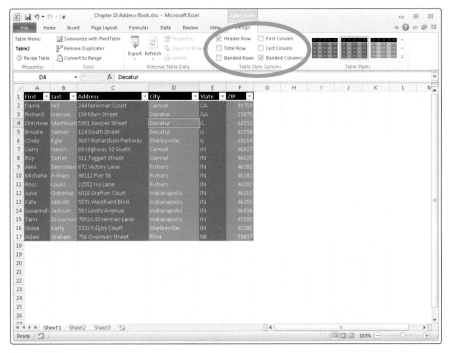

Figure 5-10

4. **Choose Home⇨Format as Table⇨Table Style Medium 10.**

   (It's one of the red styles in the Medium section. You can point to a style to see a ScreenTip that shows its name.) The options you set in Step 3 still apply.

5. **On the Table Tools Design tab, deselect the Banded Columns check box and select the Banded Rows check box.**

6. **Save the workbook.**

Leave the workbook open for the next exercise.

Add a Total row to a table

One of the advantages of making a data range into a table is the ability to show a Total row as part of the table. As you probably expect, more options for calculating totals are available when working with a numeric field, but even text fields have some totals they can display, such as a count of the number of records. You can use any function in Excel for figuring totals, but the most common ones — such as Sum, Average, and Count — are available from a menu for easy access.

In the following exercise, you add a Total row to a table.

Files needed: Address Book.xlsx from the preceding exercise

LINGO

A **Total row** performs a summary operation of your choice on any field(s) in the table.

1. **In Address Book.xlsx, click anywhere in the table and then choose Table Tools Design⇨Total Row to turn on the Total row for the table.**

   The Total row appears at the bottom of the table. Excel considers only the ZIP field in the table as numeric, so it automatically applies a SUM function to that field. (That's not very useful, but Excel doesn't know that yet.)

2. **Click cell F18 to select the automatically created total in that cell. Click the down arrow that appears and choose Count, as shown in Figure 5-11.**

   Cell F18 then shows 16, the number of records in the table.

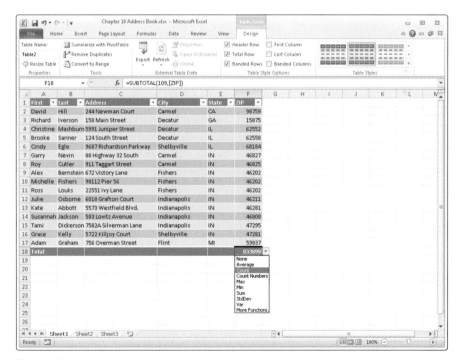

Figure 5-11

3. **Click in cell A18 and type** Count, **replacing** *Total*.

   It's important to clearly label each calculation in a worksheet, and this table is no exception.

4. **Save the workbook.**

For more practice, reopen the menu for cell F18 and try some of the other functions on the list. They won't make logical sense when calculated on zip codes, but you still get an idea of how they work.

Leave the workbook open for the next exercise.

Convert a table to a range

Some of Excel's features don't work on cells that are part of a table. If you do something that triggers an error message that the operation can't be performed on a table or if you just don't want the table anymore, you can convert the table back to a regular range.

When you convert a table to a range, you get to keep the table formatting that you have previously applied to it, but you lose the Filter arrows on each column.

In the following exercise, you convert a table to a range.

Files needed: Address Book.xlsx from the preceding exercise

1. **In Address Book.xlsx, click anywhere in the table and then choose Table Tools Design⇨Convert to Range.**

2. **Click Yes in the confirmation box that appears.**

   All the data and formatting remain, but the Filter arrows disappear from the column headings. The Table Tools Design tab is no longer available.

3. **Click in cell F18. Notice that instead of an available drop-down list is a SUBTOTAL function: =SUBTOTAL(103,Sheet1!$F$2:$F$17) as shown in the Formula bar of Figure 5-12.**

4. **Save the workbook.**

	A	B	C	D	E	F	G
1	First	Last	Address	City	State	ZIP	
2	David	Hill	244 Newman Court	Carmel	CA	98759	
3	Richard	Iverson	158 Main Street	Decatur	GA	15875	
4	Christine	Mashburn	5991 Juniper Street	Decatur	IL	62552	
5	Brooke	Sanner	124 South Street	Decatur	IL	62558	
6	Cindy	Egle	9687 Richardson Parkway	Shelbyville	IL	68184	
7	Garry	Nevin	88 Highway 32 South	Carmel	IN	46827	
8	Roy	Cutler	911 Taggart Street	Carmel	IN	46825	
9	Alex	Bernstein	672 Victory Lane	Fishers	IN	46202	
10	Michelle	Fishers	98112 Pier 56	Fishers	IN	46202	
11	Ross	Louks	22551 Ivy Lane	Fishers	IN	46202	
12	Julie	Osborne	6018 Grafton Court	Indianapolis	IN	46211	
13	Kate	Abbott	5573 Westfield Blvd.	Indianapolis	IN	46281	
14	Susannah	Jackson	583 Lovitz Avenue	Indianapolis	IN	46808	
15	Tami	Dickerson	7582A Silverman Lane	Indianapolis	IN	47295	
16	Grace	Kelly	5722 Killjoy Court	Shelbyville	IN	47281	
17	Adam	Graham	756 Overman Street	Flint	MI	59837	
18	Count					16	
19							
20							

Cell F18 formula: =SUBTOTAL(103,Sheet1!$F$2:$F$17)

Figure 5-12

Leave the workbook open for the next exercise.

TIP

You might have been surprised that cell F18 (in Step 3) contained a SUBTOTAL function and not a COUNT function. That's a remnant of the table's Total row. When you add a Total row to a table, the SUBTOTAL function is used no matter which of the operations you choose from the drop-down list. Each of the available functions has a numeric value. The COUNT function's number happens to be 103, which is why the first argument in the function in F18 is 103. The second argument is the range: F2:F17 (with absolute cell references, hence the dollar signs) on Sheet1. An advantage of the SUBTOTAL function is that it includes only visible cells, so that if any filters are applied to the table, the filtered data's subtotals are accurate.

Merging and Splitting Data

As you build a database in Excel, you may decide that you made some mistakes in how you've broken up your data into fields. Fortunately, you're not stuck, nor do you have to retype all the data. You can use Excel's features that merge and split cell contents based on criteria you specify.

Merge the contents of multiple columns

You can merge the content of two or more cells into a single cell using the CONCATENATE function. For example, if cell A2 contains *David* and B2 contains *Hill,* you could concatenate those values into a new cell that displays *David Hill.* You can then copy that function to an entire column, converting a whole column of data at once.

You can choose to leave the data in the new concatenated cells, but those cells will always contain a function that relies on the original data being present to refer to. If you want to delete the original cells that contained the concatenated data, you must copy the results of the concatenation formula to a new cell using a special Paste option, and paste the value rather than the formula.

> **LINGO**
>
> **Concatenate** means to join together end to end. In Excel, you use the CONCATENATE function to combine cell content and add literal character strings as well, if you want.

In the following exercise, you concatenate the first and last names in a data range into a new column, and then delete the original columns.

Files needed: Address Book.xlsx from the preceding exercise

1. **In Address Book.xlsx, drag across the column headers for columns C and D to select those two columns, and then choose Home⇨Insert.**

   Two new columns are inserted. See Figure 5-13.

2. **In cell C2, type** =CONCATENATE(.

Insert button

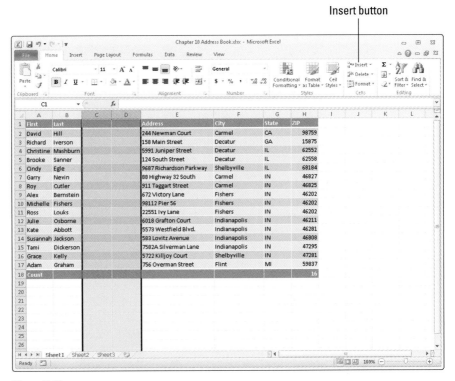

Figure 5-13

3. **Click cell A2, type ," ", (a comma, quotation marks with a space in between, and another comma), click cell B2, and press Enter.**

4. **Click cell C2, which reads *David Hill,* and view the function in the formula bar.**

   The function looks like =CONCATENATE(A2," ",B2), as shown in Figure 5-14.

5. **Drag the fill handle from cell C2 down to C17, copying the function to the rest of the names.**

6. **Double-click the divider between column headings C and D to widen column C to fit the contents.**

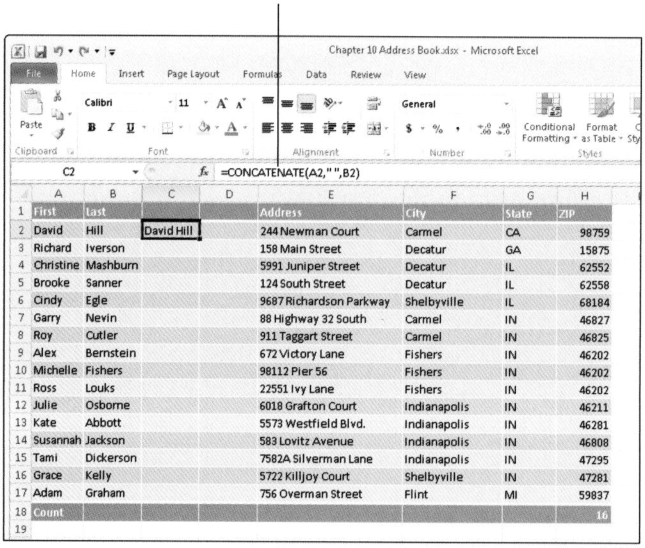

CONCATENATE function

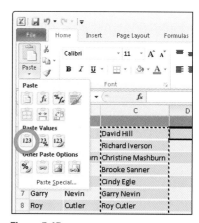

Figure 5-14

7. **Select the range C2:C17 and press Ctrl+C to copy them to the Clipboard.**

8. **Click in cell D2 and from the Home tab, click the down arrow under the Paste button and choose Values (the first icon) from the Paste Values section.**

   See Figure 5-15. The values from column C paste into column D.

9. **Double-click the divider between columns D and E to widen column D to fit the contents.**

10. **Drag across the column headers for columns A:C to select those columns.**

11. **Choose Home⇨Delete, and then click in cell A1 and type Name, defining a new column header label.**

    The completed data range appears in Figure 5-16.

Figure 5-15

	A	B	C	D	E
1	Name	Address	City	State	ZIP
2	David Hill	244 Newman Court	Carmel	CA	98759
3	Richard Iverson	158 Main Street	Decatur	GA	15875
4	Christine Mashburn	5991 Juniper Street	Decatur	IL	62552
5	Brooke Sanner	124 South Street	Decatur	IL	62558
6	Cindy Egle	9687 Richardson Parkway	Shelbyville	IL	68184
7	Garry Nevin	88 Highway 32 South	Carmel	IN	46827
8	Roy Cutler	911 Taggart Street	Carmel	IN	46825
9	Alex Bernstein	672 Victory Lane	Fishers	IN	46202
10	Michelle Fishers	98112 Pier 56	Fishers	IN	46202
11	Ross Louks	22551 Ivy Lane	Fishers	IN	46202
12	Julie Osborne	6018 Grafton Court	Indianapolis	IN	46211
13	Kate Abbott	5573 Westfield Blvd.	Indianapolis	IN	46281
14	Susannah Jackson	583 Lovitz Avenue	Indianapolis	IN	46808
15	Tami Dickerson	7582A Silverman Lane	Indianapolis	IN	47295
16	Grace Kelly	5722 Killjoy Court	Shelbyville	IN	47281
17	Adam Graham	756 Overman Street	Flint	MI	59837
18					16

Figure 5-16

12. Save the workbook.

Leave the workbook open for the next exercise.

Split a column's content into multiple columns

If you put more data in a single column than you should have, you can split the data into multiple cells. Text to Columns is the splitting feature in Excel 2010.

For splitting to work, a consistently used, separator character differentiates the data that should be in one cell from the data that should be in another. For example, if you want to separate first and last names, such as David Hill, the separator character is a space. If some names have three space-separated parts to them, the split won't work right and you have to manually correct those entries afterward. However, if most of the data falls into a consistent pattern, you can save some time by allowing Excel to split as many entries as it can.

In the following exercise, you split first and last names into separate cells.

Files needed: Address Book.xlsx from the preceding exercise

1. **In Address Book.xlsx, click the column letter B and then choose Home⇨Insert to insert a new column.**

2. **Select the range A2:A17 and then choose Data⇨Text to Columns.**

   The Convert Text to Columns Wizard – Step 1 of 3 dialog box opens. See Figure 5-17.

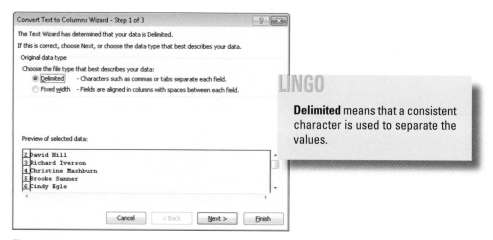

Figure 5-17

3. **Click Next to select the default Delimited data type and move on to the Convert Text to Columns Wizard – Step 2 of 3 dialog box.**

4. **Select the Space check box, deselect the Tab check box, select the Treat Consecutive Delimiters as One check box.**

   The Treat Consecutive Delimiters as One option ignores the second delimiter if there are two in a row, and it allows for data entry errors where an extra space might have been inserted. That doesn't apply to the data being used for this exercise, but it might apply in data you create for yourself later.

5. **Preview the split in the Data Preview area, as shown in Figure 5-18, and then click Next.**

   The Convert Text to Columns Wizard – Step 3 of 3 dialog box appears. In this dialog box, you can fine-tune the data types, such as Text or Date.

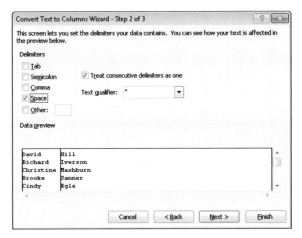

Figure 5-18

6. **Select the Text option to set the first column as Text; then click the second column in the Data Preview area and select the Text option to set the second column as Text, as shown in Figure 5-19.**

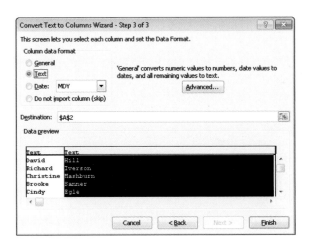

Figure 5-19

7. **Click the Finish button.**

A dialog box appears asking whether you want to replace the contents of the destination cells.

8. **Click OK, and the last names are placed into column B.**

9. **In cell A1, type** First. **In cell B1, type** Last.

The names are split into two separately named columns, as shown in Figure 5-20.

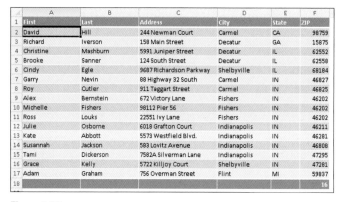

	A	B	C	D	E	F
1	First	Last	Address	City	State	ZIP
2	David	Hill	244 Newman Court	Carmel	CA	98759
3	Richard	Iverson	158 Main Street	Decatur	GA	15875
4	Christine	Mashburn	5991 Juniper Street	Decatur	IL	62552
5	Brooke	Sanner	124 South Street	Decatur	IL	62558
6	Cindy	Egle	9687 Richardson Parkway	Shelbyville	IL	68184
7	Garry	Nevin	88 Highway 32 South	Carmel	IN	46827
8	Roy	Cutler	911 Taggart Street	Carmel	IN	46825
9	Alex	Bernstein	672 Victory Lane	Fishers	IN	46202
10	Michelle	Fishers	98112 Pier 56	Fishers	IN	46202
11	Ross	Louks	22551 Ivy Lane	Fishers	IN	46202
12	Julie	Osborne	6018 Grafton Court	Indianapolis	IN	46211
13	Kate	Abbott	5573 Westfield Blvd.	Indianapolis	IN	46281
14	Susannah	Jackson	583 Lovitz Avenue	Indianapolis	IN	46808
15	Tami	Dickerson	7582A Silverman Lane	Indianapolis	IN	47295
16	Grace	Kelly	5722 Killjoy Court	Shelbyville	IN	47281
17	Adam	Graham	756 Overman Street	Flint	MI	59837
18						16

Figure 5-20

10. **Save the workbook and close it. Close Excel.**

Summing Up

Here are the key points you learned about in this lesson:

- A database is a collection of information stored in a consistent, structured way.

- Each type of information is a field, and each complete entry for an instance is a record.

- Excel stores simple databases in tables. You can use ranges, but tables offer additional sorting, filtering, and summarizing capabilities.

- To convert a range to a table, you can select the data and then choose Insert⇨Table or Home⇨Format as Table.

- Click the Filter arrow to the right of a field name in a table header to open a menu containing sorting and filtering commands.

- You can filter data in many ways, including using the Filter menu, right-clicking the data, or using filter commands on the Data tab.

- You can format a table from the Table Tools Design tab, in the Table Styles group, or by choosing Home⇨Format as Table.

- To add a Total row to a table, mark the Total Row check box on the Table Tools Design tab.

- To convert a table back to a range, choose Table Tools Design⇨Convert to Range.

- To merge data from multiple cells, use the CONCATENATE function.

- To split data into multiple cells, choose Data⇨Text to Columns.

Try-it-yourself lab

1. **Start Excel, open the file Try It Addresses.xlsx, and save it as Splits.xlsx.**

2. **Using the Text to Columns feature, split the cities, states, and zip codes into separate columns.**

   Hint: Use Comma and Space as the delimiters.

3. **Convert the range containing all the data to a table.**

4. Rename each of the column headings from the default names (Column1 through Column6) to more appropriate names.

5. Save the workbook and close Excel.

Know this tech talk

CONCATENATE: An Excel function that merges data from two or more cells into one cell.

database: A collection of information stored in a consistent, structured way.

field: A specific type of information, such as cities or zip codes.

filter: To hide data that does not match criteria you specify.

filter by selection: To hide data that does not match a selection.

record: All the stored information about one instance, such as an individual person's name and contact information.

relational database: A multi-table database, such as one created in Microsoft Access.

table: In Excel, a range that has been defined as a database.

Text to Columns: An Excel feature that splits data from one column into multiple columns.

Total row: In a table, an optional row that performs summary operations on one or more fields in the table.

Lesson 6

Exploring Financial Functions and Scenarios

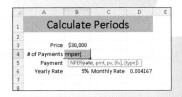

✔ The PV, FV, PMT, RATE, and NPER functions calculate parts of a loan or investment.

✔ Goal Seek helps you set variables for a formula to the exact amounts needed for the formula's result to come out a certain way.

✔ The Analysis ToolPak add-in offers additional features for performing data calculation and analysis.

✔ A moving average is more accurate as an estimator of future performance than a regular average when there are large fluctuations in the data.

✔ The Solver add-in finds optimal answers to complex questions that rely on multiple variables and constraints.

✔ Scenarios let you create and save multiple scenarios for what-if analysis.

✔ Naming a range makes it easier to refer to the range in formulas and functions.

One of the most common uses for Excel is to analyze financial data. Excel offers a huge variety of functions that can help make sense of money, and also a variety of add-ins, wizards, and other advanced features that can help, too.

In this lesson, you learn about a set of related financial functions for calculating loan payments and interest: PV, FV, PMT, RATE, and NPER. You also learn how to load add-ins, such as the Analysis ToolPak and Solver, and how to use them to find the best answers to financial questions. Finally, you learn how to save your what-if possibilities as scenarios, and how to name ranges to make it easier to refer to cells in formulas.

Exploring Financial Functions

Financial functions are some of the most useful tools for home and small business worksheets because they're all about the money: borrowing it, lending it, and monitoring it.

Here's the basic set:

- **PV:** Calculates the present value or principal amount. In a loan, it's the amount you're borrowing; in a savings account, it's the initial deposit.

- **FV:** The future value. This is the principal plus the interest paid or received.

- **PMT:** The payment to be made per period. For example, for a mortgage, it's the monthly payment; in a savings account, it's the amount you save each period. A period can be any time period, but it's usually a month.

- **RATE:** The interest rate to be charged per period (for a loan), or the percentage of amortization or depreciation per period.

- **NPER:** The number of periods. For a loan, it's the total number of payments to be made, or the points in time when interest is earned if you're tracking savings or amortization.

These financial functions are related. Each is an argument in the others; if you're missing one piece of information, you can use all the pieces you *do* know to find the missing one. For example, if you know the loan amount, the rate, and the number of years, you can determine the payment.

Take a look at the PMT function as an example. The syntax for the PMT function is as follows, with the optional parts in italic:

```
PMT(RATE, NPER, PV, FV, Type)
```

EXTRA INFO

Here is the syntax for each function. As you can see, they're all intertwined with one another:

```
PV (RATE, NPR, PMT,
    FV, Type)
FV(RATE, NPER, PMT,
    PV, Type)
PMT(RATE, NPER, PV,
    FV, Type)
RATE(NPER, PMT, PV,
    FV, Type)
NPER(RATE, PMT, PV,
    FV, Type)
```

TIP

The Type argument specifies when the payment is made: 1 for the beginning of the period, or 0 at the end of the period. Type is not a required argument, and I don't use it in the examples here.

So, for example, say the rate is 0.833 percent per month (that's 10 percent per year) for 60 months, and the amount borrowed is $25,000. The Excel formula looks like this:

```
=PMT(.00833,60,25000)
```

Enter that into a worksheet cell, and you find that the monthly payment is $531.13. You could also enter those values into cells, and then refer to the cells in the function arguments, like this (assuming you entered them into cells B1, B2, and B3):

```
=PMT(B1,B2,B3)
```

Use the PMT function

The PMT function calculates the payment amount on a loan, given the rate, number of periods, and the present value. Use this function to answer the question: "What would my monthly payment be?"

In this exercise, you calculate a loan payment.

Files needed: Loans.xlsx

1. **Open Loans.xlsx and save it as Loans Practice.xlsx.**

2. **On the PMT worksheet, from cell B5, choose Formulas⇨Insert Function.**

3. **In the Insert Function dialog box that appears, from the Or Select a Category drop-down list, choose Financial.**

4. **Select PMT from the Select a Function list, as shown in Figure 6-1, and then click OK.**

   The Function Arguments dialog box opens.

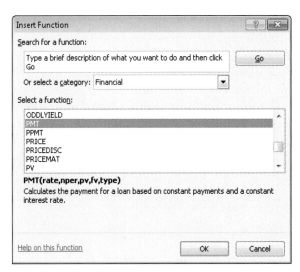

Figure 6-1

5. **Drag the dialog box to the side so you can see columns B through D on the worksheet; in the dialog box, click in the Rate text box and then click cell D6 in the worksheet.**

Interest rates on loans are commonly discussed as a yearly rate, but when calculating a payment, you need to use the monthly rate. The amount in cell D6 is the yearly rate (cell B6) divided by 12.

6. **In the dialog box, click in the Nper text box, and then click cell B4 on the worksheet.**

7. **In the dialog box, click in the Pv text box, and then click cell B3 on the worksheet, as shown in Figure 6-2.**

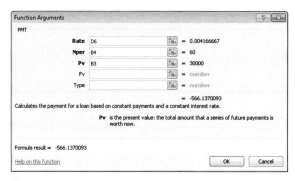

Figure 6-2

8. **Click OK. The calculated payment –$566.14 appears in cell B5. It is a negative number (and therefore appears in red and in parentheses) because the amount entered in cell B3 is positive.**

If you want the value in cell B5 to appear as a positive number, make the amount in cell B3 negative. If you want them both to appear as positives, enclose the function in B5 in an ABS (absolute value) function. To do this, change the entry in B5 to `=ABS(PMT(D6,B4,B3))`.

9. **Save the changes to the workbook.**

Leave the workbook open for the next exercise.

Use the NPER function

The NPER function calculates the number of payments (in other words, the length of the loan), given the rate, the present value, and the payment amount. Use this function to answer the question: "How long will it take to pay this off?"

In this exercise, you calculate the number of periods for a loan.

Files needed: Loans Practice.xlsx from the preceding exercise

1. **In Loans Practice.xlsx, click the NPER worksheet tab, click cell B4, and type** =NPER(.

   A ScreenTip appears below the cell to prompt you for the arguments. See Figure 6-3. The first argument, rate, is bold in the ScreenTip.

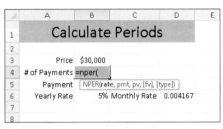

Figure 6-3

2. **Type** D6 **and then type a comma.** The ScreenTip makes the next argument prompt (pmt) bold. The formula now looks like this: =NPER(D6,.

3. **Type** B5 **and then type a comma. The ScreenTip makes the next argument prompt (pv) bold.** The formula now looks like this: =NPER(D6,B5,.

4. **Type** B3 **and then press Enter.** The function is complete. The number of payments is 69.18744.

You can't have a fractional payment in real life, so you might want to use the ROUNDUP function to round up the value in cell B4 to the nearest whole number. To do so, enclose the current function in a ROUNDUP function like this: =ROUNDUP(NPER(D6,B5,B3),0). The comma and zero near the end are required; the zero says to use no decimal places.

5. **Click the PMT worksheet tab and note the payment amount calculated for a loan of 60 months: $566.14.**

6. **Click the NPER worksheet tab and change the value in cell B5 to $566.14.** The number of payments in cell B4 changes to 60; Figure 6-4 shows the completed worksheet.

7. **Save the changes to the workbook.**

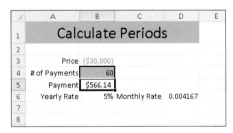

Figure 6-4

Leave the workbook open for the next exercise.

Use the PV function

The PV function calculates the starting value of a loan (assuming it starts in the present moment) given the rate, the number of periods, and the payment amount. Use this function to answer the question: "How much can I borrow?"

In this exercise, you calculate the present value for a loan.

Files needed: Loans Practice.xlsx from the preceding exercise

1. **In Loans Practice.xlsx, click the PV worksheet tab, and then in cell B3, type** =PV(D6,B4,B5).

2. **Press Enter.**

   The function is complete, and the value is ($26,495.35), which is negative. You can tell it's negative because of the parentheses.

3. **Select cell B3 and note the function in the formula bar is** =PV(D6,B4,B5).

4. **Change the value in cell B6 from 5% to 3.5%.**

   The amount in B3 changes to ($27,484.99). You can borrow more money if you get an interest rate lower than 5%.

5. **Change the value in cell B4 from 60 to 72.**

   The amount in B3 changes to ($32,428.79). You can borrow more money if you increase the length of the loan. Figure 6-5 shows the completed worksheet.

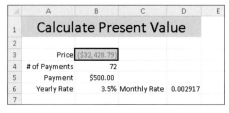

Figure 6-5

6. **Save the changes to the workbook.**

Leave the workbook open for the next exercise.

Analyzing Data

Besides using functions, you can analyze data in Excel in other ways. In the following sections, you learn about some of these methods, including using Goal Seek, using Solver, and calculating a moving average.

Using Goal Seek to find a value

When you create formulas that rely on values from multiple cells, you can usually experiment with various values to approximate a certain desired value in the formula's result. For example, suppose you have a PMT (payment) function set up and are trying to determine the maximum amount you can spend on a car if your payment has to be less than $400. You can enter different amounts for the PV argument until you find the one that results in the PMT function being exactly $400.

You don't have to use the trial-and-error method to find the formula result you're after. You may prefer to use the Goal Seek feature in such situations to automatically set a certain variable to a certain amount in order to reach a certain goal.

In this exercise, you use Goal Seek to find the loan amount when the payment is a certain value.

Files needed: Loans Practice.xlsx from the preceding exercise

1. **In Loans Practice.xlsx, click the PMT worksheet tab and select cell B5.2. Choose Data⇨What-If Analysis⇨Goal Seek.**

   The Goal Seek dialog box opens.

3. **In the Set Cell box, B5 is already entered, so leave that as-is; in the To Value box, type -400, making sure you type a – sign at the beginning to make it negative.**

   Here's an exception: If you used the ABS function to change the value in B5 to a positive number earlier, do not make the number negative here.

4. **In the By Changing Cell box, type B3, as shown in Figure 6-6.**

5. **Click OK. The value in cell B3 changes to $21,196, as shown in Figure 6-7. Click OK to accept the new values.**

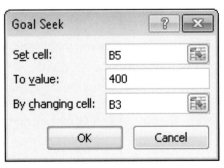

Figure 6-6

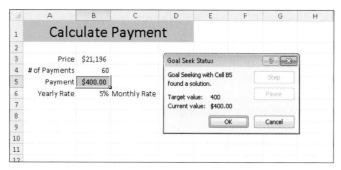

Figure 6-7

6. Save the workbook and close it.

Leave Excel open for the next exercise.

Loading an add-in

Excel has some tools that are rather specialized, and rather than bog down the application with them for everyone, Microsoft issued them as add-ins for Excel. You can load them only if you need them. An add-in is an optional feature that can be enabled or disabled in the application.

In this exercise, you load the Analysis ToolPak and the Solver add-ins, which you need for upcoming exercises.

Files needed: None

1. Choose File⇨Options ⇨ Add-Ins.

A list of active and inactive add-ins appears. See Figure 6-8.

2. In the Manage drop-down list toward the bottom of the window, choose Excel Add-Ins if it's not already selected and then click the Go button.

The Add-Ins dialog box opens.

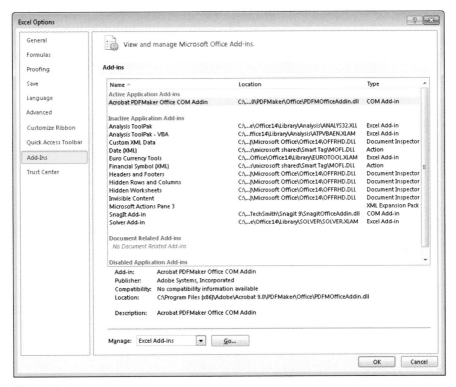

Figure 6-8

3. **Select the Analysis ToolPak check box.**

   (You don't need to select the Analysis ToolPak – VBA check box.)

4. **Select the Solver add-in if it is not already selected.**

   You'll use Solver later in this lesson. See Figure 6-9.

5. **Click OK and then click the Data tab on the Ribbon.**

   Notice that a new Analysis group appears, with a Data Analysis button in it. See Figure 6-10. You use this button in later exercises to select data analysis features.

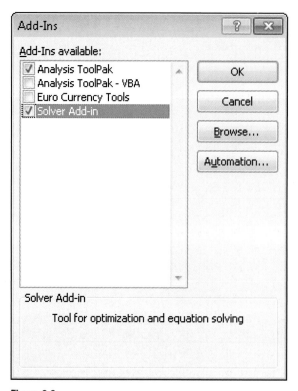

Figure 6-9

Add-ins

Figure 6-10

Leave Excel open for the next exercise.

Calculating a moving average

When you look at all the data in an Excel worksheet, you may find some values in a data series that are not congruent with the surrounding ones. For example, you may see a particularly good or bad month for sales in an organization that usually has fairly consistent sales revenue. Excel helps you get a clearer picture of the data with its Moving Average feature in the Analysis ToolPak.

Calculating a moving average manually

You could calculate moving averages on your own, but it would be time-consuming. For example, suppose you wanted a moving average of the following numbers: 3, 5, 4, 7, 10, with an interval of 3. To calculate the moving average manually:

> **LINGO**
>
> A **moving average** is a sequence of averages computed from parts of a data series. A moving average smoothes out fluctuations in data to show a pattern or trend more clearly.

1. **Take the average of the first number (in this case, 3) with the two numbers that come before it. No two numbers come before 3, so this produces nothing.**

2. **Take the average of the second number (in this case, 5) with the two numbers that come before it. Again, no two numbers come before 5, so this produces nothing.**

3. **Take the average of the third number (in this case, 4) with the two numbers that come before it (in this case, 3 and 5): (3+5+4)÷3=4, so the first number in the moving average is 4.**

4. **Take the average of the fourth number (in this case, 7) with the two numbers that come before it (in this case, 5 and 4): (5+4+7)÷3=5$^1/_3$, so the second number in the moving average is 5.33.**

5. **Take the average of the fifth number (in this case, 10) with the two that come before it (in this case, 4 and 7): (4+7+10)÷3=7, so the third number in the moving average is 7.**

Based on those calculations the moving averages for this data are 4, 5.33, and 7. Overall the trend of this data is an increase of approximately 1.5 per movement, because there is about 1.5 difference between the three averages.

Calculating a moving average in Excel

I had you calculate a moving average manually in the preceding exercise to give you an appreciation of how much easier moving averages are to calculate using Excel.

In this exercise, you use the Moving Average feature of the Analysis ToolPak to calculate a moving average.

Files needed: Analysis.xlsx

1. **Open Analysis.xlsx, save it as Analysis Practice.xlsx, and display the Revenue sheet if it's not already displayed.**

2. **Choose Data⇨Data Analysis. In the Data Analysis dialog box that appears, select Moving Average, as shown in Figure 6-11, and then click OK.**

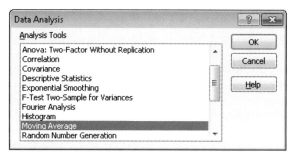

Figure 6-11

3. **In the Moving Average dialog box that appears, type** C1:C13 **in the Input Range box.**

   Alternatively, you can select the range C1:C13 behind the dialog box.

   TIP

   Excel fills in the dollar signs around the cell addresses automatically, creating absolute references.

4. **Select the Labels in First Row check box and then type** 3 **in the Interval box.**

5. **In the Output Range box, type** D2:D13 **(or select that range on the worksheet behind the dialog box) and then select the Chart Output check box.**

   The completed dialog box resembles Figure 6-12.

EXTRA INFO

The higher the interval, the more numbers adjacent to each value in the data series will be considered in the averaging, and the smoother the results will be. However, the higher the interval, the fewer usable values there will be in the results because Excel throws out a number of results at the beginning of the data series equal to the interval you chose minus 1. So, for example, if you use an interval of 3, the first two rows will not have a moving average calculated for them.

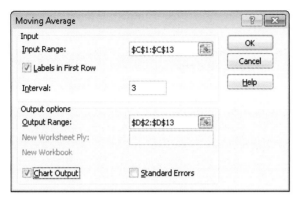

Figure 6-12

6. **Click OK and notice that the moving average values are filled into the range D4:D13 (cells D2 and D3 show the #N/A error message), and a chart is created on the worksheet (see Figure 6-13).**

Expected errors

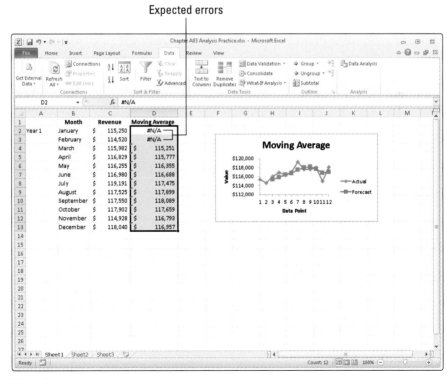

Figure 6-13

7. **Drag the border of the chart frame to expand it so you can see the chart more clearly.**

The blue line (Actual) is plotted from the Revenue column. The red line (Forecast) is plotted from the Moving Average column. See Figure 6-14. The Forecast line is much smoother because the moving average minimizes the variations.

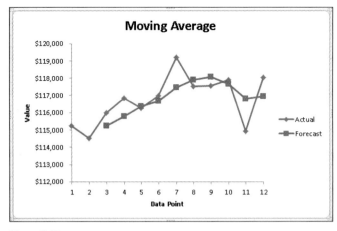

Figure 6-14

8. **Click cell D4 and notice the =AVERAGE(C2:C4) formula in the formula bar. Click cell D5 and notice the =AVERAGE(C3:C5) formula in the formula bar.** This is congruent with the manual moving averaging you did earlier.

9. **Save the workbook.**

Leave the workbook open for the next exercise.

Using Solver to analyze complex problems

Using Solver to analyze complex problems works something like Goal Seek (as you see in the "Using Goal Seek to find a value" section). With Goal Seek, you find a certain value in one cell based on changing one other cell. Excel's Solver tool is somewhat like Goal Seek except that it solves problems that have multiple variables and constraints.

LINGO

A **constraint** is a rule that limits the range of values a cell may contain. For example, in a grade book worksheet, a constraint might be that scores on a test must not be negative numbers.

Suppose you run a factory that has a certain number of employees, and can produce different products, each of which has different manufacturing parts and labor costs and can be sold for a different price. Which products should you make, and how many, in order to produce the most profit? Solver can provide an answer to complex questions like this.

In this exercise, you use Solver to determine the optimal number of two products to produce.

Files needed: Analysis Practice.xlsx from the preceding exercise

1. **Click the Production tab, and take a moment to familiarize yourself with the scenario outlined there, as shown in Figure 6-15.**

   • Each product takes both materials and labor to produce.

   • Each product has a fixed cost to produce that is based on the materials plus labor cost.

   • There is a limited number of man-hours per day because there are only 15 employees (see cell B3).

   • The profit for each product (cells F14 and F15) is the sales price minus all the manufacturing costs.

   • You need to determine which combination of product production will generate the maximum value in the Total Profit cell (F17).

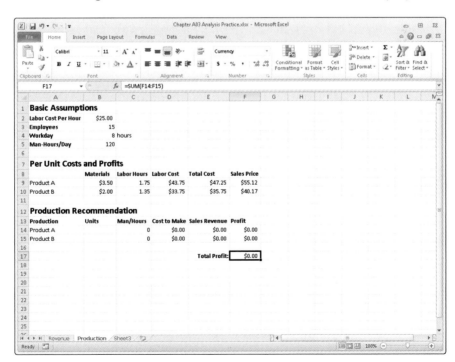

Figure 6-15

2. **In cell B14, type** 75, **as an experiment.** The worksheet shows how much profit would be made if you made 75 units of product A and none of product B.

3. **Notice in cell C17 that Man/Hours is over the 120 limit specified in cell B5. That won't work.**

4. **Type** 68 **in cell B14.** Now Man/Hours is 119, which is within the limit.

5. **Type** 38 **in each of the cells B14 and B15.** Cell F17 now shows what the profit would be if you made equal numbers of each product, and kept the Man/Hours less than 120.

As you can see, with so many factors involved, this is a very thorny problem to figure out on your own. Solver will make it much easier.

6. **Choose Data⇨Solver, and the Solver Parameters dialog box opens.**

7. **In the Set Objective box, type** F17 **and make sure the Max option button is selected in the To area.** (Cell F17 contains the total profit, and you want to maximize it.)

8. **In the By Changing Variable Cells box, type** B14:B15.

(These are the two cells that you want to find the correct values for, the number of units to produce of each product.) The dialog box looks like Figure 6-16.

Figure 6-16

9. **Click the Add button to add a constraint, and in the Add Constraint dialog box that opens, type** C17 **in the Cell Reference box. The drop-down list is already set to Less Than Or Equal To (<=), so leave it as-is.**

Figure 6-17

10. **In the Constraint box, type** B5 **(see Figure 6-17) and then click OK to add the constraint to the Subject to the Constraints list.**

11. **Click the Solve button in the Solve Parameters dialog box.**

The values in cells B14 and B15 change, and the Solver Results dialog box opens. See Figure 6-18. Solver has determined that the maximum profit will be obtained by making 88 units of Product B and none of Product A.

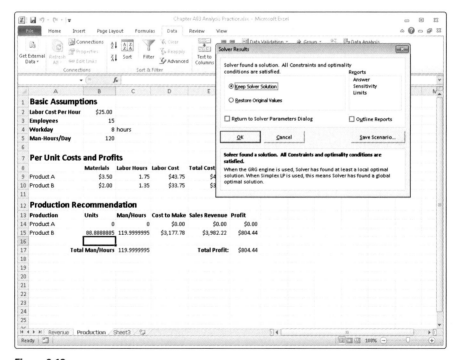

Figure 6-18

12. **In the Solver Results dialog box, click OK to keep the Solver solution.**

    With the current data, it made more sense to not make any of Product A. But what if you needed to produce at least half as many of product A as you do Product B? Modify Solver to accommodate that additional constraint.

13. **Choose Data⇨Solver to open the Solver Parameters dialog box and then click the Add button to open the Add Constraint dialog box.**

14. **In the Cell Reference box, type B14 and choose >= from the drop-down list.**

15. **In the Constraint box, type =B15/2 and then click OK.** The new constraint is added, as shown in Figure 6-19.

Figure 6-19

16. **Click the Solve button in the Solver Parameters dialog box.** The Solver Results dialog box appears, and the values in cells B14 and B15 change to reflect the new constraints. See Figure 6-20.

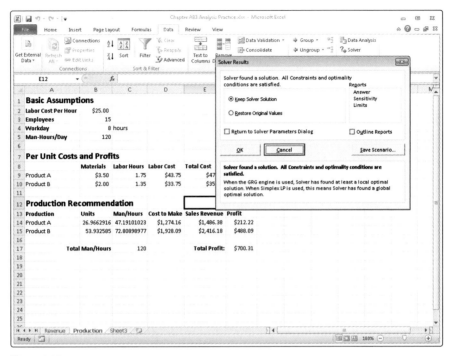

Figure 6-20

17. **In the Solver Results dialog box, click the Save Scenario button to open the Save Scenario dialog box.**

You learn more about scenarios in the next exercise.

18. **Type 2X Product B in the Scenario Name field, as shown in Figure 6-21, and then click OK.**

19. **Click OK again to dismiss the Solver Results dialog box. Then save the workbook.**

Leave the workbook open for the next exercise.

Figure 6-21

Creating Scenarios

As you see in the earlier exercises, what-if analysis can be very useful. You can try different possibilities to see which one gives you the results you want. After you try a certain combination of values, you may want to revisit that combination at a later time. Using scenarios in Excel makes it possible to easily do so.

LINGO

A **scenario** is a stored set of values for particular cells. At the end of the preceding exercise, for example, you saved the Solver results as a scenario. You can recall this scenario at any time from the Scenario Manager. You can also create new scenarios and store them for later use.

Recalling a stored scenario

If you already have a scenario stored, you can easily recall it with the Scenario Manager.

In this exercise, you open a stored scenario.

Files needed: Analysis Practice.xlsx from the preceding exercise

1. **On the Production tab, in cell B14, type** 0, **replacing the value there. In cell B15, type** 88, **replacing the value there.**

2. **Choose Data⇨What-If Analysis⇨Scenario Manager.** The 2X Product B scenario is there from the preceding exercise. See Figure 6-22.

Figure 6-22

3. **Click the 2X Product B scenario if it is not already selected and then click the Show button.** The stored scenario is loaded into the appropriate cells on the worksheet.

4. **Click the Close button.** The Scenario Manager closes.

5. **Save the workbook.**

Leave the workbook open for the next exercise.

Creating a scenario

When you were using Solver, you saw one way of creating a scenario — to save the Solver results as one. You can also manually create new scenarios.

In this exercise, you create a new scenario that looks at what would happen if the labor cost per hour changed.

Files needed: Analysis Practice.xlsx from the preceding exercise

1. **Choose Data⇨What-If Analysis⇨Scenario Manager to open the Scenario Manager dialog box.**

2. **Click the Add button, and the Add Scenario dialog box opens, as shown in Figure 6-23.**

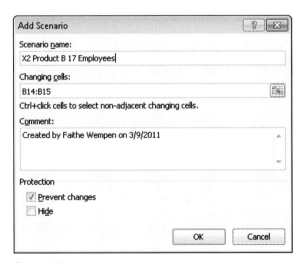

Figure 6-23

3. **In the Scenario Name box, replace the current name with** Labor Cost Decrease; **in the Changing Cells box, replace the current entry with** B2.

Figure 6-24

4. **Click OK, and in the Scenario Values dialog box that opens, change 25 (the current value in B2) to 20, as shown in Figure 6-24, and then click OK again.**

The Scenario Manager dialog box reappears.

5. **Click the Show button.**

The value in cell B2 changes to 20, and the cells that depend on that value also change.

6. **Click the Close button to close the Scenario Manager dialog box.**

For more practice, re-run Solver to update the quantities in cells B14 and B15 to reflect the new labor cost. The quantities will stay the same.

7. **Save the workbook.**

Leave the workbook open for the next exercise.

Working with Named Ranges

Naming a range can be helpful because you can refer to the range by a friendly name, rather than by the cell addresses, when constructing formulas and functions. That way you don't have to remember the exact cell addresses; you can construct formulas based on meaning.

For example, instead of remembering that the number of employees is stored in cell B3, you could name cell B3 *Employees.* Then in a formula that uses B3's value, such as =B3*2, you could use the name instead, such as =Employees*2.

Naming a range

Here are the three ways to name a range, each with pros and cons:

- ✔ **If the default names are okay to use, you can choose Formulas⇨Create from Selection.** With this method, Excel chooses the name for you based on text labels it finds in an adjacent cell (above or to the left of the current cells). This method is very fast and easy, and works well when you have to create a lot of names at once and when the cells are well-labeled with adjacent text.

- ✔ **You can select the range and then type a name in the Name box** (the area immediately above the column A heading, to the left of the Formula bar). With this fast and easy method, you get to choose the name. However, you have to do each range separately; you can't do a big batch at a time like you can by choosing Formulas⇨Create from Selection.

- ✔ **If you want to more precisely control the options for the name, choose Formulas⇨Define Name.** This method opens a dialog box from which you can specify the name, the scope, and any comments you might want to include.

In this exercise, you name several ranges using three methods.

Files needed: Analysis Practice.xlsx from the preceding exercise

1. **On the Production tab, select the range A3:B4 and then choose Formulas⇨Create from Selection to open the Create Names from Selection dialog box.**

2. **Select the Left Column check box (see Figure 6-25) and then click OK.**

   Cells C3 and C4 are assigned names based on the text in cells B3 and B4.

Figure 6-25

3. **Choose Formulas⇨Name Manager. The Name Manager dialog box opens.**

   The names appear on the list that you just created. See Figure 6-26.

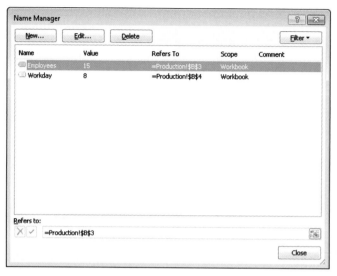

Figure 6-26

4. **Click Close to close the Name Manager dialog box.**

5. **Click cell F9; in the Name box above column A, type** SalesPriceA **(as shown in Figure 6-27) and press Enter.**

6. **Click cell F10; in the Name box, type** SalesPriceB **and press Enter.**

7. **Click cell F17 and choose Formulas⇨Define Name.**

   The New Name dialog box opens. The Total_Profit name is suggested for you. That name works well enough, so you don't need to change it.

8. **Choose Production from the Scope drop-down list, as shown in Figure 6-28.** This name applies only to this worksheet.

9. **Click OK to create the name and then choose Formulas⇨Name Manager.** The Name Manager dialog box reopens.

10. **Examine the list of all the named ranges you have created, and then click Close to close the dialog box.**

Name box

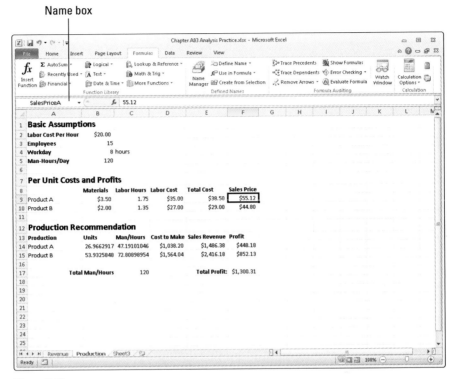

Figure 6-27

TIP

All the ranges you created in this exercise consist of a single cell, but ranges can consist of any number of cells. When a range contains multiple cells and you use the name in a formula, Excel treats it as if you had specified the range with the starting and ending cell addresses, such as A3:B6.

11. Save the workbook.

Leave the workbook open for the next exercise.

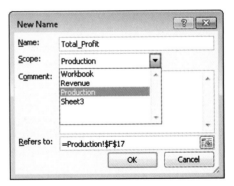

Figure 6-28

Using a named range in a formula

The main reason for naming a range is to refer to it in a formula. You can substitute the range name for the cell addresses in any situation where using a range would be appropriate.

WARNING!

Range names that refer to multiple cells may produce an error in a formula where a multi-celled range would not be an appropriate argument. For example, if the Sales range referred to B4:B8, the formula =Sales would result in an error because there's no math operation specified. (The formula =B4:B8 would produce the same error.) However, =SUM(Sales) would work just fine, as would =SUM(B4:B8).

In this exercise, you use range names in formulas.

Files needed: Analysis Practice.xlsx from the preceding exercise

1. **Click cell B5 to select it and then replace its formula with** =Employees*Workday.

2. **Select cell E14, click in the formula bar, and edit the formula as follows:** =B14*SalesPriceA.

3. **Select cell E15, click in the formula bar, and edit the formula as follows:** =B15*SalesPriceB.

4. **Save the workbook and close it.**

5. **Exit Excel.**

 *Summing Up*

Here are the key points you learned about in this lesson:

- ✔ The functions PV, FV, PMT, RATE, and NPER are all for calculating different parts of a loan's terms. PV is present value; FV is future value. PMT is payment amount. RATE is interest rate. NPER is number of periods.

- ✔ The Goal Seek feature helps you adjust the value in one cell by solving for a particular value in another dependent cell. To access Goal Seek, choose Data⇨What-If Analysis⇨Goal Seek.

- ✔ Some features in Excel are add-ins. To load an add-in, choose File⇨ Add-Ins, and in the Manage box, select Excel Add-Ins, and click Go.

- ✔ One of the Data Analysis add-in features is Moving Average, which calculates a sequence of averages to smooth out fluctuations in data.

- ✔ Another add-in is Solver, which is like Goal Seek except it solves problems that have multiple variables and constraints.

- ✔ A scenario is a stored set of values for particular cells. You can save and load scenarios to try and re-try different possibilities. Access them from Data⇨What-If Analysis⇨Scenario Manager.

- ✔ You can name ranges and then use the names in formulas and functions instead of the cell references. One way to name a range is to select it and then type a name in the Name box (to the left of the Formula bar).

Try-it-yourself lab

1. **Start Excel, and create a worksheet that uses the RATE function to calculate the interest rate on a loan given a present value of $150,000, a term of 360 payments, and a payment of $1,000. Make the present value negative in the worksheet so the rate comes out positive.**

 In the cell where you place the RATE function, you may need to increase the number of decimal places shown in order to see the rate correctly. Choose Home⇨Increase Decimal. You may also want to format the rates as percentages; choose Home⇨Percentage.

2. **(Optional) Look up the PPMT function in the Excel Help system, and then use it to create an amortization table for the loan. If you don't know what an amortization table is, research it online.** Figure 6-29 shows an example of the completed project.

	A	B	C	D	E	F
1	Loan					
2						
3	Rate	0.59%	Yearly	7%		
4	Value	($150,000)				
5	Periods	360				
6	Payment	$1,000				
7						
8						
9	#	Payment	Principal	Interest	Balance	
10					($150,000)	
11	1	$1,000	$122.46	$877.54	($149,877.54)	
12	2	$1,000	$123.08	$876.92	($149,754.46)	
13	3	$1,000	$123.70	$876.30	($149,630.76)	
14	4	$1,000	$124.32	$875.68	($149,506.45)	
15	5	$1,000	$124.94	$875.06	($149,381.51)	
16	6	$1,000	$125.57	$874.43	($149,255.94)	
17	7	$1,000	$126.19	$873.81	($149,129.74)	
18	8	$1,000	$126.83	$873.17	($149,002.92)	
19	9	$1,000	$127.46	$872.54	($148,875.46)	
20	10	$1,000	$128.10	$871.90	($148,747.36)	
21	11	$1,000	$128.73	$871.27	($148,618.63)	
22	12	$1,000	$129.37	$870.63	($148,489.26)	
23	13	$1,000	$130.02	$869.98	($148,359.24)	
24	14	$1,000	$130.66	$869.34	($148,228.57)	
25	15	$1,000	$131.31	$868.69	($148,097.26)	
26	16	$1,000	$131.96	$868.04	($147,965.30)	
27	17	$1,000	$132.62	$867.38	($147,832.68)	
28	18	$1,000	$133.27	$866.73	($147,699.40)	

◄ ◄ ► ►◄ Sheet1 / Sheet2 / Sheet3 / ◌ /

Figure 6-29

Excel has an interest calculation function, IPMT, but you don't have to use it to calculate the interest. You can just subtract the principal amount from the payment.

As you are entering the arguments for the PPMT function, make sure you use absolute references for any of the cells that shouldn't change when that function is copied. That way you can easily fill in the rest of the amortization table by copying.

Know this tech talk

add-in: An optional feature that can be enabled or disabled in an application.

constraint: A rule that limits the range of values a cell may contain.

FV: A function that calculates the future value of a loan or savings account.

Goal Seek: A feature that forces a certain cell to be a certain value by changing the values in dependent cells.

moving average: A sequence of averages computed from parts of a data series.

NPER: A function that calculates the number of periods in a loan.

PMT: A function that calculates the payment to be made per period for a loan.

PV: A function that calculates the present value or principal amount for a loan or savings account.

RATE: A function that calculates the interest rate to be charged per period, or the percentage of amortization or depreciation per period.

scenario: A stored set of values for particular cells in a worksheet.

Solver: An Excel add-in that solves for a certain value by manipulating one or more variables or constraints.

Working with Math, Statistical, and Text Functions

✔ You can exponentiate a number by any multiple with the POWER function.

✔ You can quickly determine a number's square root with the SQRT function.

✔ The ROUND functions enable you to round numbers to a certain number of decimal places.

✔ You can calculate sine, cosine, and tangent with Excel's trigonometry functions SIN, COS, and TAN.

✔ The AVERAGE and MEDIAN functions help you find the average and midpoint values in data series.

✔ The MAX and MIN functions report the highest and lowest values in a series of numbers.

✔ The COUNT function counts the number of values in a specified range.

✔ You can change the case of text with the UPPER, LOWER, and PROPER functions.

✔ The TRIM function removes extra spaces in text strings, and the CLEAN function removes non-printing characters from text strings.

✔ You can combine the contents of two or more cells with the CONCATENATE function.

*E*xcel offers hundreds of functions in various categories. In this lesson, I show you a sampling of the functions in three of those categories: math, statistics, and text. You learn how to do exponentiation and square roots using functions; how to compute sines, cosines, and tangents; and how to format and manipulate text by using functions.

Using Math Functions

Excel uses basic math operators in formulas, and you're probably already familiar with these:

- ✔ **Addition:** +
- ✔ **Subtraction:** –
- ✔ **Multiplication:** *
- ✔ **Division:** /
- ✔ **Exponentiation:** ^

If you want to go beyond these basic calculations, you must rely on functions. In the next several exercises, you explore Excel's math functions and try a few examples.

Use the POWER and SQRT functions

The POWER function takes the number to the *n*th power, where *n* is a number you specify. For example, if cell A1 contains 7, and you enter =POWER(A1,2) in some other cell, the result is 49, which is 7 to the 2nd power (7×7). The function =POWER(A1,3) would result in 343, which is $7 \times 7 \times 7$.

LINGO

Exponentiation is another name for power. You can do exponentiation with the ^ math operator in Excel instead of using the POWER function if you prefer. For example, instead of =POWER(A1,2), you could use =A1^2.

Square root is the opposite of exponentiation; it's the number that, when multiplied by itself, equals the original value. For example, 4 is the square root of 16 because 4 x 4 = 16.

The SQRT function finds the square root of a number. For example, if cell A1 contains 49, the function =SQRT(A1) would produce a result of 7.

In this exercise, you practice using the POWER and SQRT functions.

Files needed: Functions.xlsx

1. **Open Functions.xlsx, save it as Functions Practice.xlsx, and click the Power worksheet tab to display that sheet.**

2. **In cell A3, type** =SQRT(B3) **and then press Enter. Click cell A3 again and drag the fill handle down to cell A12 to copy the function.** See Figure 7-1.

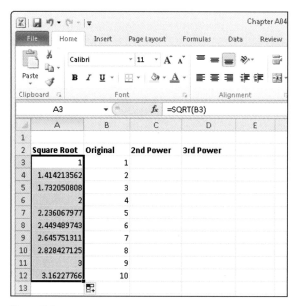

Figure 7-1

3. **In cell C3, type** =POWER(B3,2) **and then press Enter. Click cell C3 again and drag the fill handle down to cell C12 to copy the function.** See Figure 7-2.

4. **In cell D3, type** =POWER(B3,3) **and then press Enter. Click cell D3 again and drag the fill handle down to cell D12 to copy the function.** See Figure 7-3.

5. **Save the workbook.**

Leave the workbook open for the next exercise.

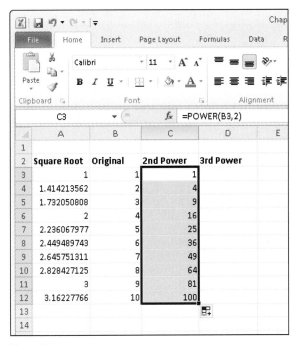

Figure 7-2

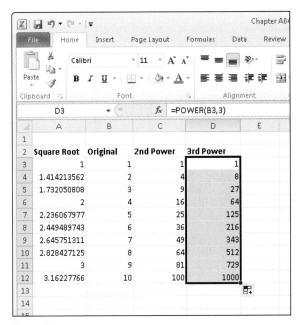

Figure 7-3

Use the ROUND functions

The ROUND function rounds a number either up or down, depending on the number, to a specified number of decimal points. For example, if cell A1 contains 3.244, the function =ROUND(A1,2) rounds this number to two decimal places, resulting in 3.24. The final 4 is rounded down to 0 because the value of that digit (4) is less than 5. If the value of the digit removed is greater than or equal to 5, the number is rounded up. If the number does not have as many decimal places as the function specifies, the ROUND function makes no change to the number.

LINGO

To **round** a number is to limit a number to a certain number of decimal places, increasing the last visible decimal place digit by one if the numbers removed were greater than or equal to 5. For example, when rounding 1.252 to 2 decimal places, the result would be 1.25 because the removed number (2) is less than 5. However, rounding 1.256 to 2 decimal places would result in 1.26 because the removed number (6) is greater than 5.

If you want to round a number down, regardless of whether the digit being rounded is greater than or less than 5, use the ROUNDDOWN function. Conversely, to round up no matter what the number is, use ROUNDUP.

In this exercise, you practice using rounding functions.

Files needed: Functions Practice.xlsx from the preceding exercise

1. **Click the Rounding worksheet tab to switch to that sheet.**

2. **In cell B3, type** =ROUND(A3,1) **and then press Enter. Click cell B3 again and drag the fill handle down to cell B9 to copy the function.** See Figure 7-4.

3. **In cell C3, type** =ROUNDUP(A3,1) **and then press Enter. Click cell C3 again and drag the fill handle down to cell C9 to copy the function.** See Figure 7-5.

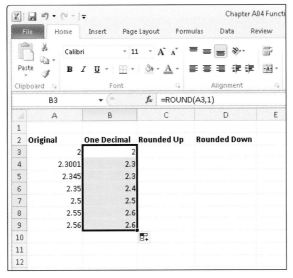

Figure 7-4

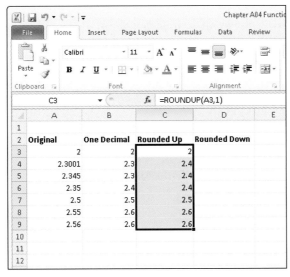

Figure 7-5

4. **In cell D3, type** =ROUNDDOWN(A3,1) **and then press Enter. Click cell D3 again and drag the fill handle down to cell D9 to copy the function.** See Figure 7-6.

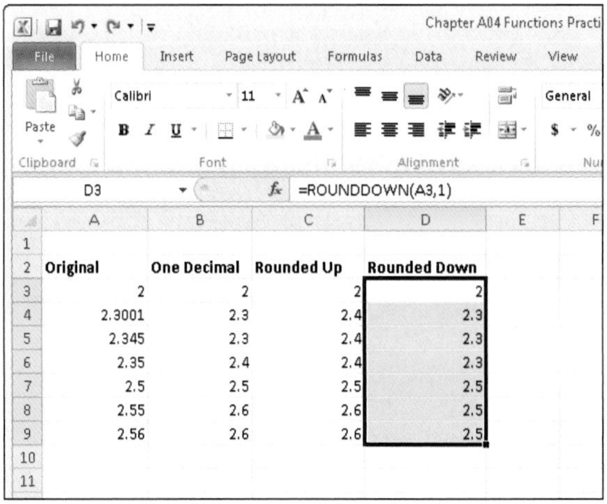

Figure 7-6

5. **Save the workbook.**

Leave the workbook open for the next exercise.

Use trigonometry functions

Sine, cosine, and tangent are three essential calculations used in trigonometry. Excel has functions for each of them: SIN, COS, and TAN. You can use them to create a reference table for solving trigonometry problems, or for solving individual trig problems.

In this exercise, you practice using trigonometry functions.

Files needed: Functions Practice.xlsx from the preceding exercise

1. **Click the Trig worksheet tab to switch to that sheet.**

2. **In cell B3, type** =SIN(A3) **and then press Enter. In cell C3, type** =COS(A3) **and then press Enter. In cell D3, type** =TAN(A3) **and then press Enter.** See Figure 7-7.

3. **Select the range B3:D3 and drag the fill handle down to cell D21, copying the functions.** See Figure 7-8.

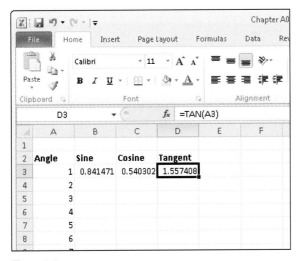

Figure 7-7

	A	B	C	D	E
1					
2	**Angle**	**Sine**	**Cosine**	**Tangent**	
3	1	0.841471	0.540302	1.557408	
4	2	0.909297	-0.41615	-2.18504	
5	3	0.14112	-0.98999	-0.14255	
6	4	-0.7568	-0.65364	1.157821	
7	5	-0.95892	0.283662	-3.38052	
8	6	-0.27942	0.96017	-0.29101	
9	7	0.656987	0.753902	0.871448	
10	8	0.989358	-0.1455	-6.79971	
11	9	0.412118	-0.91113	-0.45232	
12	10	-0.54402	-0.83907	0.648361	
13	11	-0.99999	0.004426	-225.951	
14	12	-0.53657	0.843854	-0.63586	
15	13	0.420167	0.907447	0.463021	
16	14	0.990607	0.136737	7.244607	
17	15	0.650288	-0.75969	-0.85599	
18	16	-0.2879	-0.95766	0.300632	
19	17	-0.9614	-0.27516	3.493916	
20	18	-0.75099	0.660317	-1.13731	
21	19	0.149877	0.988705	0.151589	
22	20	0.912945	0.408082	2.237161	
23	21	0.836656	-0.54773	-1.5275	
24					
25					

Figure 7-8

4. **Save the workbook.**

Leave the workbook open for the next exercise.

TIP

Many other math functions are available. To find a complete list of Excel's math-based functions, choose Formulas➪Math & Trig. Then click the formula you're interested in using to open a dialog box where you can enter its arguments.

Using Statistical Functions

Statistical functions help you interpret a data set, providing useful information about the data that might not be obvious at a glance. When many people hear *statistics,* they automatically think about advanced statistical analysis like standard deviation and variance (and Excel offers many functions to do those calculations), but statistics is a much larger tent than that and also includes more basic calculations such as averages, medians, and counts as well.

Use the AVERAGE and MEDIAN functions

Average and median are two ways of looking at what consists of a common score or response. Neither is better than the other; they are simply two different ways of analyzing data.

In this exercise, you practice using the AVERAGE and MEDIAN functions.

Files needed: Functions Practice.xlsx from the preceding exercise

1. **Click the Stats worksheet tab to switch to that sheet.**

2. **In cell B2, type** =AVERAGE(, **drag across the range B10:B35, and press Enter.** Excel adds the closing parenthesis for you automatically. The average for test 1 appears in cell B2.

3. **Click cell B2 to see the formula in the formula bar.** See Figure 7-9.

4. **In cell B3, type** =MEDIAN(B10:B35) **and press Enter.** (You could drag across the range again as you did in Step 2, but typing is sometimes easier.)

> **LINGO**
>
> An **average** sums all the values and then divides that total by the number of values. A **median** is the middle value in the list of values when arranged from large to small (or vice versa; it's the same either way). For example, in the list 1, 5, and 6, the average is 4 (1+5+6 divided by 3), and the median is 5 (the middle number).

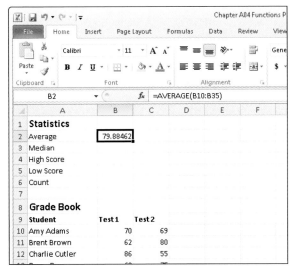

Figure 7-9

5. Click cell B3 to see the formula in the Formula bar. See Figure 7-10.

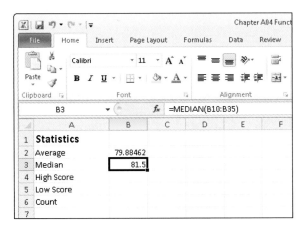

Figure 7-10

6. Save the workbook.

Leave the workbook open for the next exercise.

Use the MAX, MIN, and COUNT functions

The MIN, MAX, and COUNT functions provide a specific piece of information about a data set.

In this exercise, you practice using the COUNT, MIN, and MAX functions.

Files needed: Functions Practice.xlsx from the preceding exercise

1. **On the Stats tab, in cell B4, type** =MAX(B10:B35) **and then press Enter.** The largest value from the range appears in cell B4.

2. **Click cell B4 again to see the completed function in the Formula bar.** See Figure 7-11.

LINGO

MIN determines the lowest (minimum) value in the set, and **MAX** determines the highest (maximum). **COUNT** counts the number of cells in a range that contains numeric values.

EXTRA INFO

There are other counting functions, and each one puts a slightly different spin on things. For example, COUNTA counts the number of non-blank cells in the range, regardless of whether they contain text or numbers, and COUNTBLANK counts the number of blank cells. COUNTIF counts the number of cells that meet a condition you specify, and DCOUNT counts the cells containing numbers that also match conditions you specify.

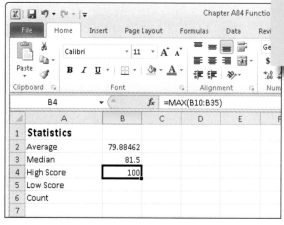

Figure 7-11

3. **In cell B5, type** =MIN(B10:B35) **and then press Enter.** The smallest value from the range appears in cell B5.

4. **In cell B6, type** =COUNT(B10:B35) **and then press Enter.**

5. **Click cell B6 again to see the completed function in the formula bar. See Figure 7-12.**

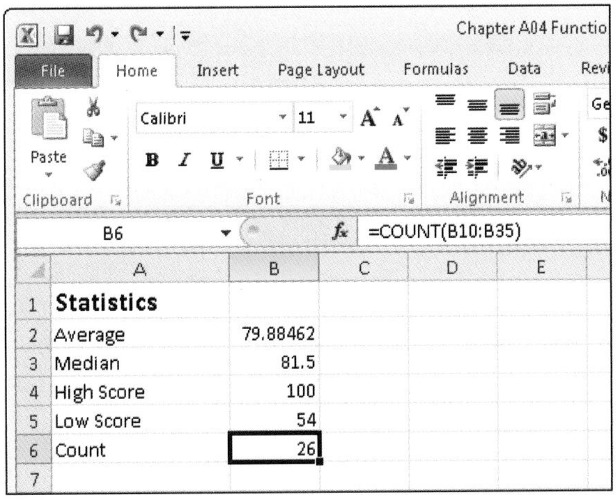

	A	B	C	D	E
1	**Statistics**				
2	Average	79.88462			
3	Median	81.5			
4	High Score	100			
5	Low Score	54			
6	Count	26			
7					

B6 f_x =COUNT(B10:B35)

Figure 7-12

For more practice, repeat these steps for the data in column C, placing the functions in cells C2:C6.

6. **Save the workbook.**

Leave the workbook open for the next exercise.

Formatting Data with Text Functions

Functions usually work with numbers, but some functions are designed specifically for use with text. For example, if you have a list of data in which the capitalization is not consistent, you could use the UPPER function to make all the text uppercase.

EXTRA INFO

Many other statistical functions are available in Excel, including several that are specific to calculating probability, such as standard deviation and variance. For example, for standard deviation, Excel 2010 breaks variants into separate functions: STDEV.S (based on a sample) and STDEV.P (based on an entire population). For compatibility with Excel 2007 and earlier, Excel 2010 also supports a simpler and more generic version: STDEV, which calculates standard deviation based on a sample and ignores logical values and text. An STDEVA version is the same except it includes logical values and text.

Text functions can be used to

- ✓ **Standardize capitalization.** Use the UPPER, LOWER, and PROPER functions to correct data entry errors or apply capitalization conventions.

- ✓ **Clean up text.** Use CLEAN and TRIM to remove extra spaces or unwanted characters that may end up in your worksheet when you bring text into Excel from other sources.

- ✓ **Evaluate a text string.** The LEFT, MID, or RIGHT function can report on the characters at certain positions in a cell; LEN can report the length of the text string overall, and the T function tells whether a cell's content is a text string at all.

- ✓ **Merge cell contents.** With the CONCATENATE function, you can join the content of two or more cells into a single cell.

Replacing cell content using a text function is typically a multi-step process. When you modify a cell's content with a text function, you have to place the new entry in a separate cell from the original. Then, if you want the new entry to appear in the original location, you have to copy the function to the Clipboard and then use Paste Special to paste its value back to the original location. Finally, you can delete the function that you used to make the change. Some of the upcoming exercises demonstrate this process.

Standardize capitalization

Often when different people enter data into a worksheet, they have different ideas about the correct capitalization, or they simply get sloppy about entering data consistently. You can clean up data by standardizing the capitalization using a text function. The UPPER function converts all text to uppercase, LOWER converts all text to lowercase, and PROPER capitalizes only the first letter in each word, as if each word were a proper noun.

In this exercise, you practice using the PROPER and LOWER functions to standardize text capitalization.

Files needed: Functions Practice.xlsx from the preceding exercise

1. **Click the Text worksheet tab to display that worksheet.**

2. **In cell G3, type** =PROPER(A3) **and then press Enter.**

   The name Amy appears in G3. Amy doesn't change in cell A3 because it was already capitalized correctly. See Figure 7-13.

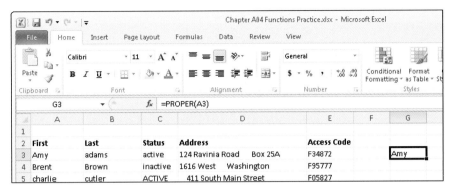

Figure 7-13

3. **Select cell G3 and drag the fill handle to cell H3, copying the function.** Notice that because the reference to cell A3 was relative, H3 now contains =PROPER(B3).

4. **Select the range G3:H3 and drag the fill handle down to cell H26, copying the function to all the intervening cells.** All the names appear in consistently capitalized form in columns G and H. See Figure 7-14.

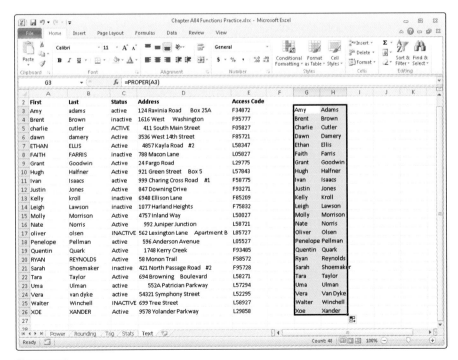

Figure 7-14

5. **Press Ctrl+C to copy the selected cells to the Clipboard and then click cell A3.**

6. **From the Home tab, click the down arrow on the Paste button, as shown in Figure 7-15, and choose the first icon in the Paste Values section.**

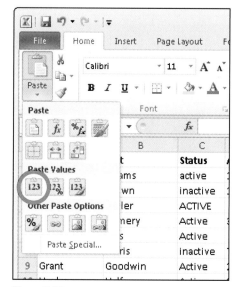

This pastes the results of the functions, rather than the functions themselves.

7. **Select G3:H26 again and then press the Delete key to clear their contents.**

8. **In the now-empty cell G3, type =LOWER(C3) and then press Enter.**

Cell G3 displays the word *active* — the same as what's in cell C3 — because C3 already contained a lowercase entry.

Figure 7-15

9. **Select cell G3 and drag the selection handle down to cell G26, copying the function.**

All the statuses from column C appear in column G in consistently lower-cased format. See Figure 7-16.

10. **Press Ctrl+C to copy the selection to the Clipboard and then click cell C3.**

11. **From the Home tab, click the down arrow on the Paste button and choose the first icon in the Paste Values section, pasting the values.**

12. **Select the range G3:G26 and then press the Delete key to remove the functions from column G.**

TIP

You might be thinking, "Why not use Ctrl+X for Cut instead of copying in Step 10?" Then you wouldn't have to delete the range in Step 12. That won't work, though, because Paste Values is not available as an option in Step 11 if you choose Cut in Step 10.

13. **Save the workbook.**

Leave the workbook open for the next exercise.

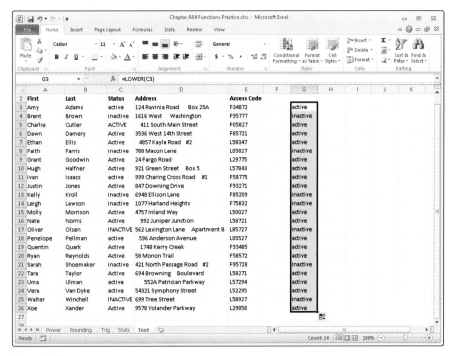

Figure 7-16

Clean up text

Sometimes when you bring in text to Excel from other sources, you end up with extra characters. These could be multiple extra spaces, or they could be non-printing "junk" characters such as tabs, page break characters, paragraph breaks, line breaks, and non-ASCII characters. Non-printing characters sometimes occur when you import data from obscure data formats, for example, or when Excel misidentifies the data type when importing data.

Excel gives you two functions for cleaning up text. The TRIM function removes extra spaces anywhere that they occur in the entry, replacing them with a single space. The CLEAN function removes any non-printing characters from the entry.

If unwanted blank spaces are at the beginning of a text entry, the TRIM function removes all except one of them in each spot. One exception, though: If blank spaces are at the beginning of the entry, it removes them all. That's actually very handy because then you don't have to worry about some entries having a blank space at the beginning that you would have to manually remove.

In this exercise, you clean up some text entries using the TRIM function.

Files needed: Functions Practice.xlsx from the preceding exercise

1. **On the Text worksheet, in cell G3, type =TRIM(D3) and then press Enter.**

   The same text in cell D3 appears in cell G3, except without the extra spaces.

2. **Click cell G3 and check the formula in the Formula bar.**

   See Figure 7-17.

Figure 7-17

3. **Drag the fill handle from cell G3 down to cell G26.**

   All the addresses are cleaned up, with extra spaces removed.

4. **With the range G3:G26 selected, press Ctrl+C to copy to the Clipboard and then click cell D3.**

5. **From the Home tab, click the down arrow on the Paste button and choose the first icon in the Paste Values section.**

   The cleaned-up addresses are pasted into column D. See Figure 7-18.

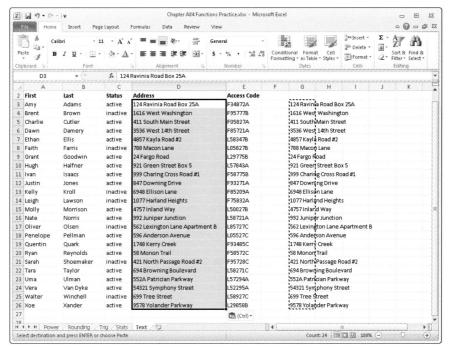

Figure 7-18

6. **Select the range G3:G26 and then press the Delete key to clear those cells.**

7. **Save the workbook.**

Leave the workbook open for the next exercise.

Extract characters

The LEFT, RIGHT, and MID functions extract a character from a specific point in the text string. LEFT extracts from the beginning, RIGHT from the end, and MID from the midpoint. You can specify the number of characters to include. These functions are handy when you need to distill text entries down to just a few characters at the beginning or end of the string, or to truncate text strings that are more than a certain number of characters.

In this exercise, you extract the suffix character (A, B, or C) from a list of access codes.

Files needed: Functions Practice.xlsx from the preceding exercise

1. **On the Text worksheet, in cell F2, type** Code Type.

2. **In cell F3, type** =RIGHT(E3,1) **and then press Enter.**

The RIGHT function has two arguments. The first one specifies the cell containing the text to be evaluated, and the second one specifies the number of characters to extract. The LEFT and MID functions take the same arguments.

3. **Click cell F3 again and notice its function in the Formula bar. See Figure 7-19.**

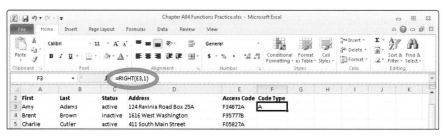

Figure 7-19

4. **Drag the fill handle down to F26 to complete the column, as shown in Figure 7-20.**

5. **Save the workbook.**

Leave the workbook open for the next exercise.

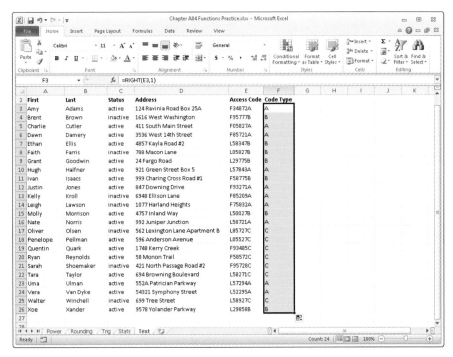

Figure 7-20

Concatenate text

In some worksheets, you may find that you have split data into multiple columns that would make more sense in a single column. For example, perhaps you entered first and last names in separate cells, but now you prefer to have them both in a single cell. To fix such problems, you can use the CONCATENATE function.

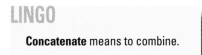

LINGO

Concatenate means to combine.

When concatenating values from cells, you specify the cells as you normally would — by their addresses (such as cell A1). In between the cell contents, you probably want to insert some literal text, such as a blank space. You enclose any literal text in quotation marks within the function's arguments; so if you wanted to include a space, you'd enclose a single space in quotation marks like this: " ".

In this exercise, you concatenate first and last names into a single column.

Files needed: Functions Practice.xlsx from the preceding exercise

1. **On the Text worksheet, in cell G3, type** =CONCATENATE(.

2. **In cell A3, type a comma, type a quotation mark, press the spacebar, type another quotation mark, and then type a comma (this looks like** , " " , **).**

3. **Click cell B3 and then press Enter.** Excel inserts the closing parenthesis automatically for you.

4. **Click cell G3 and look at the** =CONCATENATE(A3," ",B3) **function in the Formula bar.** See Figure 7-21.

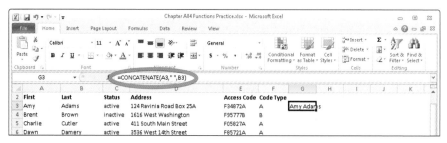

Figure 7-21

5. **Drag the fill handle down to G26, copying the function.**

   All the names appear in column G.

6. **Press Ctrl+C to copy the selection to the Clipboard and then click cell A3.**

7. **From the Home tab, click the down arrow on the Paste button and choose the first icon in the Paste Values section, as shown in Figure 7-22.**

   The names are pasted into column A.

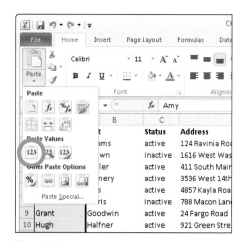

Figure 7-22

8. Select the range G3:G26 and then press the Delete key to clear those cells.

9. Click the column heading for column B to select that column and then choose Home⇨Delete to remove it.

10. Double-click between column headings A and B to auto-resize column A to fit the widest entry.

11. Click cell A2 and type Name, **replacing the earlier entry in that cell.**

Figure 7-23 shows the completed worksheet.

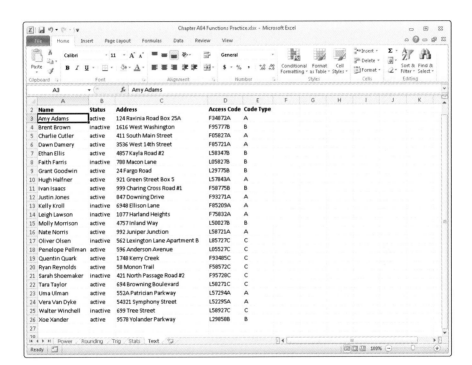

Figure 7-23

12. **Save the worksheet and close it. Exit Excel.**

 *Summing Up*

Here are the key points you learned about in this lesson:

- ✔ The POWER function multiplies a number (the first argument) by itself, the number of times specified in its second argument. For example, =POWER(A1,3) multiples A1 × A1 × A1.

- ✔ The SQRT function finds the square root of the number specified in its argument; it takes only one argument.

- ✔ The ROUND function rounds a number (the first argument) to the number of decimal places specified in its second argument. For example, =ROUND(A1,3) rounds the number in A1 to 3 decimal places.

- ✔ The ROUNDUP and ROUNDDOWN functions round in a specific direction, but otherwise work like ROUND.

- ✔ The SIN, COS, and TAN functions perform the trigonometric functions of sine, cosine, and tangent, respectively.

- ✔ AVERAGE sums all the values and divides by the total number of values.

- ✔ MEDIAN finds the midpoint value when the list of values is arranged from smallest to largest, or largest to smallest.

- ✔ The MIN and MAX functions find the smallest and largest values in a data set, respectively.

- ✔ The COUNT function counts the number of numeric values in a range. COUNTA counts the number of non-blank cells, regardless of content type.

- ✔ The UPPER and LOWER functions convert text to uppercase or lowercase, respectively. The PROPER function capitalizes the first letter of each word.

- ✔ To remove extra spaces, use TRIM. To remove non-printing characters, use CLEAN.

- ✔ To extract a certain number of characters from one end of a text string, use the LEFT or RIGHT function. The MID function extracts a certain number of characters from the center.

- ✔ To combine the contents of multiple cells, use the CONCATENATE function and separate the pieces to be concatenated by commas, like this: =CONCATENATE(A1,A2). If you want a space between the cell's contents, include a space, in quotation marks, as an argument like this: =CONCATENATE(A1," ",A2).

Try-it-yourself lab

In this lab, you try some of the functions that were mentioned in this lesson but not included in exercises:

1. **Start Excel, open Cleanup.xlsx, and save it as Cleanup Practice.xlsx.**

   This file contains some non-printing junk characters that you can get rid of with the CLEAN function.

2. **In column B, use the CLEAN function to clean up the data from column A. Then using Copy and Paste Special, replace the data in column A with the new values from the function results from column B.**

3. **Delete the contents of column B.**

4. **In column B, use the LEN function to find the length of each of the text strings in column A.**

   Hint: They are all between 13 and 17 characters.

5. **In cell A8, use the COUNTA function to count the number of non-blank cells in the range A1:A7. Reduce the number of decimal places displayed to zero.**

6. **Save the workbook and close Excel.**

Know this tech talk

average: To sum the values in a series and then divide the total by the number of values.

concatenate: To combine the contents of two or more cells into a single cell.

exponentiation: Multiplying a number by itself.

median: The midpoint value in a list of numbers arranged from smallest to largest, or largest to smallest.

round: To limit a number to a certain number of decimal places, increasing the last visible decimal place digit by one if the numbers removed were greater than or equal to 5.

square root: The number that, when multiplied by itself, produces the desired value. For example, 3 is the square root of 9 because $3 \times 3 = 9$.

Lesson 8

Creating and Formatting Charts

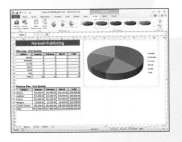

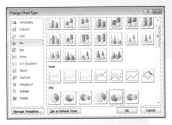

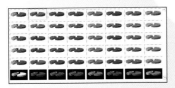

✔ Charts help you present data in a more interesting and understandable way.

✔ Pie charts show how parts relate to a whole.

✔ Column charts compare multiple data series across two axes.

✔ Switching rows and columns can present the same data but emphasize a different aspect.

✔ Placing a chart on its own tab allows it space to be easily viewed.

✔ A legend explains what each color or pattern in a chart represents.

✔ A data table appears under a chart, showing the data on which the chart is based.

✔ Data labels show the exact values of data points.

✔ Chart styles apply formatting presets to charts for quick and easy formatting.

1 s a picture really worth a thousand words? Just ask anyone who has been faced with a spreadsheet full of numbers to analyze. Creating charts that summarize data is a quick way to make sense of data — or to present data to someone else.

In this lesson, you learn how to create several types of charts, and how to add and remove chart elements such as legends, data labels, and data tables. You learn how to move and resize charts, how to place a chart on its own separate tab in a workbook, and how to apply a variety of formatting to a chart.

Creating a Basic Chart

Excel offers various chart types, each suited for a different type of data analysis: Pie charts show how parts contribute to a whole, line and column charts compare values over time, stock charts show daily pricing information, and so on. You don't have to know a lot about charts to get started creating them, though, so I want to knock out a few simple charts right off the bat and then spend the rest of the lesson manipulating them in various ways.

Create a pie chart

Pie charts are good for situations in which the relationship among the values being charted is the most significant thing. For example, suppose Kris sold 15 cars, Dave sold 7, and Tom sold 8. If the important thing is that Kris sold 50 percent of all the cars, a pie chart is ideal. Pie charts are limited in that they can handle only one data series. For example, you couldn't use a single pie chart to show Kris, Dave, and Tom's sales for several different periods; you'd have to do a separate pie chart for each period.

LINGO

A **pie chart** shows a circle divided into slices. The relative size of each slice represents a data point's contribution to the whole. Each pie chart shows one **data series** — that is, only one related set of numeric values.

In the following exercise, you create a basic pie chart.

Files needed: Publishing.xlsx

1. **Start Excel, if needed, open Publishing.xlsx, and save it as Publishing Plan.xlsx.**

2. **Select cells A5:A10. Hold down the Ctrl key and select cells E5:510.**

   The first selection is the labels for the chart; the second selection is the data. The labels and the data do not have to be contiguous.

3. **Choose Insert⇨Pie⇨Pie in 3-D.**

   (That's the first icon in the 3-D section of the menu; see Figure 8-1.)

   A floating pie chart appears on the worksheet.

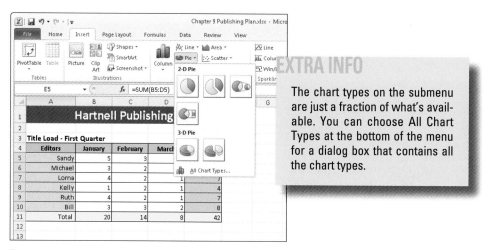

EXTRA INFO

The chart types on the submenu are just a fraction of what's available. You can choose All Chart Types at the bottom of the menu for a dialog box that contains all the chart types.

Figure 8-1

4. **Point at the chart's border (but not on a selection handle) and drag it to place it to the right of the Title Load data.** See Figure 8-2.

PRACTICE

For more practice, select the new chart and press the Delete key to remove it. Then re-create the chart by choosing All Chart Types in Step 3 and then choosing a different chart type. Repeat this a few times, each time picking a different chart type; then repeat Steps 3–4 exactly as written to finalize the chart.

Leave the workbook open for the next exercise.

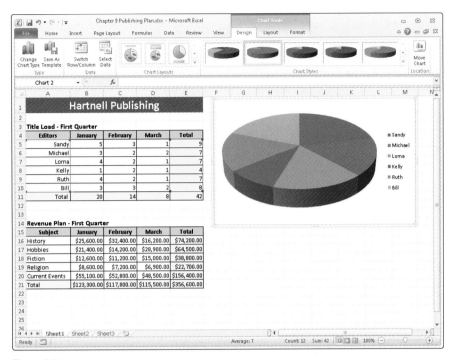

Figure 8-2

Create a column chart

A column chart is good for showing multiple data series on a two-axis grid, like in geometry class. For example, in Figure 8-2, notice that each editor has different values for each month. Depending on how you plot the data, each month could be a data series or each editor could be a data series. (You can switch back and forth between plotting by rows or by columns after you create the chart. You learn that later in this lesson in the section "Switch rows and columns.")

In the following exercise, you create a basic column chart.

Files needed: Publishing Plan.xlsx from the preceding exercise

1. **In Publishing Plan.xlsx, select the range A15:D20 and then choose Insert➪Column➪3-D Clustered Column.**

   A new column chart appears in the center of the worksheet.

2. **Drag the chart by its border (but not by a selection handle) to place it below the pie chart. See Figure 8-3.**

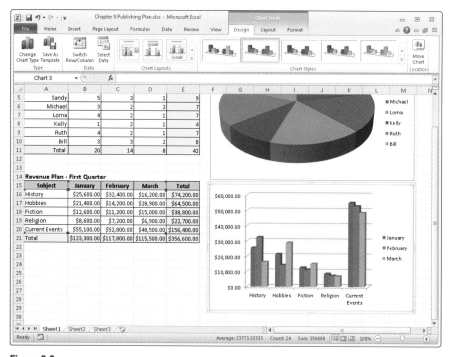

Figure 8-3

3. **Save the workbook.**

Leave the workbook open for the next exercise.

EXTRA INFO

Chart selection handles are different from the selection handles for most other graphic objects. Instead of squares or circles representing the selection handles, tiny dots are at certain points on the frame that mark where the selection handle areas are. These are in the centers of each side and in the corners of the frame.

LINGO

Column charts, as the name implies, use vertical bars — or columns — to represent the data points. A related chart type, the **bar chart**, is the same thing except the bars run horizontally rather than vertically. Some other related chart types include the **line chart**, which shows a connecting line between the data points rather than a bar beneath them; the **scatter chart**, which is a line chart without the line (only the data points); and the **area chart**, which fills in the space between the bars.

Changing a Chart

Now that you have a couple charts under your belt, take a closer look at some chart types. Figure 8-4 shows four chart types created from the same data, so you can compare their look and presentation. In the next few sections, you learn about the elements of a chart, switch chart types, and make some changes to your charts.

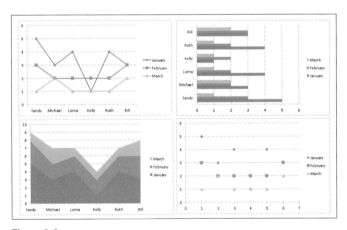

Figure 8-4

Understand the elements of a chart

Each chart has many elements, which is significant because you can customize each element separately. Learning the names for the elements of a chart helps you understand what's going on later in the lesson, in "Adding and Positioning Chart Elements," when I cover customization. Figure 8-5 points out some key elements of a chart, and Table 8-1 describes them.

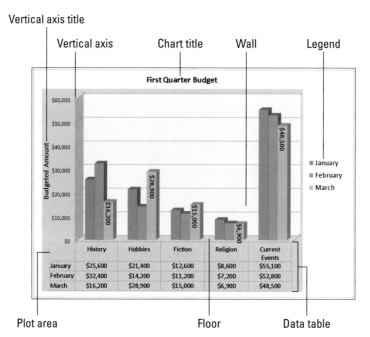

Vertical axis title

Vertical axis   Chart title   Wall   Legend

Plot area   Floor   Data table

Figure 8-5

Table 8-1	The Elements of a Chart	
Element	**What It Is**	**Usage**
Chart area	The entire contents of the chart frame	Everything in Figure 8-5 is considered part of the chart area.
Chart title	A title that identifies the chart	Use if it's not already obvious what the chart represents
Data point	A single bar, line, column, pie slice, and so on	Each column is a data point in Figure 8.5.
Data series	All the bars (lines, columns, and so on) of a common color	All the blue columns are a data series in Figure 8.5.
Data table	An optional table that appears below the chart, showing the data that comprises it	Used mostly when a chart is on a separate tab
Floor	On a 3-D chart, the area that the 3-D bars rest on	A floor can give a 3-D chart an additional appearance of being three-dimensional.

Element	What It Is	Usage
Horizontal axis	The axis that runs side to side	In Figure 8-5, the horizontal axis shows the book types.
Legend	The key that tells what each data series represents	The legend can appear at the right (as in Figure 8-5) or in any other position around the plot area.
Plot area	The area of the chart that contains the data, the axes, and the data table (if present)	In Figure 8-5, the plot area is shaded to distinguish it from the chart area.
Vertical axis	The axis that runs up and down	In Figure 8-5, vertical axis shows the numeric values and is the value axis.
Vertical axis title	A text label that explains what the vertical axis represents	In Figure 8-5, the vertical axis title is Budgeted Amount.
Wall	The area directly behind the data	In Figure 8-5, the wall is shaded light gray to distinguish it from the plot area.

Edit the chart data range

You can decide after initially creating a chart that you want a different data range to be plotted in it. For example, you might want to add or remove a data series or exclude certain data points.

In the following exercise, you change the data range on a chart.

Files needed: Publishing Plan.xlsx from the preceding exercise

1. **In Publishing Plan.xlsx, select the column chart.** The range B16:D20 becomes outlined with a blue border, with blue square selection handles in the corners, as shown in Figure 8-6.

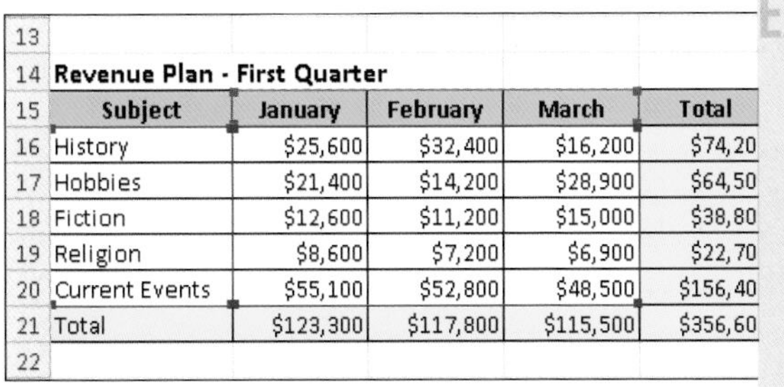

13				
14	**Revenue Plan - First Quarter**			
15	**Subject**	**January**	**February**	**March**	**Total**
16	History	$25,600	$32,400	$16,200	$74,20
17	Hobbies	$21,400	$14,200	$28,900	$64,50
18	Fiction	$12,600	$11,200	$15,000	$38,80
19	Religion	$8,600	$7,200	$6,900	$22,70
20	Current Events	$55,100	$52,800	$48,500	$156,40
21	Total	$123,300	$117,800	$115,500	$356,60
22					

EXTRA INFO

Other colored outlines are also on the data range. The purple outline marks the data series labels, and the green outline marks the category labels. These outlines can also be dragged to change the ranges used.

Figure 8-6

2. **Drag the bottom-right corner selection handle of the blue-selected area upward so the blue outline excludes the Current Events row (row 20).** The chart changes immediately to show the new range. See Figure 8-7.

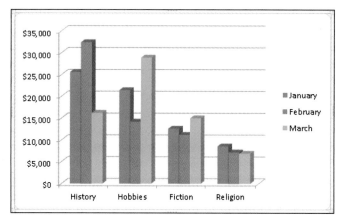

Figure 8-7

3. **Choose Chart Tools Design⇨Select Data, and the Select Data Source dialog box opens.**

4. **Click the Collapse Dialog button to the right of the Chart Data Range box (see Figure 8-8).** The dialog box collapses.

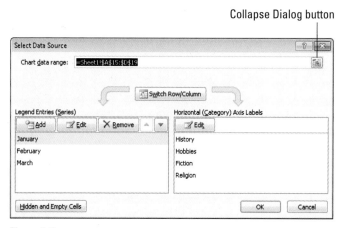

Figure 8-8

5. **Re-select the desired range A15:D20, and then press Enter to reopen the Select Data Source dialog box.**

6. **Click OK to accept the new chart range.** The Current Events data is shown again in the chart.

7. **Save the workbook.**

Leave the workbook open for the next exercise.

Change the chart type

You can change a chart's type, rather than completely re-creating a chart, if you decide you didn't choose the right type initially. In fact, it's so easy to change the chart type that you might want to experiment with several chart types before you make the final decision of which one to use.

In the following exercise, you change the chart type for two charts.

Files needed: Publishing Plan.xlsx from the preceding exercise

1. **In Publishing Plan.xlsx, select the pie chart and then choose Chart Tools Design⇨Change Chart Type, and the Change Chart Type dialog box opens.**

2. **In the Pie section, click the Exploded Pie in 3-D type (the fifth icon in the series), as shown in Figure 8-9, and then click OK.**

   The pie chart changes to show the new type. All the slices are exploded, as in Figure 8-10.

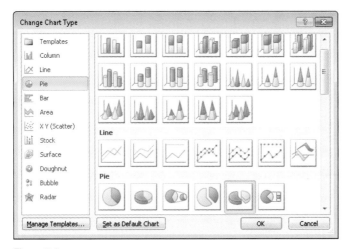

Figure 8-9

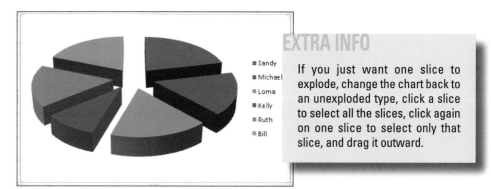

EXTRA INFO

If you just want one slice to explode, change the chart back to an unexploded type, click a slice to select all the slices, click again on one slice to select only that slice, and drag it outward.

Figure 8-10

3. **Click the column chart on the worksheet, right-click the chart's border, and choose Change Chart Type to open the Change Chart Type dialog box.**

4. **In the list of categories at the left, click Area; then click Stacked Area in 3-D and click OK.**

   The chart changes to the new type, as shown in Figure 8-11.

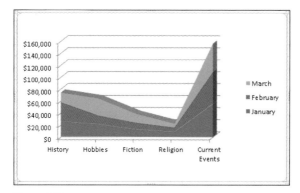

Figure 8-11

PRACTICE

Using the same process as in Steps 3–4, change the chart to a Clustered Horizontal Cone (which is one of the bar chart types). See Figure 8-12. It's okay for now that the value axis (the horizontal axis) scrunches up the values so they aren't readable, because you fix that in a later exercise.

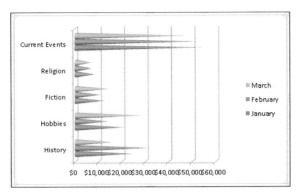

Figure 8-12

> **5. Save the workbook.**

Leave the workbook open for the next exercise.

Switch rows and columns

Numbers don't lie, but presenting the numbers in different ways can make your audience think about the numbers differently. For example, in Figure 8-12, the Clustered Horizontal Cone chart invites the audience to consider each book category separately, comparing that category's performance over three months. If you wanted the audience to compare the different categories with one another for each month, you could switch the rows and columns so that the series become the categories rather than the months. That's what you do in the following exercise.

In the following exercise, you switch a chart's rows and columns.

Files needed: Publishing Plan.xlsx from the preceding exercise

> **1. In Publishing Plan.xlsx, select the cone chart and then choose Chart Tools Design⇨Switch Row/Column.**
>
> The chart changes to show the categories as the series. See Figure 8-13.

Charts that consist of a single data series, such as pie charts, change to something unusable if you try to switch their rows/columns.

Switch Row/Column button

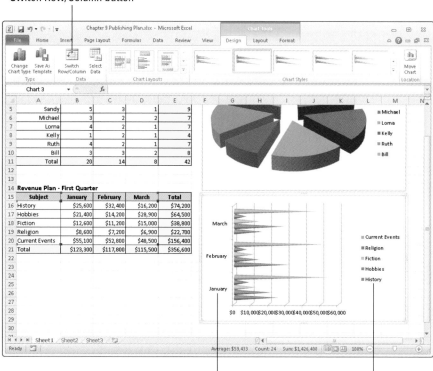

Months on vertical axis   Book categories as series

Figure 8-13

2. **Click the pie chart and then choose Chart Tools Design⇨Switch Row/ Column.** The chart changes to a single pie with only one big slice.

3. **Choose Chart Tools Design⇨Switch Row/Column again to change the pie chart back to its original appearance.**

4. **Save the changes to the workbook.**

Leave the workbook open for the next exercise.

Resize a chart

You can resize a chart by dragging a selection handle on the border of its frame in any direction. Selection handles are marked with small dots; the side selection handles are in the center of each side, and the corner selection handles are in each corner. You can also specify an exact size for a chart's frame using the Height and Width text boxes on the Chart Tools Format tab.

In the following exercise, you resize charts.

Files needed: Publishing Plan.xlsx from the preceding exercise

1. **In Publishing Plan.xlsx, select the pie chart; then point the mouse pointer at the bottom-right corner of the chart's frame, so the mouse pointer becomes a double-headed arrow.**

2. **Drag inward so the bottom-right corner of the chart aligns with the bottom-right corner of cell K11.** See Figure 8-14.

Drag the chart corner

Figure 8-14

3. **Select the cone chart and then on the Chart Tools Format tab, in the Shape Height box, type** 2.5".

4. **In the Shape Width box, type** 5.25".

The chart's frame adjusts to the specified dimensions. See Figure 8-15.

Shape Height

Shape Width

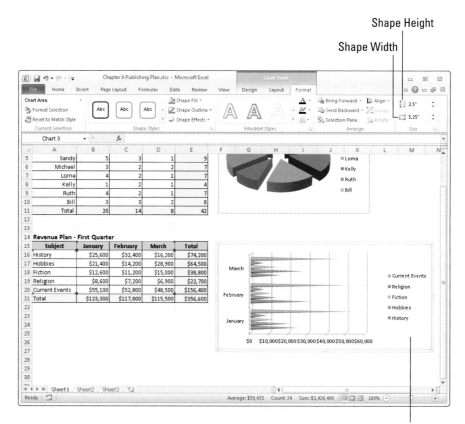

Change chart dimensions

Figure 8-15

    5. Save the workbook.

Leave the workbook open for the next exercise.

Move a chart to its own tab

On a crowded worksheet, you may not have much room for a chart, and as a result, the chart might need to be resized down to a size where it's not as easy to read as it might otherwise be. To solve this problem, you might want to move a chart to its own sheet.

TIP

When a chart is on its own sheet, a data table is sometimes useful to remind the reader what data the chart represents, such as the one you saw in Figure 8-5. See "Add a data table" later in this lesson to learn how to add one.

In the following exercise, you move a chart to its own tab.

Files needed: Publishing Plan.xlsx from the preceding exercise

1. **In Publishing Plan.xlsx, right-click the frame of the cone chart and choose Move Chart.** The Move Chart dialog box opens.

2. **Select the New Sheet option, and in the New Sheet text box, type** Revenue Plan Chart. See Figure 8-16.

Figure 8-16

3. **Click OK.** The chart is placed on its own sheet in the workbook. See Figure 8-17.

   Notice that the chart still has a chart frame where the white of the chart area background intersects the gray of the worksheet background.

4. **Right-click the chart's frame and choose Move Chart.** The Move Chart dialog box reopens.

Chart frame

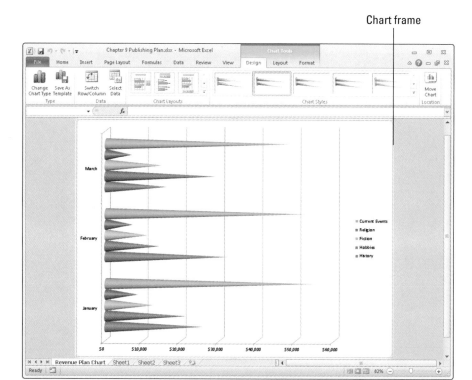

Figure 8-17

5. **Select the Object In option, and choose Sheet2 from the Object In drop-down list. Click OK.**

   The chart moves to Sheet2 as a floating object.

6. **Move the chart on Sheet2 so its upper-left corner aligns with the upper-left corner of cell A1.**

   To move a chart, drag its border, but not on a selection handle.

7. **Resize the chart on Sheet2 so that the chart covers cells A1:M22.**

   See Figure 8-18. To resize a chart, drag one of the selection handles on its border.

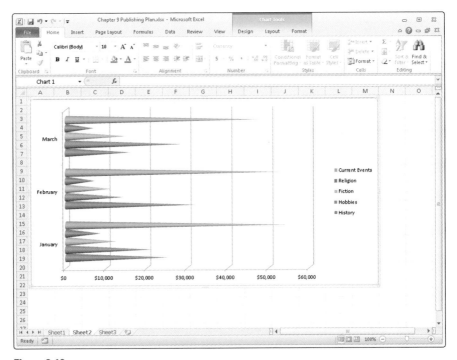

Figure 8-18

8. **Save the workbook.**

Leave the workbook open for the next exercise.

Adding and Positioning Chart Elements

As I hint earlier in the lesson, when reviewing the elements of a chart (see Figure 8-5), each element is individually customizable. You can turn elements on and off, change their positions, and so on. In the next exercises, you add and position a legend, data table, and data labels.

Add a legend

By default, a legend is positioned to the right of the chart, but you can place it anywhere. When a legend is placed at the top or bottom of a chart, it is laid out horizontally, whereas when it's placed at the side of a chart, it's laid out vertically.

In the following exercise, you remove and then re-add a legend on a chart, and position it below the chart.

Files needed: Publishing Plan.xlsx from the preceding exercise

LINGO

The **legend** is the key that tells what each color (or pattern, or shade of gray) represents on a chart. Legends are useful for pie charts, for example, and for most multi-series charts, such as the bar, column, and cone charts you have worked with throughout this lesson. A legend is not particularly useful on a chart that contains only one series, such as a bar chart that consists of a single set of bars, all the same color.

1. **In Publishing Plan.xlsx, on Sheet2, click the legend to select it.** Selection handles appear around the legend. See Figure 8-19.

Legend

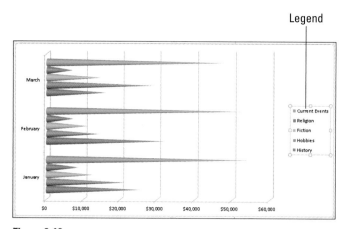

Figure 8-19

2. **Press the Delete key to remove the legend.** The chart expands horizontally to fill in the space.

3. **Choose Chart Tools Layout⇨Legend⇨Show Legend at Bottom. See Figure 8-20.** The legend appears at the bottom of the chart.

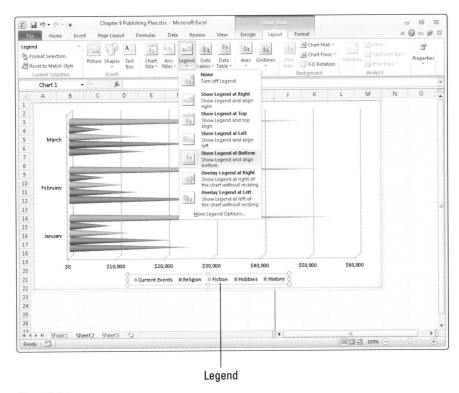

Legend

Figure 8-20

For more practice, try each of the other legend positions on the menu.

4. **Select the legend and drag it to the right, so its right edge aligns with the right edge of the chart's plot area.** See Figure 8-21.

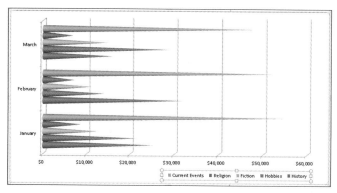

Figure 8-21

     5. Save the workbook.

Leave the workbook open for the next exercise.

Add a data table

In the following exercise, you add a data table with a legend key to a chart.

Files needed: Publishing Plan.xlsx from the preceding exercise

    1. In Publishing Plan.xlsx, on Sheet2, click the legend and press the Delete key.

    You don't need the legend because the data table you create provides colored squares for each series that duplicate the functionality of a legend.

    2. Choose Chart Tools Layout⇨Data Table⇨Show Data Table with Legend Keys.

    The data table appears below the chart, as shown in Figure 8-22.

    3. Save the workbook.

Leave the workbook open for the next exercise.

LINGO

A **data table** repeats the data on which the chart is based. A data table is helpful when the cells containing the data and the chart are not simultaneously visible onscreen.

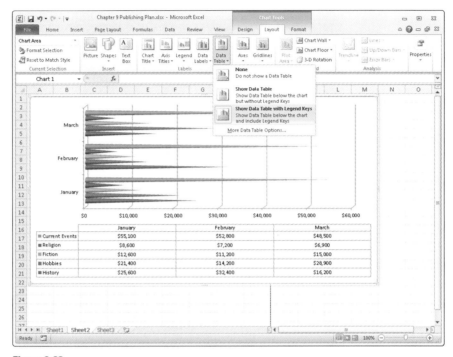

Figure 8-22

Add data labels

On a pie chart, you can either show the exact value of each slice or the percentage of the whole that it represents. Depending on what you want to show with the chart, one or the other may be more valuable.

In the following exercise, you add a data table with a legend key to a chart.

Files needed: Publishing Plan.xlsx from the preceding exercise

LINGO

Data labels show the individual values on each data point. Data labels are used whenever the exact value of a data point is significant. You can add data labels for the entire chart, a single series, or a single data point.

1. **In Publishing Plan.xlsx, on Sheet2, click one of the light blue cones on the chart (one of the Current Events cones).** All the light blue cones become selected.

2. **Choose Chart Tools Layout⇨Data Labels⇨Show.** The data labels appear for only the selected series. See Figure 8-23.

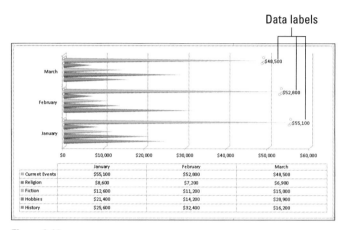

Figure 8-23

3. **Click the Sheet1 tab and select the pie chart. Drag the bottom-right corner of the chart frame down to cell M19 to enlarge the chart so it's easier to work with.**

4. **Choose Chart Tools Layout⇨Data Labels⇨Center.** Data labels appear in the centers of each slice.

5. **Choose Chart Tools Layout⇨Data Labels⇨More Data Label Options.** The Format Data Labels dialog box opens.

6. **Select the Percentage check box, deselect the Value check box, and select the Category Name check box.** Each slice shows the person's name and the percentage, as shown in Figure 8-24.

   You may need to move the dialog box to see the slices at this point.

7. **Click the Close button to close the dialog box.**

   You no longer need the legend on this chart because the data labels serve the same purpose.

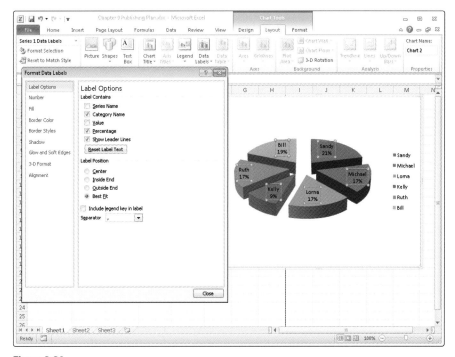

Figure 8-24

8. **Choose Chart Tools Layout⇨Legend⇨None.**

    This is an alternate way of turning off the legend; you can also select the legend and press the Delete key, as you did in an earlier exercise.

9. **Save the workbook.**

Leave the workbook open for the next exercise.

Formatting a Chart

Chart formatting can make a big difference in a chart's attractiveness and readability. Depending on the look you're after, you may prefer to make blanket formatting changes to the entire chart by applying a chart style, or to select and make changes to individual elements. For each individual part of the chart, you can change its fill color, its outline, and its text (including font, size, color, attributes, alignment, and so on).

Apply chart styles

In the following exercise, you change the style of two charts.

Files needed: Publishing Plan.xlsx from the preceding exercise

1. **In Publishing Plan.xlsx, on Sheet1, click the pie chart's frame to select the chart and then choose Chart Tools Design⇨More in the Chart Styles group.**

   A gallery of chart styles opens. See Figure 8-25.

LINGO

Chart styles are collections of formatting presets that you can apply to the entire chart at once. Each chart style can be applied in a variety of color combinations, all based on the theme colors for the workbook.

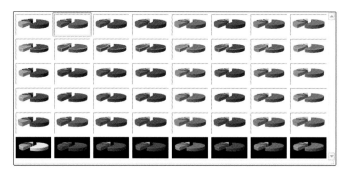

Figure 8-25

2. **Click Style 36 (the all-red sample in the next-to-last row).**

   The style changes to the colors and shape style represented by that sample. Point to a style to see a ScreenTip that tells its style number.

PRACTICE

For more practice, try several of the other chart styles.

3. **Click the More button again, to reopen the gallery, and click Style 42 (the black-background style that uses multiple colors). Point to a style to see a ScreenTip that tells its style number.**

4. **Click the Sheet2 tab and then choose Chart Tools⇨Layout⇨Data Table⇨None to turn off the data table so the chart style is displayed better.**

5. **Choose Chart Tools Design⇨More button in the Chart Styles group to open the palette of styles.**

6. **Click Style 40 (the orange style in the next-to-last row).** The chart changes to use that style. See Figure 8-26.

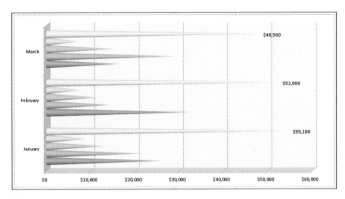

Figure 8-26

7. **Save the workbook.**

Leave the workbook open for the next exercise.

Format text on a chart

When you resize a chart, some of the text in it resizes also. If you want certain text to be larger or smaller in relation to the chart size, though, you can manually change its font size. You can also change the font's color, typeface, and attributes.

One of the most commonly done text-resizing changes is to make the legend text larger because by default, Excel's legends are a bit small.

In the following exercise, you resize the text on a chart.

Files needed: Publishing Plan.xlsx from the preceding exercise

1. **In Publishing Plan.xlsx, on Sheet1, click the pie chart's frame to select the chart and then click the data label on one of the pie slices.** All the labels on all the pie slices are selected.

2. **Choose Home⇨Increase Font Size until the font size is 12 point. Choose Home⇨Bold to make the text bold.**

3. **Click the text on the largest slice (Sandy 21%).**

4. **On the Home tab, click the down arrow to the right of the Font Color button, opening its color palette; then, click the Yellow square in the Standard colors section.**

   The selected data label (and only that one) becomes yellow. Figure 8-27 shows the completed formatting.

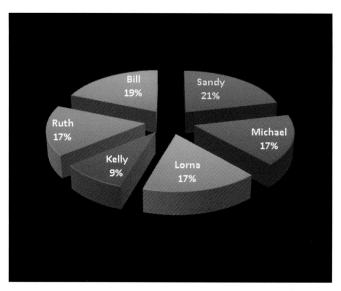

Figure 8-27

5. **Click the Sheet2 tab, select the chart, and choose Chart Tools Layout⇨Legend⇨Show Legend at Right to redisplay the legend.**

6. **Click the legend to select it, and on the Home tab, open the Font Size drop-down list and choose 12.**

7. **Click one of the month names on the left.** All three month names are selected in a single frame.

8. **Choose Home⇨Increase Font Size until the font size for the month names is 12 point. Choose Home⇨Orientation⇨Angle Counterclockwise, and the month names rotate by 45 degrees, as shown in Figure 8-28.**

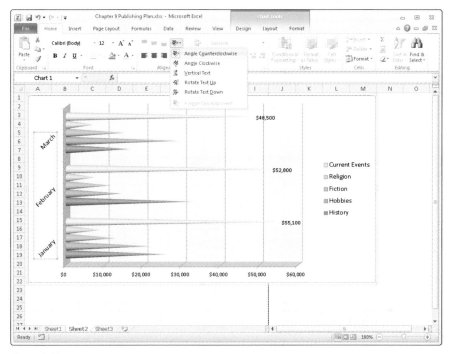

Figure 8-28

9. **Save the workbook.**

Leave the workbook open for the next exercise.

Change the color of a chart element

Each element of a chart can be recolored individually. This includes the data points and series, the chart's walls, its plot area, the entire chart area, the legend, and all the text used for every purpose.

One of the most common color changes is to change the colors of one or more of the data series in a bar chart, or to change one or more pie slice colors in a pie chart.

Usually when you change the color of a data bar (or other data-related object), you want to change the color for the entire series, not just for one individual data point. If you have a legend that shows what each color means and then you change the color of the whole series, the legend updates automatically. However, if you change the color of only one data point, the legend still shows the color for the other bars in the series, and that one data point does not match up with anything in the legend.

In the following exercise, you change the colors of some elements in a chart.

Files needed: Publishing Plan.xlsx from the preceding exercise

1. **In Publishing Plan.xlsx, on Sheet2, click the chart's legend to select it.**

   On the Chart Tools Format tab, in the Current Selection group, the Chart Elements box shows *Legend.* The Chart Elements box provides the name of the selected element.

2. **Choose Series "History" from the Chart Elements drop-down list.** The bars that represent History are selected. See Figure 8-29.

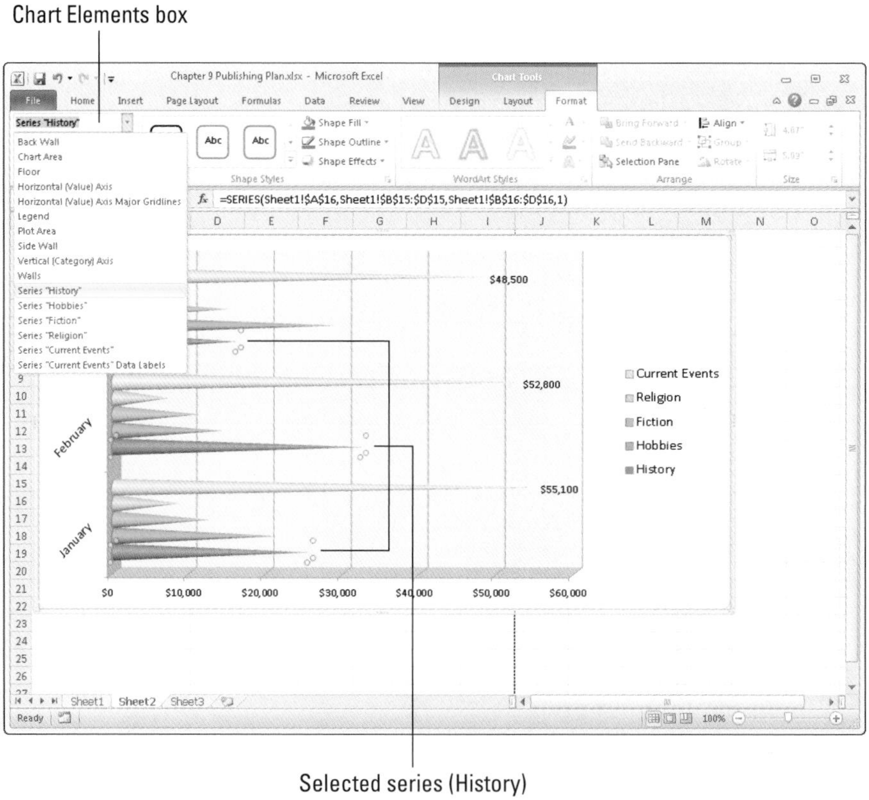

Chart Elements box

Selected series (History)

Figure 8-29

3. **Choose Chart Tools Format⇨Shape Fill⇨Blue, Accent 1.** (You can point to a fill color to see a ScreenTip that tells its name.)

   All the bars in the selected series change to that color, as does the legend key for that series.

4. **Click the legend to select it. Note that Legend appears again in the Chart Elements drop-down list.**

5. **Choose Chart Tools Format⇨More in the Shape Styles group, opening a palette.**

6. **Click Moderate Effect, Red, Accent 2.** (It's the red sample in the next-to-last row.)

   The legend formats to that shape style, which includes a red gradient background. See Figure 8-30.

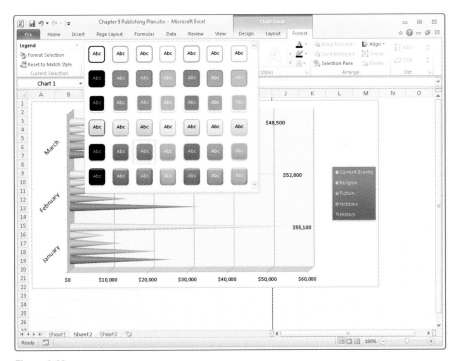

Figure 8-30

7. **With the legend still selected, choose Chart Tools Format⇨Shape Outline⇨Red Accent 2, Darker 50%.** (You can point to a fill color to see a ScreenTip that tells its name.)

8. **Choose Back Wall from the Chart Elements drop-down list.**

9. **Choose Chart Tools Format➪Format Selection.** The Format Wall dialog box opens.

10. **On the Fill tab, click Gradient Fill and from the Preset Colors drop-down list, choose Wheat.**

    The chart's back wall changes to the gradient fill. See Figure 8-31.

Choose chart element   Apply Gradient Fill

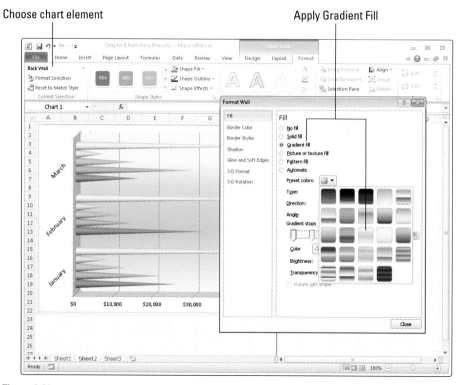

Figure 8-31

11. **Click Close to close the dialog box.**

12. **Save the workbook and close it. Exit Excel.**

Summing Up

Here are the key points you learned about in this lesson:

- ✔ To insert a chart, select the data, click the appropriate chart type on the Insert tab, and then select a subtype from the menu that appears.
- ✔ To change a chart's data range, choose Chart Tools Design⇨Select Data.
- ✔ To change the chart type, choose Chart Tools Design⇨Change Chart Type.
- ✔ To switch rows and columns, choose Chart Tools Design⇨Switch Row/Column.
- ✔ To resize a chart, drag a selection handle on its frame. To move a chart, drag the frame anywhere except on a selection handle.
- ✔ To move a chart to its own tab, right-click its frame and choose Move Chart.
- ✔ To add, remove, or modify a legend, choose Chart Tools Layout⇨Legend.
- ✔ To add or remove a data table, choose Chart Tools Layout⇨Data Table.
- ✔ To add or remove data labels, select the data series or points to affect and then choose Chart Tools Layout⇨Data Labels.
- ✔ To apply a style to a chart, on the Chart Tools Design tab, click a style in the Chart Styles group. Open the full gallery with the More button, if needed.
- ✔ To format text on a chart, use the commands in the Font group on the Home tab.
- ✔ To modify an element of a chart, select it and then choose Chart Tools Format⇨Format Selection.

Try-it-yourself lab

1. Start Excel, open the file Try It Publishing.xlsx, and save it as Charts.xlsx.

2. On a new Monday Sales tab, create a column chart using the Clustered Column type that shows each week's sales for Mondays only. Do not include a legend.

3. Change the bar colors on the chart to Chart Style 28.

4. On a new Overall tab, create a column chart that uses the Stacked Column in 3-D type and includes all the data on Sheet1.

5. Add a data table to the Overall chart that includes a legend key and then remove the separate legend.

6. Format each chart to make them as attractive as possible. This may include increasing font sizes and changing colors or chart styles.

7. Save the workbook and close Excel.

Know this tech talk

area chart: Like a line chart, except the space below the line is filled in as an area.

bar chart: A column chart that runs horizontally rather than vertically.

chart style: A collection of formatting presets you can apply to an entire chart at once.

column chart: A chart that uses vertical bars to represent data points on a two-dimensional or three-dimensional grid.

data labels: Labels that show the individual values on each data point.

data series: A related set of numeric values in a chart.

data table: A table under a chart that repeats the data on which the chart is based.

legend: The color key that tells what each color, pattern, or shade represents on a chart.

line chart: Like a column chart, except dots represent the data points, and the dots are connected by a line.

pie chart: A circle that's divided into wedges that represent parts of the whole.

scatter chart: Like a line chart, but there's no line; data points are represented by dots.

value axis: The axis that contains the numeric values.

Lesson 9
Working with PivotTables

- PivotTables allow you to analyze and summarize data without disturbing the original data set.

- Sorting data in a PivotTable makes it easier to look up data in chronological order.

- Filtering a PivotTable limits its scope to certain values you specify.

- Using summary functions in a PivotTable allows you to average data, count records, or perform other calculations.

- A PivotChart presents PivotTable information in a graphical way.

*P*ivotTables are summary grids that display information in different ways from the default way it is presented on the worksheet. They enable you to glean meaningful information from a data set by summarizing, sorting, and filtering the data, without disturbing the original data set. In this lesson, you learn how to create PivotTables and PivotCharts, format them, and use the summarizing, sorting, and filtering options to manipulate the data to extract useful facts from it.

Creating a PivotTable

You create PivotTables within the workbook that contains the data you want to analyze. The PivotTable typically is placed on its own worksheet. After creating the PivotTable, you can drag fields onto it.

Create a PivotTable from worksheet data

To create a PivotTable, start with a worksheet that already contains data in row-and-column format. A table like the ones you created in Lesson 5 would be appropriate, for example. Typically the field names should appear at the top, across a single row, with the records beneath those headings. After making sure the data is ready, you can insert a PivotTable to summarize it.

EXTRA INFO

Excel's PivotTable feature is especially useful when you work with a large data set that's not conducive to browsing. You can also create PivotCharts, which summarize, sort, and filter data similarly to PivotTables, but do so in a graphical format.

LINGO

A **PivotTable** is a customizable table view of some data that exists elsewhere in your workbook. A PivotTable isn't a real table in the same sense as a table you create by converting a range to a table (by choosing Insert⇨Table). A PivotTable doesn't actually store the data it displays, and you can't edit the data from within it; it's simply a view. A finished PivotTable is also called a **report**.

A **field** is a type of data within the range being analyzed. For example, if you're analyzing a data range where the column headings describe what's in the rows beneath them, each column heading would be a field, such as Product, Price, or Quantity Sold.

In this exercise, you create a PivotTable.

Files needed: Data.xlsx

1. **Open Data.xlsx and save it as Data Pivot.xlsx.**

2. **On Sheet1, select the range A1:E29 and then choose Insert⇨ PivotTable.** The Create PivotTable dialog box opens. See Figure 9-1.

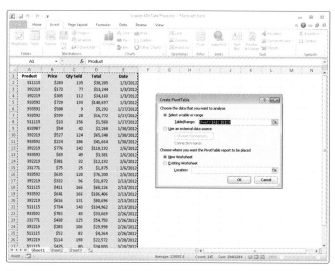

Figure 9-1

3. **Click OK to accept the default settings.**

   The default settings use the selected range and place the PivotTable on a new worksheet. A new sheet appears. A PivotTable empty placeholder appears at the left, and on the right is a PivotTable Field List task pane. See Figure 9-2.

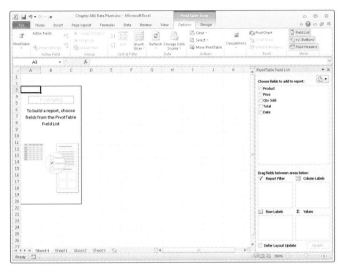

Figure 9-2

4. **In the PivotTable Field List task pane, drag the Product field from the top section of the pane to the Row Labels area at the bottom.**

   The product codes appear in the PivotTable, in a single column on the left. See Figure 9-3. Notice that each product appears only once in this summary; in the original data, each product appeared multiple times.

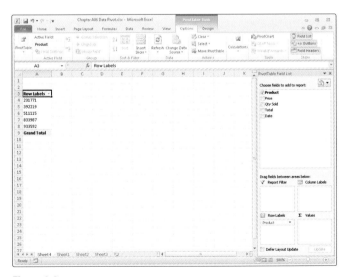

Figure 9-3

5. **Drag the Date field to the Column Labels area at the bottom.** The dates appear across the top of the PivotTable, in a single row. See Figure 9-4.

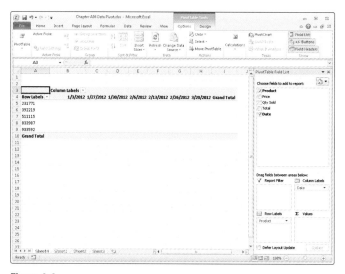

Figure 9-4

6. **Drag the Total field to the Values area at the bottom.** The totals appear at the intersection of the row and column labels on the PivotTable. See Figure 9-5.

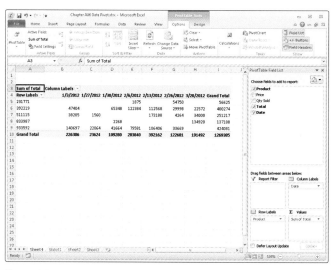

Figure 9-5

7. **In the Values area at the bottom of the task pane, click Sum of Total and choose Remove Field (see Figure 9-6).**

The field is removed from the PivotTable.

8. **In the upper part of the task pane, click the Qty Sold and Price check boxes.**

These fields are added to the Values area at the bottom of the task pane, just as if you had dragged them there, and to the PivotTable. This is an alternate method for specifying fields for the Values part of the report. See Figure 9-7.

TIP

Notice in Figure 9-7 that an additional item has been added in the Column Labels area of the task pane: Values. This allows sub-headings based on the Values fields under the main column headings for Date.

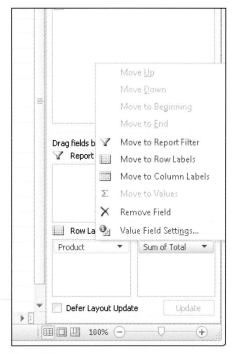

Figure 9-6

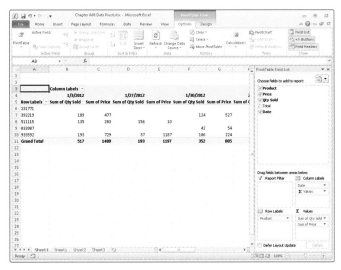

Figure 9-7

9. **Save the workbook.**

Leave the workbook open for the next exercise.

Format PivotTables

Sometimes when you create a PivotTable from existing data, the PivotTable might not pick up the formatting correctly from the original data. For example, currency values may not be formatted as currency anymore, and font sizes and colors may be lost. You can easily reapply any formatting you like.

In this exercise, you format a PivotTable.

Files needed: Data Pivot.xlsx from the preceding exercise

1. **Rename the worksheet tab** *PivotTable* **by double-clicking the worksheet tab for the PivotTable's sheet, typing** PivotTable, **and pressing Enter.**

2. **In the Values section of the task pane, click Sum of Price, as shown in Figure 9-8, and choose Value Field Settings.**

   The Value Field Settings dialog box opens. See Figure 9-9.

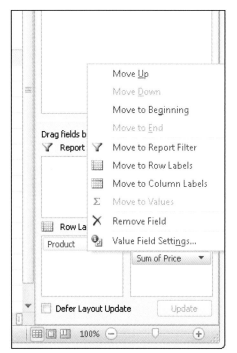

Figure 9-8

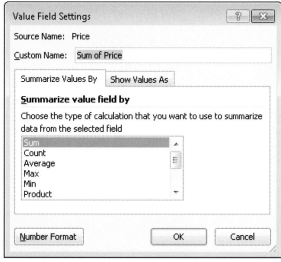

Figure 9-9

3. **Click the Number Format button.**

The Format Cells dialog box opens. This is a custom version of the dialog box, with only the Number tab.

4. **Select Currency in the Category list. In the Decimal Places box, click the down-increment arrow twice to decrease the number of decimal places to 0, as shown in Figure 9-10, and then click OK.**

Figure 9-10

5. **Click OK again to close the Value Field Settings dialog box, and the numbers in the Sum of Price columns appear as currency.**

6. **Choose PivotTable Tools Options⇨Field Headers to toggle off the field headers.** See Figure 9-11.

7. **Click cell B4 and type** Quantity Sold, **replacing the previous entry.**

All the cells containing this same heading also change (cells D4, F4, H4, and so on).

8. **Select row 4 by clicking its row header and then choose Home⇨ Center to horizontally center all the headings in that row.** See Figure 9-12.

Field Headers button

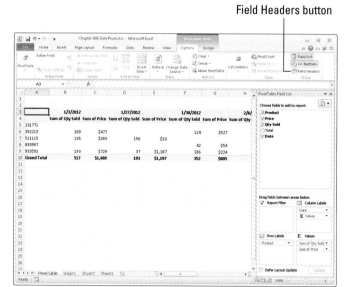

Figure 9-11

Center button

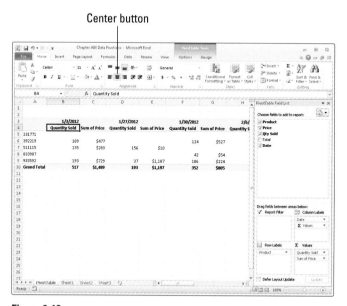

Figure 9-12

9. **Select row 3 by clicking its row header and then choose Home⇨ Increase Font Size twice to increase the font size in that row to 14 pt.**

10. **Select the range A5:Q9 and then choose Home⇨Borders⇨All Borders.** See Figure 9-13.

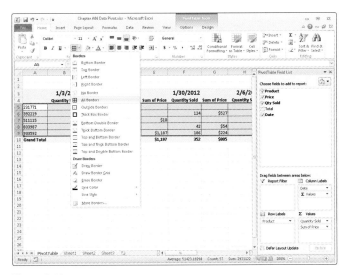

Figure 9-13

11. **Click away from the PivotTable to deselect it. Notice that the PivotTable Tools tabs no longer appear on the Ribbon.**

12. **Save the workbook.**

Leave the workbook open for the next exercise.

Sorting and Filtering PivotTable Data

Like tables, PivotTables can be sorted and filtered to make the meaning of the data more apparent. In the following exercises, you learn how to sort and filter a PivotTable.

Sort a PivotTable

LINGO

You can sort by any field, in either ascending or descending order.

In this exercise, you sort a PivotTable.

Files needed: Data Pivot.xlsx from the preceding exercise

An **ascending** sort sorts from oldest to newest, or from A to Z. In an ascending sort, symbols and numbers (0 to 9) come before letters. A **descending** sort sorts from newest to oldest, or from Z to A. In a descending sort, numbers (9 to 0) and symbols come after letters.

1. **Click inside the PivotTable to re-select it and then choose PivotTable Tools Options⇨Field Headers to turn on the display of field headers.** (You turned them off in the preceding exercise.)

2. **Click the down arrow on the Column Labels field header and choose Sort Newest to Oldest.** See Figure 9-14.

   The dates are reordered in the PivotTable.

3. **Click the down arrow on the Row Labels field header and choose Sort Smallest to Largest.** See Figure 9-15.

   The product numbers are sorted in ascending order.

4. **Save the workbook.**

Leave the workbook open for the next exercise.

LINGO

A **report filter** is an overall filter that applies to the entire PivotTable.

Filter a PivotTable

One way to filter a PivotTable is to apply a report filter. You can apply a report filter by adding a field to the Report Filter section of the PivotTable Field List task pane and then specifying the values (or range of values) to include. You must use this method if you want to filter by a field that's not part of the PivotTable. For example, you might want to filter by a specific date, but not include the Date field in the PivotTable grid itself.

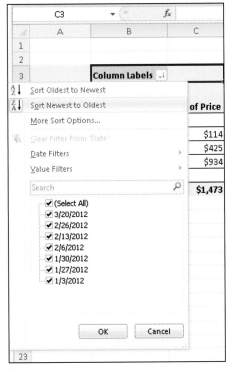

Figure 9-14

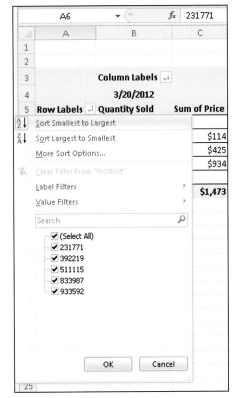

Figure 9-15

In this exercise, you filter a PivotTable.

Files needed: Data Pivot.xlsx from the preceding exercise

1. **In the PivotTable Field List task pane, drag the Total field to the Report Filter section.**

   A filter row appears in row 1. See Figure 9-16.

TIP

Dragging a field to the Report Filter section is useful for filtering by a field that doesn't appear already in the PivotTable.

2. **Click the down arrow in cell B1 and select the Select Multiple Items check box.**

   Each of the values now appears with a check box next to it.

3. **Deselect the check boxes for all values less than $5,000, as shown in Figure 9-17, and click OK to apply the filter.**

   The data is filtered to show only totals more than $5,000, and the filter in cell B1 appears as (Multiple Items). A funnel (filter) symbol appears next to Total in the task pane. See Figure 9-18.

4. **Save the workbook.**

Leave the workbook open for the next exercise.

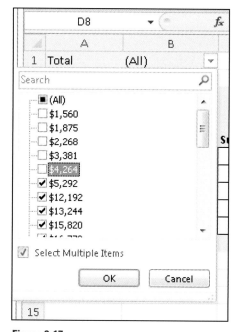

Figure 9-16   Figure 9-17

Filter row

Filter symbol

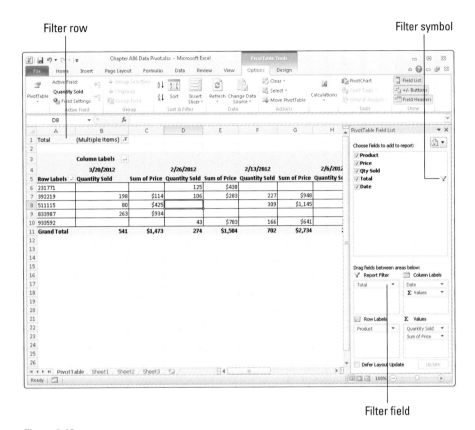

Filter field

Figure 9-18

Filter individual column and row fields

Another way to filter a PivotTable is to select specific values for individual fields by using the Column Labels or Row Labels menus. Each filter you apply for different fields combines with other filters already in place so that only records that match all the criteria you specify appear.

In this exercise, you filter individual fields on a PivotTable.

Files needed: Data Pivot.xlsx from the preceding exercise

1. **Click the down arrow on the Column Labels field header, point to Date Filters, and choose After, as shown in Figure 9-19.**

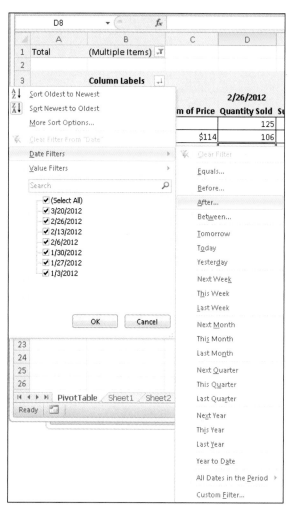

Figure 9-19

2. **In the Date Filter (Date) dialog box that appears, type** 1/31/2012, **as shown in Figure 9-20, and click OK.**

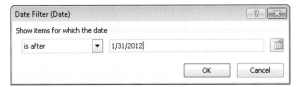

Date Filter (Date)	?	X

Show items for which the date

is after	▼	1/31/2012	📅

	OK	Cancel

Figure 9-20

3. **Scroll the worksheet to the right to confirm that no dates appear that are earlier than 1/31/2012. Then scroll back so column A is visible again.**

4. **Save the workbook.**

Leave the workbook open for the next exercise.

Modifying a PivotTable

PivotTables are famous for their flexibility. No matter how you want to analyze your data, a PivotTable can probably accommodate your wishes. In this section, you learn how to change the summary functions that the PivotTable uses and how to set PivotTable options.

Change the summary functions

When you include numeric values in a PivotTable, Excel automatically assigns a summary function of SUM to the field. You may have noticed in the file you've been working with, for example, that the Price field was assigned Sum of Price, and the Quantity field was assigned Sum of Quantity. (You changed the latter's heading to different text, but the data still sums the quantities.)

Sometimes, though, sum is not a meaningful statistic for a particular field. For example, when summarizing orders, Sum of Price is not helpful. A more useful statistic might be the average price. You can choose any of these math operations for the summary: SUM, AVERAGE, MAX, MIN, PRODUCT, COUNT (numbers), STDEV (standard deviation), or VAR (variance).

In this exercise, you change a field's summary function.

Files needed: Data Pivot.xlsx from the preceding exercise

1. **In the PivotTable Field List task pane, in the Values section, click Sum of Price, as shown in Figure 9-21, and choose Value Field Settings.**

   The Value Field Settings dialog box opens.

2. **On the Summarize Values By tab, click Average, and in the Custom Name box, delete the word *of* so that the name reads Average Price.** See Figure 9-22.

3. **Click OK to apply the change.**

4. **Save the workbook.**

Leave the workbook open for the next exercise.

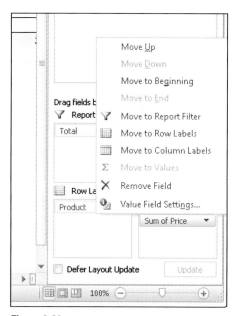

Figure 9-21

Change PivotTable options

You can set many options for a PivotTable — so many that covering them all would consume a whole lesson! The commands on the PivotTable Tools Options tab enable you to take actions, such as moving the PivotTable, displaying or hiding the field list and field headers, and more. In addition, the PivotTable Options dialog box provides dozens of other settings you can control.

In this exercise, you set PivotTable options.

Files needed: Data Pivot.xlsx from the preceding exercise

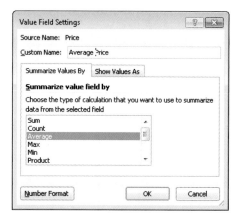

Figure 9-22

1. **On the PivotTable Tools Options tab, click the Field List button to deselect it, and the PivotTable Field List task pane closes.**

2. **Click the Field Headers button to deselect it.**

    The field headers disappear from the PivotTable. Figure 9-23 shows the PivotTable Tools Options tab.

Figure 9-23

3. **Choose PivotTable Tools Options⇨Move PivotTable, and the Move PivotTable dialog box opens.**

4. **Behind the dialog box, click the Sheet1 worksheet tab and then click cell G2.**

    In the Location text box in the Move PivotTable dialog box, a new location is filled in: Sheet1!$G$2. See Figure 9-24.

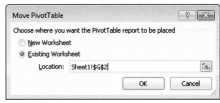

Figure 9-24

5. **Click OK.**

    The PivotTable moves to Sheet1.

    Notice that some of the columns aren't wide enough, and some entries are truncated. See Figure 9-25.

6. **Choose Home⇨Format⇨AutoFit Column Width, and the column widths adjust in the PivotTable.**

7. **Click PivotTable Tools Options⇨Options to open the PivotTable Options dialog box.**

8. **In the Name box at the top, type** Sales Information, **replacing the default entry. See Figure 9-26.**

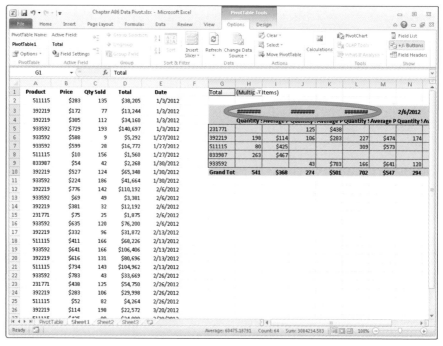

Figure 9-25

Figure 9-26

9. **Click the Totals & Filters tab, deselect both check boxes in the Grand Totals section, and click OK.**

   The Grand Total row and column are hidden.

10. **Save the workbook.**

Leave the workbook open for the next exercise.

Creating a PivotChart

PivotCharts enable you to easily experiment with charting different data. You could do this with regular charts, too, but with PivotCharts, you can more easily select different data and filter the data to include.

LINGO

A **PivotChart** is like a PivotTable except it appears in graphical chart format rather than as a report. Actually each PivotChart also has an associated PivotTable, where the data used to make the chart is stored. You could think of a PivotChart as an optional extension of a PivotTable.

Define a PivotChart

Creating a PivotChart is very much like creating a PivotTable. The main difference is that instead of clicking the PivotTable button on the Insert tab, you open the PivotTable button's drop-down list and choose PivotChart.

In the following steps, you create a PivotChart.

Files needed: Data Pivot.xlsx from the preceding exercise

1. **On the Sheet1 tab, select the range A1:E29.**

2. **On the Insert tab, click the down arrow on the PivotTable button and choose PivotChart.** See Figure 9-27.

   The Create PivotTable with PivotChart dialog box opens. See Figure 9-28.

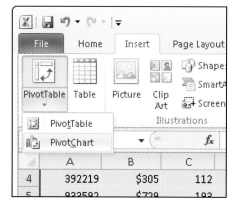

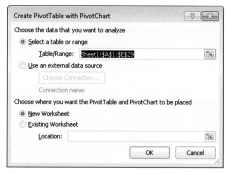

Figure 9-28

Figure 9-27

3. **Click OK to accept the default settings in the dialog box; a new work-sheet is created, and on it, an empty PivotTable and PivotChart.** See Figure 9-29.

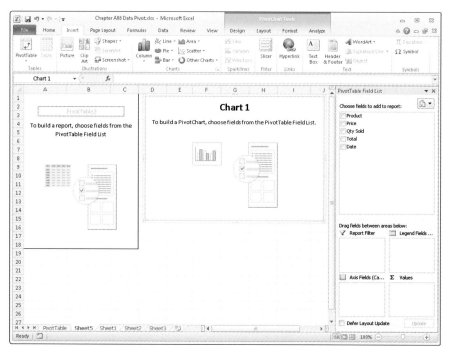

Figure 9-29

4. **In the PivotTable Field List task pane, drag the Product field to the Axis Fields area at the bottom.**

5. **Drag the Qty Sold field to the Values area at the bottom.**

   The chart shows the quantities sold by product, and a PivotTable appears to the left of the chart showing the data being used for the chart. See Figure 9-30.

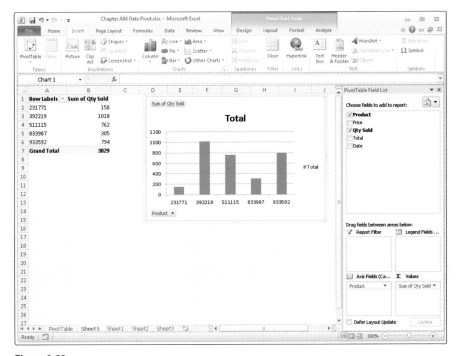

Figure 9-30

6. **Drag the Date field to the Legend Fields area, and the PivotChart and the PivotTable both change to show the new data.** See Figure 9-31.

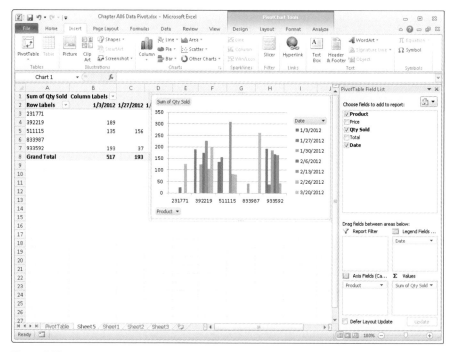

Figure 9-31

7. In the Legend Fields area, click Date and choose Remove Field.

The PivotTable and PivotChart go back to the way they were in
Figure 9-30.

8. Save the workbook.

Leave the workbook open for the next exercise.

Filter a PivotChart

Just like with a PivotTable, you can filter a PivotChart to show only certain
values. For example, you can filter a chart to show only certain dates, or only
certain products.

In the following steps, you filter a PivotChart.

Files needed: Data Pivot.xlsx from the preceding exercise

1. **In the PivotTable Field List task pane, drag the Date field to the Report Filter area.**

   A Date button with drop-down list arrow appears in the chart. See Figure 9-32.

Date field added as filter

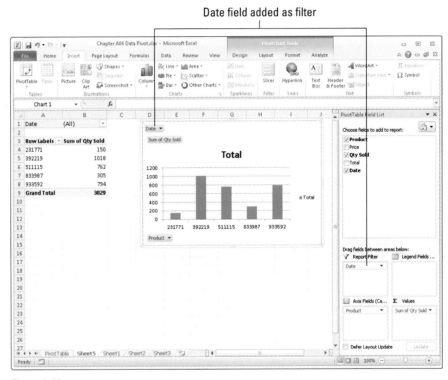

Figure 9-32

2. **Click the Date button on the chart, and the menu shown in Figure 9-33 appears.**

3. **Click 1/3/2012 and then click OK.**

   The chart changes to show only the products sold for that date. See Figure 9-34.

Figure 9-33

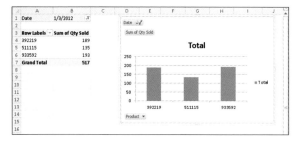

Figure 9-34

4. **Click the Date button again and select the Select Multiple Items check box so that individual check boxes appear for each date.**

5. **Select the 1/27/2012 and 1/30/2012 check boxes so that all the dates in January are selected, as shown in Figure 9-35, and then click OK.**

   The chart changes to show the products for the chosen dates.

Figure 9-35

6. **In the Report Filter area of the task pane, click Date and choose Remove Field, and the filter is removed from the chart.**

7. **Save the workbook.**

Leave the workbook open for the next exercise.

Format a PivotChart

Formatting a PivotChart is much like formatting any other chart (see Lesson 8), except you use Ribbon tabs related to PivotCharts. The commands are mostly the same.

Here are the three main PivotChart Tools tabs for formatting:

- ✔ **PivotChart Tools Design:** You can change the chart type, layout, and style from this tab.

- ✔ **PivotChart Tools Layout:** From this tab, you can modify the individual elements of the chart, including the legend, title, and so on.

- ✔ **PivotChart Tools Format:** Use this tab to modify the attributes of individual chart items. For example, change the font for a title or color a bar on the chart differently from the others.

In addition, the PivotChart Tools Analyze tab provides controls for displaying and hiding the field buttons and field list.

In the following steps, you format a PivotChart.

Files needed: Data Pivot.xlsx from the preceding exercise

1. **With the PivotChart selected, choose PivotChart Tools Analyze⇨Field List to turn off the field list.**

2. **Choose PivotChart Tools Analyze⇨Field Buttons to turn off the field buttons.**

   The PivotChart looks very much like a regular chart. See Figure 9-36.

3. **Choose PivotChart Tools Design⇨Change Chart Type.**

   The Change Chart Type dialog box opens.

4. **In the list at the left, click Pie; click the Pie in 3-D sub-type (the second icon in the Pie section), as shown in Figure 9-37; and click OK.**

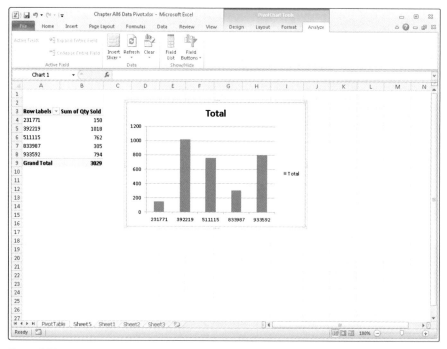

Figure 9-36

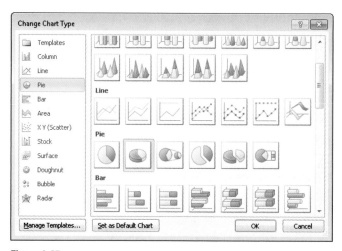

Figure 9-37

5. **Choose PivotChart Tools Layout⇨Chart Title⇨None, as shown in Figure 9-38, and the chart's title is removed.**

6. **Choose PivotChart Tools Layout⇨Data Labels⇨Outside End, as shown in Figure 9-39, and data labels are added to the chart.**

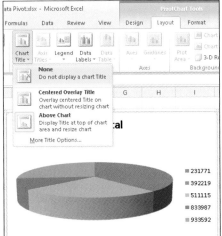

Figure 9-38

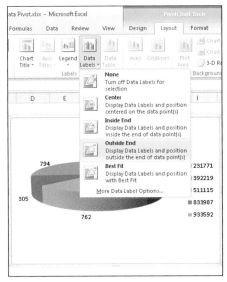

Figure 9-39

7. **Choose PivotChart Tools Layout⇨3-D Rotation.**

   The Format Chart Area dialog box opens with the 3-D Rotation options displayed.

8. **Click the Perspective up-arrow button until the setting is 0.1°, as shown in Figure 9-40.**

   This decreases the tilt on the pie so it's easier to read.

9. **Click the Close button and then click the red pie slice on the chart twice to select only that slice.**

10. **Choose PivotChart Tools Format⇨Shape Fill and then click the Orange, Accent 6 theme color.**

    (It's the orange square in the top line of the Theme Colors section.)

    The red slice changes to orange. See Figure 9-41.

Figure 9-40

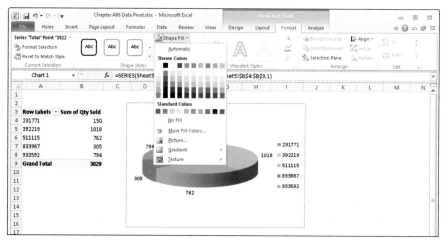

Figure 9-41

11. Save the workbook and close it.

12. Exit Excel.

Summing Up

Here are the key points you learned about in this lesson:

- ✔ PivotTables are summary grids that display information in different ways, to help users understand their meaning.

- ✔ When analyzing data in a PivotTable, a field is a type of data that is consistent for each record. For example, for a list of products, Product Number would be a field because each product has one.

- ✔ To create a PivotTable, select the data and choose Insert⇨PivotTable. Then use the PivotTable Field List task pane to add fields to the PivotTable.

- ✔ To sort a PivotTable, open the menu for the field on the PivotTable and choose one of the Sort commands.

- ✔ To filter a PivotTable, drag a field to the Report Filter section of the task pane. Alternatively, you can open the menu for the field on the PivotTable and select a filter.

- ✔ To change which summary function is used for a value, click a field in the Values area of the task pane, choose Value Field Settings, and in the dialog box that appears, choose a different function.

- ✔ A PivotChart is like a PivotTable except it's a chart instead of a report. To create one, select the data and on the Insert tab, choose PivotTable⇨PivotChart.

- ✔ You can filter a PivotChart by dragging a field to the Report Filter area of the task pane.

- ✔ To format a PivotChart, use the commands on the PivotChart Tools tabs: Analyze, Design, Layout, and Format.

Try-it-yourself lab

In this lab, you try some of the functions that I mention in this lesson but didn't include in the exercises:

1. **Reopen the original Data.xlsx file for this lesson and save it as Try It Pivot.xlsx.**

2. **Using the range A1:E29, create a new PivotTable and PivotChart that looks like Figure 9-42.**

This chart is a Stacked Column chart that shows only dates in February. The Grand Totals for both rows and columns have been turned off, and the field headers (on the PivotTable) and field buttons (on the PivotChart) have been hidden.

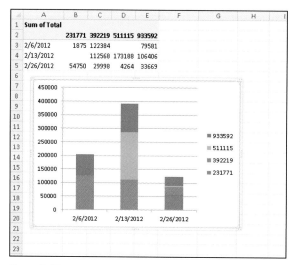

Figure 9-42

3. **Save and close the workbook.**

4. **Exit Excel.**

Know this tech talk

field: A type of data in a data range that stores data records, such as ID, Product Name, or Price.

PivotChart: A chart layout associated with a PivotTable, in which you can easily customize and modify the fields being plotted.

PivotTable: A customizable table view that displays and analyzes information from a range in a worksheet.

report: A completed PivotTable or PivotChart.

Correcting and Validating Data

✔ Formula error checking helps find and fix common errors in formulas and functions.

✔ Showing formulas in their cells makes it easy to browse the formulas in an entire worksheet at once.

✔ Evaluating a formula provides a step-by-step picture of how a formula arrives at its result.

✔ Tracing precedents and dependents helps you determine how a formula arrives at its result.

✔ Data validation helps minimize data entry errors by limiting what data a cell accepts.

Despite your best efforts, your worksheets may contain errors. And they may not be your fault! Other users might introduce errors into your work, for example, if you allow them editing privileges. Excel has lots of features to help you fix errors, and in this lesson, you learn how to fix them and create validation rules that prevent some data entry mistakes.

Finding and Fixing Errors in Formulas

In a large or complicated workbook with multiple dependent formulas and functions, the location of errors that prevent the workbook from delivering accurate results isn't always obvious. Excel offers a variety of error-correction tools, which you learn about in the following sections.

Use formula error checking

Excel has an Error Check utility that analyzes an entire worksheet and reports the errors it finds, one by one, for you to deal with. These are some of the errors Error Check may find:

- **Circular references:** A cell's formula refers to that cell, which places it into an endless loop. For example, if you place =C3 in cell C3, you get a circular reference.

- **#NAME errors:** This error occurs when the formula references a named range or cell address that's invalid. For example, if you have a named ELX range, but you accidentally type ELY in a formula, this error would occur.

- **#VALUE errors:** This error occurs when the formula can't calculate a valid result. You might get this error if one of the cells you're trying to perform a math operation upon contains text, for example.

- **Inconsistent formulas:** In a table or a range that contains a series of similar formulas in adjacent cells, if one of the cells in that range contains a formula that's unlike the others, Excel may flag it for closer inspection. This isn't necessarily an error; it's just a warning.

In this exercise, you correct errors in a worksheet.

Files needed: Errors.xlsx

1. **Open Errors.xlsx. Click OK to close the circular reference warning. Save the workbook as Errors Fixed.xlsx.**

2. **On the Formulas tab, click the down arrow on the Error Checking button and point to Circular References.**

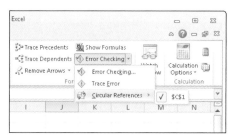

   A list of the circular reference errors appears.

   See Figure 10-1. In this example, you see that cell C1 contains a circular reference.

   Figure 10-1

3. **Click $C$1 on the list of circular references.**

   The cell cursor moves to cell C1. In the Formula bar, cell C1 contains =COM and so does the Name box. This cell has been named COM, so the formula =COM is equivalent to =C1. That's why the result shows $0. See Figure 10-2.

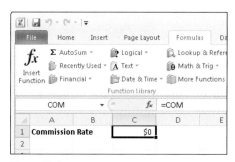

4. **In C1, type 15, replacing the current entry, and the circular reference error is corrected.**

   Figure 10-2

5. **Choose Formulas⇨Error Checking.**

   The Error Checking dialog box opens. See Figure 10-3. The first error it finds is an inconsistent formula in cell G5. You'd expect the formula to be =F5-E5, but there's a typo in it, so it reads =F4-E5 instead.

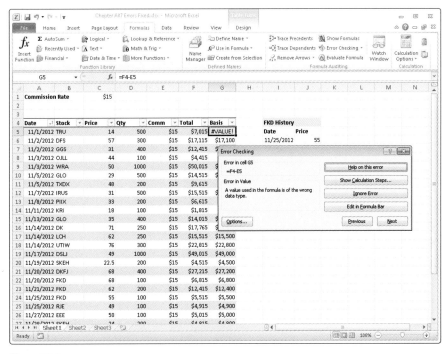

Figure 10-3

6. Click the Edit in Formula Bar button, and then in the Formula bar change F4 to F5 and press Enter.

The error is corrected.

7. In the Error Checking dialog box, click Resume.

The next error is an inconsistent formula in G14. This formula should be =F14-E14, but there is a typo in it, so it reads =F14-E13. See Figure 10-4.

8. Click the Restore to Calculated Column Formula button.

The error is corrected.

The next error appears in cell E30. In this cell, cell C3 (named COM) has been referred to incorrectly as COMM. See Figure 10-5.

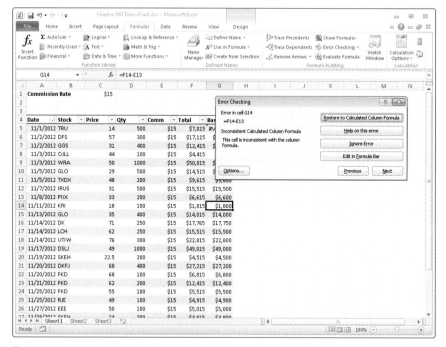

Figure 10-4

9. Click the **Edit in Formula Bar** button so that the insertion point moves to the Formula bar and then press the Backspace key to remove the extra letter **M** from the end of the cell name.

10. In the Error Checking dialog box, click the **Resume** button.

A dialog box appears that error checking is complete.

11. Click **OK**.

12. **Save the workbook.**

Leave the workbook open for the next exercise.

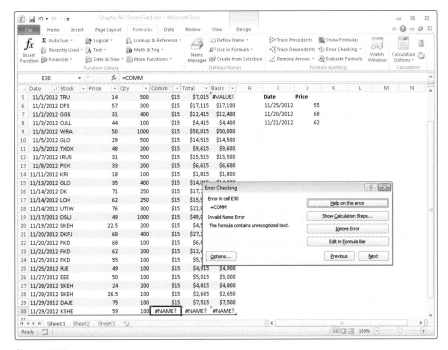

Figure 10-5

Show formulas

By default, Excel shows a formula's result in the cell itself and the formula behind that result in the Formula bar when the cell is selected. When you search for an error, it may be tedious to click each cell individually to see its formula. You may find it easier to temporarily show all the formulas at once in their cells.

In this exercise, you display and hide formulas in cells.

Files needed: Errors Fixed.xlsx from the preceding exercise

1. **Choose Formulas⇨Show Formulas.**

   The formulas appear in the cells. See Figure 10-6. Notice that the columns widen as needed to show the formulas.

TIP

Ctr+` (the accent mark above the Tab key) also toggles between showing and hiding formulas.

	A	B	C	D	E	F	G
1	Commission Rate		15				
2							
3							
4	Date	Stock	Price	Qty	Comm	Total	Basis
5	41214	TRU	14	500	=COM	=C5*D5+E5	=F5-E5
6	41215	DFS	57	300	=COM	=C6*D6+E6	=F6-E6
7	41215	GGS	31	400	=COM	=C7*D7+E7	=F7-E7
8	41216	OJLL	44	100	=COM	=C8*D8+E8	=F8-E8
9	41216	WRA	50	1000	=COM	=C9*D9+E9	=F9-E9
10	41218	GLO	29	500	=COM	=C10*D10+E10	=F10-E10
11	41218	TXDX	48	200	=COM	=C11*D11+E11	=F11-E11
12	41220	IRUS	31	500	=COM	=C12*D12+E12	=F12-E12
13	41221	PIIX	33	200	=COM	=C13*D13+E13	=F13-E13
14	41224	KRI	18	100	=COM	=C14*D14+E14	=F14-E14
15	41226	GLO	35	400	=COM	=C15*D15+E15	=F15-E15
16	41227	DK	71	250	=COM	=C16*D16+E16	=F16-E16
17	41227	LCH	62	250	=COM	=C17*D17+E17	=F17-E17
18	41227	UTIW	76	300	=COM	=C18*D18+E18	=F18-E18
19	41230	DSLJ	49	1000	=COM	=C19*D19+E19	=F19-E19
20	41232	SKEH	22.5	200	=COM	=C20*D20+E20	=F20-E20
21	41233	DKFJ	=J7	400	=COM	=C21*D21+E21	=F21-E21
22	41233	FKD	68	100	=COM	=C22*D22+E22	=F22-E22
23	41234	FKD	=J8	200	=COM	=C23*D23+E23	=F23-E23
24	41238	FKD	=J6	100	=COM	=C24*D24+E24	=F24-E24
25	41238	RJE	49	100	=COM	=C25*D25+E25	=F25-E25
26	41240	EEE	50	100	=COM	=C26*D26+E26	=F26-E26

Figure 10-6

2. **Choose Formulas⇨Show Formulas again to return to normal viewing.**

Leave the workbook open for the next exercise.

Evaluate individual formulas

When you troubleshoot a complicated formula that refers to several cells, you may find it helpful to walk through the formula's execution one step at a time, as if you were solving a math problem by hand. The Evaluate Formula feature does just that — it walks you through a formula, showing the interim results at each step.

In this exercise, you evaluate a formula.

Files needed: Errors Fixed.xlsx from the preceding exercise

1. **Click cell F5, examine its formula in the Formula bar, and then choose Formulas➪Evaluate Formula to open the Evaluate Formula dialog box.**

   The first cell reference in the formula (C5) is underlined. See Figure 10-7.

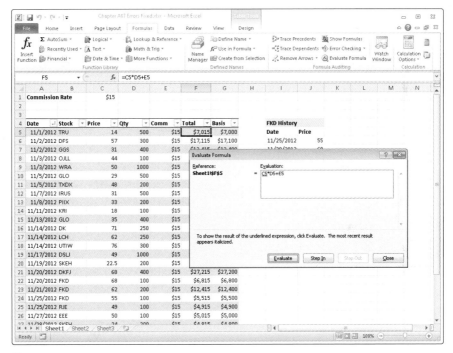

Figure 10-7

2. **Click the Evaluate button.**

   In place of C5 in the formula, the result of C5 appears, and D5 becomes underlined. See Figure 10-8.

Figure 10-8

3. Click the Step In button.

A box appears below the formula showing that D5 contains a *constant* (that is, a number, rather than another formula). See Figure 10-9.

4. Click the Step Out button.

The values for both C5 and D5 appear in the formula in the dialog box. See Figure 10-10.

5. Click the Evaluate button.

The first math operation in the formula is performed (14 x 500), and the result is shown in the dialog box (7000+E5).

6. Click the Evaluate button.

The value of E5 is substituted for the cell reference: 7000+15.

7. Click the Evaluate button.

The next math operation is performed (7000+15), and the result appears in the dialog box. See Figure 10-11. You've just seen step-by-step how Excel arrived at the value.

Figure 10-9

Figure 10-10

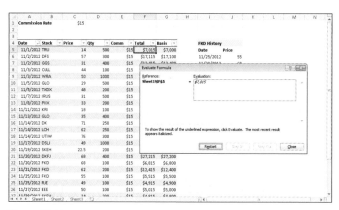

Figure 10-11

8. **Click the Close button to close the dialog box.**

9. **Save the workbook.**

Leave the workbook open for the next exercise.

Trace precedents and dependents

Some formulas in complex worksheets can be difficult to troubleshoot when you don't get the expected results because they may refer to cells that in turn, refer to other cells. To facilitate the process of troubleshooting in such situations, Excel enables you to trace the precedents and dependents of a formula.

In this exercise, you trace the precedents and dependents of a formula.

Files needed: Errors Fixed.xlsx from the preceding exercise

1. **Click cell F5, which contains the formula =C5*D5+E5, and then choose Formulas⇨Trace Precedents.**

   A blue arrow appears pointing from cell C5 to cell F5, with a blue dot in cells C5, D5, and E5 to indicate that each of those cells is included.

2. **Choose Formulas⇨Trace Precedents again, and another arrow is added to show the next level of precedents: from cell C1 to cell E5.**

   This happens because the formula in E5 refers to C3. See Figure 10-12.

> ## LINGO
>
> A **precedent** is a cell that contributes to a formula's calculation — in other words, a backward reference. For example, in the formula =A1+A2, cells A1 and A2 are precedents of that formula. If cell A1, in turn, contains the formula =C1+C2, cells C1 and C2 and precedents of A1. A **dependent** is a cell that depends upon a certain cell's content to report its own result — in other words, a forward reference. For example, if cell G9 contains =F9+10, cell G9 depends on F9.

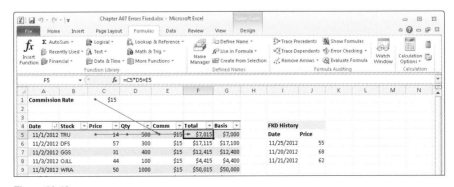

Figure 10-12

3. **Choose Formulas⇨Remove Arrows to make the arrows disappear and then choose Formulas⇨Trace Dependents.** Two arrows appear: from cell F5 to cell G5, and from F5 to cell F32.

This happens because F5 is referenced in formulas in those two cells.

4. **Choose Formulas⇨Trace Dependents again.**

Nothing happens, and an error sound plays (if you have sound support enabled on your PC), indicating that there are no further dependents.

5. **Choose Formulas⇨Remove Arrows.** The arrows are cleared.

6. **Save and close the workbook.**

Leave Excel open for the next exercise.

Validating Data

When you use Excel to store database data, it can be a challenge to maintain consistency in the data formatting and content, especially if multiple people help with the data entry. For example, some people might enter states with the full name, such as Indiana, whereas others might enter states with their abbreviations, such as IN. You might also end up with duplicate data records, which can be difficult to find just by browsing through the data. In the following sections, you learn several ways to make your data more consistent.

Create data validation rules

In this exercise, you create data validation rules.

Files needed: Validation.xlsx

1. **Open Validation.xlsx, save it as Validation Checked.xlsx, and on the Commissions tab, select the range A3:A50.**

LINGO

Validation rules can help ensure consistency by limiting what can be entered into certain cells. You can restrict a cell to a certain type of data, such as dates, numbers, or text, and you can specify a certain number of characters (or text length) for an entry.

TIP

In Step 1 (and also Step 7), you select extra rows at the bottom so that if you enter new records later, the rules also apply to them. You could select all the way down to row 100, or even further, if you had a lot more records to enter. You could even apply the validation rule to the entire column.

2. **Choose Data⇨Data Validation; the Data Validation dialog box opens.**

3. **From the Allow drop-down list, choose Date.**

4. **In the Start Date text box, type** 11/1/2012; **in the End Date text box, type** 12/1/2012. See Figure 10-13.

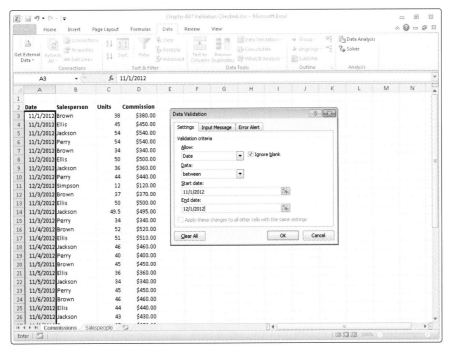

Figure 10-13

5. **Click OK; in cell A22, type** 1/2/2003 **and press Enter.** An error appears because the rule is violated. See Figure 10-14.

6. **Click the Cancel button.**

7. **Select the range C3:C50 and then choose Data⇨Data Validation to open the Data Validation dialog box.**

Figure 10-14

8. **From the Allow drop-down list, choose Whole Number; from the Data drop-down list, choose Greater Than or Equal To.**

9. **In the Minimum box, type** 0. See Figure 10-15.

Figure 10-15

10. **Click the Error Alert tab and in the Title text box, type** Entry Error.

11. **In the Input Message box, type** Units must be in whole numbers. See Figure 10-16.

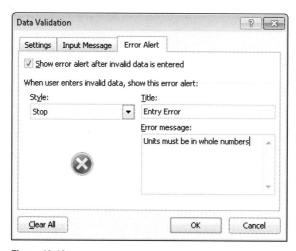

Figure 10-16

12. Click OK; in cell C45, type 12.5 **and press Enter.**

The custom Entry Error dialog box opens, as shown in Figure 10-17. (You created this dialog box in steps 10–12.)

13. Click the Cancel button.

Figure 10-17

For more practice, create a validation rule for the names in column B using the List type of rule, and specify the list on the Salespeople tab as the range from which to draw the valid names. To do this, start a new data validation rule for B3:B50 on the Commissions tab and set the Allow value to List. Set the Source to the salespeople's names on the Salespeople tab (A1:A4 on that tab).

14. Save the workbook.

Leave the workbook open for the next exercise.

Circle invalid data

You can create data validation rules either before or after you enter data. If you create the validation rules on cells that already contain data, the existing data in them may violate the rules. You can check for violations via the Circle Invalid Data feature.

In this exercise, you circle invalid data.

Files needed: Validation Checked.xlsx from the preceding exercise

1. On the Data tab, click the down arrow on the Data Validation button, as shown in Figure 10-18, and then choose Circle Invalid Data.

Excel circles data that violates the data validation rules. See Figure 10-19.

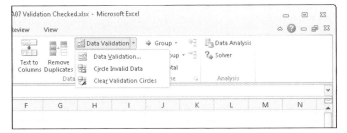

Figure 10-18

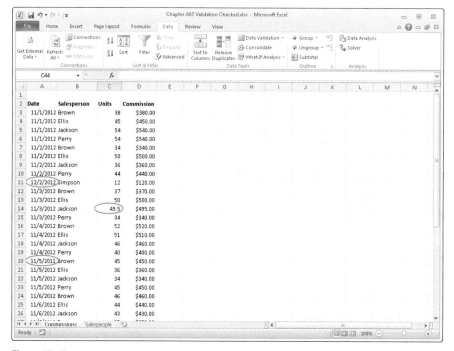

Figure 10-19

> 2. **Change the value in cell A11 to 11/2/2012; change the value in cell A20 to 11/5/2012; change the value in cell C14 to 49.**
>
>   The circles disappear on these cells.
>
> 3. **Save the workbook.**

Leave the workbook open for the next exercise.

Copy validation rules

You can copy validation rules from one cell to another using Copy and Paste Special. This method is handy when you need to extend the range that contains the data in a list, for example, or if you created the validation rules in the wrong range to begin with.

In this exercise, you copy validation rules.

Files needed: Validation Checked.xlsx from the preceding exercise

1. **Select cell A3 and then press Ctrl+C to copy it.**

2. **Select the range A51:A60.** (Column A already has the validation rules in place for rows up through 50 from a previous exercise.)

3. **On the Home tab, click the down arrow on the Paste button, as shown in Figure 10-20, and choose Paste Special.**

   The Paste Special dialog box opens.

4. **Select the Validation option, as shown in Figure 10-21, and then click OK.**

   The validation rule is copied.

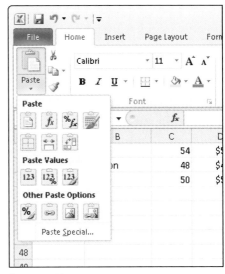

Figure 10-20

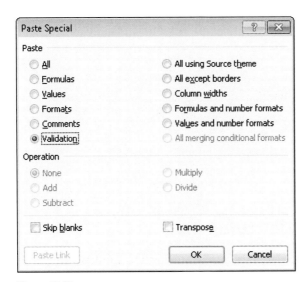

Figure 10-21

5. **Select cell A51, type** 12/01/2012, **and press Enter.**

   An error box appears, which proves that the rule was copied successfully. Any date formatted in a way that Excel recognizes as a date will work.

6. **Click the Cancel button.**

7. **Save the workbook.**

Leave the workbook open for the next exercise.

Remove duplicate data

In a long list of worksheet data, you might find that the existence of duplicate data isn't obvious. For example, if each salesperson on each date should have only one sales record and you have dozens of records, you might not be able to tell at a glance which records duplicate both the Salesperson and Date fields.

Excel's Find Duplicates feature makes it easy to identify records (rows) that have identical values in the fields (columns) that you specify.

In this exercise, you find and remove duplicate data.

Files needed: Validation Checked.xlsx from the preceding exercise

1. **Select cell A3 and choose Data⇨Remove Duplicates, and the Remove Duplicates dialog box opens.** See Figure 10-22.

Figure 10-22

2. **Deselect the Units and Commission check boxes.**

TIP

You're looking for records that have the same Salesperson and Date; they might or might not have the same Units or Commission.

3. **Click OK, and a message box appears saying that a duplicate was found and removed.** See Figure 10-23.

4. **Click OK to close the message box.**

5. **Save the workbook and close it.**

6. **Close Excel.**

Microsoft Excel

1 duplicate values found and removed; 41 unique values remain.

OK

Was this information helpful?

Figure 10-23

Summing Up

Here are the key points you learned about in this lesson:

- ✔ On the Formulas tab are several tools for finding and fixing errors.
- ✔ Choosing Formulas⇨Error Checking finds many different types of formula errors.
- ✔ To show formulas in cells, choose Formulas⇨Show Formulas or press Ctrl+`.
- ✔ To evaluate a formula, choose Formulas⇨Evaluate Formula.
- ✔ To trace a formula's precedents or dependents, choose Formulas⇨Trace Precedents or Formulas⇨Trace Dependents, respectively.
- ✔ A data validation rule restricts what can be entered into a cell. Choose Data⇨Data Validation to set up rules.
- ✔ Choose Data⇨Data Validation⇨Circle Invalid Data to find cells that violate data validation rules.
- ✔ To copy a validation rule, use Paste Special and select the Validation option.
- ✔ Choose Data⇨Remove Duplicates to clean out duplicate entries from a data list.

Try-it-yourself lab

In this lab, you make corrections to a worksheet that has several problems in its formulas.

1. **Reopen Try It Errors.xlsx file and save it as Try It Fixed.xlsx.**
2. **Find and fix the circular reference.**
3. **Correct the problem with the function name in column E.**
4. **Correct the problem with the calculation of Roommates 2 and 3's share of the expenses.**
5. **Correct the problem with the formula in cell B12 not containing the right range.**
6. **Save the workbook and close it.**
7. **Exit Excel.**

Know this tech talk

circular reference: An error in which a cell's formula refers to its own cell address.

dependent: A cell that depends on a certain cell's content to report its own result.

#NAME error: An error that occurs when a formula references an invalid named range or cell address.

precedent: A cell that contributes to a formula's calculation.

validation rule: A rule that limits what can be entered into a certain cell.

#VALUE error: An error that occurs when a formula can't calculate a valid result.

Lesson 11

Protecting and Sharing Data

- ✔ Protect a worksheet to prevent changes from being made to it.

- ✔ Unlocking cells makes them editable when the rest of the worksheet is protected.

- ✔ Encrypting a workbook password-protects it to secure sensitive information.

- ✔ Mark a workbook as final to discourage further editing of an approved draft.

- ✔ A digital signature verifies that a document comes from a recognized source and has not been tampered with.

- ✔ Tracking changes made to a workbook enables you to manage changes from multiple users.

1. **How can you prevent changes to a worksheet in general, while allowing a certain cell on it to remain editable?**

Find out on page 309

2. **How do you prevent others from deleting worksheets from a workbook?**

Find out on page 313

3. **How do you remove the password on an encrypted workbook?**

Find out on page 314

4. **How do you remove personal information from a workbook, such as author name?**

Find out on page 315

5. **How can you enable a workbook to be accessed simultaneously by multiple users?**

Find out on page 324

1 n Lesson 10, you saw that Excel offers features to guard against your own mistakes, but it also includes features that minimize other people's ability to mess up your worksheets. Suppose that you want to share a workbook with others and track the changes made to it; in this lesson, you see how Excel helps you do so. You also learn how to encrypt a workbook with a password, and how to digitally sign it and mark it as the final draft.

Protecting Ranges

Excel offers a variety of tools and commands for protecting your work from being altered, either accidentally or on purpose. Furthermore, you don't have to protect the entire workbook, or even the entire sheet, just to get protection on certain cells. You can protect a little or a lot.

Locking and unlocking cells

By default, every cell on a worksheet is set to be locked. You don't notice this because the worksheet itself is unprotected, so the locking of the individual cells doesn't take effect. Only when the worksheet is protected does a cell's Locked status become important.

Because of this, locking cells actually works backward from the way you might think. On a given worksheet, you unlock the cells that you want to still be able to change when the worksheet is protected. Then you protect the worksheet, and the protection doesn't apply to the cells you unlocked.

In this exercise, you unlock some cells.

Files needed: Loans Unlock.xlsx

1. **Open Loans Unlock.xlsx and save it as Loans Protection.xlsx.**
2. **Click the Payments tab and select the range B3:B4; then right-click the selection and choose Format Cells to open the Format Cells dialog box.**

3. **Click the Protection tab, deselect the Locked check box (see Figure 11-1), and then click OK.**

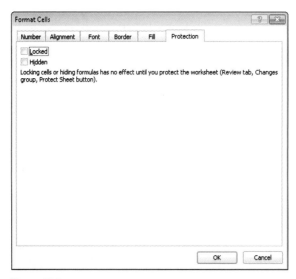

Figure 11-1

Locking is an on/off toggle. To relock a cell, select the Locked check box.

4. **Click the Amount tab and select the range B4:B5; then right-click the range and choose Format Cells.**

5. **In the Format Cells dialog box, click the Protection tab, deselect the Locked check box, and click OK.**

6. **Save the workbook.**

Leave the workbook open for the next exercise.

Protecting a worksheet

When you protect a worksheet, you make it uneditable, except for any cells that have been unlocked (as described in the preceding exercise). Protection is not an all-or-nothing thing; you can choose specific editing actions to allow or disallow on a protected worksheet. For example, you might choose to allow data to be edited, but no rows or columns to be added or removed.

You can also specify a protection password for the sheet. That way, anyone who knows the password can unprotect it. If you decline to use a password, anyone may unprotect the sheet.

As you plan protection for a worksheet, think about why you want to protect it. Are you more concerned about avoiding accidental changes? If so, no password is necessary. Are you worried about unauthorized users making intentional changes that would ruin the sheet? Use a password.

In this exercise, you protect a worksheet.

Files needed: Loans Protection.xlsx from the preceding exercise

1. **Click the Payments worksheet tab and choose Review⇨Protect Sheet.**

   The Protect Sheet dialog box opens.

2. **In the Password to Unprotect Sheet text box, type** Unprotect.

3. **Select the Format Cells, Format Columns, and Format Rows check boxes (see Figure 11-2) and then click OK.**

   The Re-Enter Password dialog box opens.

4. **Type** Unprotect **and click OK.**

5. **Click cell B5 and try to type something. An error message appears. Click OK to clear it.**

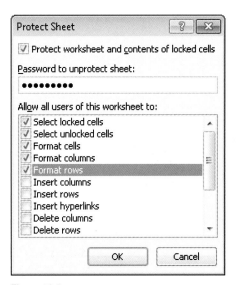

Figure 11-2

6. **With cell B5 still selected, click the Home tab. In the drop-down list in the Number group, choose Currency.** See Figure 11-3.

   Excel lets you change the cell's formatting.

7. **Click cell B4 (which is unlocked) and on the Home tab, in the drop-down list in the Number group, choose General.**

   Excel lets you change the cell's formatting, too.

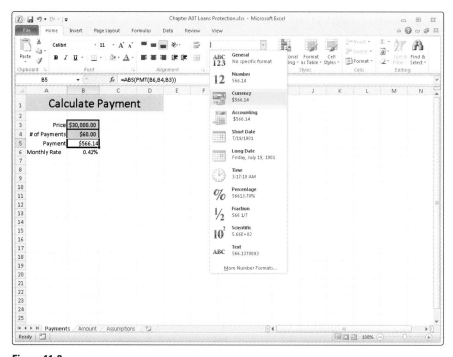

Figure 11-3

8. **In cell B4, type** 45, **replacing the previous value; Excel lets you change the cell's content, as shown in Figure 11-4.**

9. **Choose Review⇨Unprotect Sheet to open the Unprotect Sheet dialog box.**

10. **Type** Unprotect **and click OK; worksheet-level protection is removed.**

11. **Save the workbook.**

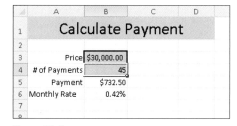

Figure 11-4

Leave the workbook open for the next exercise.

Protecting a workbook

When you protect an entire workbook, you can choose to protect either or both of these aspects:

- ✔ **Structure:** Nobody can add or delete worksheets, rows, columns, or cells.

- ✔ **Windows:** The workbook opens with the worksheet windows arranged in a certain way.

> Protecting a workbook doesn't protect any individual cells from having their content altered; that's a function of whether the cells are unlocked and whether the worksheet is protected. (I cover both in earlier exercises in this lesson.)

In this exercise, you protect (and then unprotect) a workbook from having structural changes made to it.

Files needed: Loans Protection.xlsx from the preceding exercise

1. **Choose Review➪Protect Workbook; the Protect Structure and Windows dialog box opens.**

2. **In the Password (Optional) box, type** Unprotect **(see Figure 11-5) and click OK.**

3. **In the Confirm Password dialog box that opens, type** Unprotect **and click OK.** The workbook is protected.

    On the Home tab, the Insert Sheet and Delete sheet commands are unavailable.

4. **Choose Review➪Protect Workbook; the Unprotect Workbook dialog box opens.**

5. **Type** Unprotect **(see Figure 11-6) and click OK; the workbook-level protection is removed.**

6. **Save the workbook.**

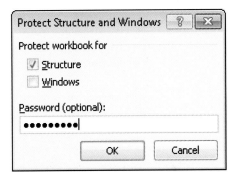

Figure 11-5

Figure 11-6

Leave the workbook open for the next exercise.

Securing Workbooks

In the preceding section, you learned various techniques for limiting people's ability to change the content of a workbook. Next, you learn about some ways to further safeguard a workbook, such as assigning a password to open a workbook, removing personal details from it, marking it as final, and adding a digital signature that assures others that it hasn't been tampered with.

Encrypting and decrypting a workbook

In this exercise, you encrypt a workbook, open it using the password, and decrypt it.

Files needed: Loans Protection.xlsx from the preceding exercise

LINGO

Encrypting a workbook means password-protecting it so that nobody can open it except those who know the password. The password is the key that unlocks the encryption, but encryption is much more than just the password; the file's content is actually modified so that it can't be opened in Excel and it can't be browsed from outside of Excel. **Decrypting** is the action of removing encryption from a workbook.

1. **Choose File⇨Info⇨Protect Workbook⇨Encrypt with Password.** See Figure 11-7. The Encrypt Document dialog box opens.

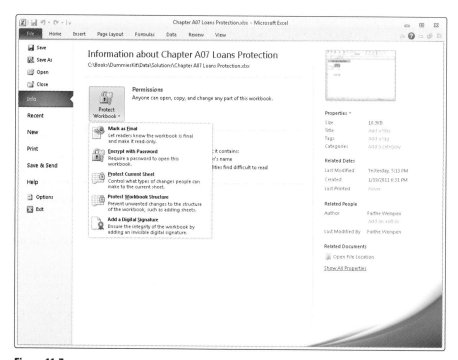

Figure 11-7

2. **Type** Unprotect **(see Figure 11-8) and click OK; the Confirm Password dialog box opens.**

3. **Type** Unprotect **and click OK.**

4. **Close the workbook. If prompted to save changes, click Save.**

5. **Choose File➪Recent➪Loans Protection; the Password dialog box opens.** See Figure 11-9.

6. **Type** Unprotect **and click OK.**

7. **Choose File➪Info➪Protect Workbook➪Encrypt with Password; the Encrypt Document dialog box opens.**

8. **Select the password in the Password box, press the Delete key to clear it, click OK, and press the Esc key to exit Backstage view.**

9. **Save the workbook.**

Figure 11-8

Figure 11-9

Leave the workbook open for the next exercise.

Using the Document Inspector

The Document Inspector checks a workbook for a number of types of content that may cause problems if you decide to share the workbook with others. These include personal information (such as the author's name), hidden content, comments, and headers/footers. If Excel finds any such content, it informs you and allows you to make a decision regarding whether to remove the content.

In this exercise, you inspect a workbook and remove some of the questionable content.

Files needed: Loans Protection.xlsx from the preceding exercise

1. **Choose File➪Info➪Check for Issues➪Inspect Document.** See Figure 11-10.

   The Document Inspector dialog box opens. See Figure 11-11.

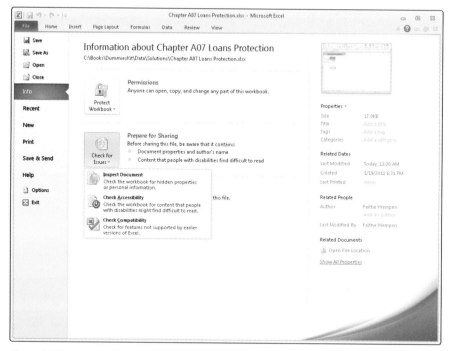

Figure 11-10

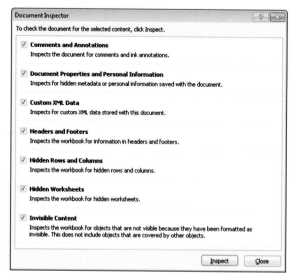

Figure 11-11

2. Click the Inspect button.

The results of the inspection appear. See Figure 11-12.

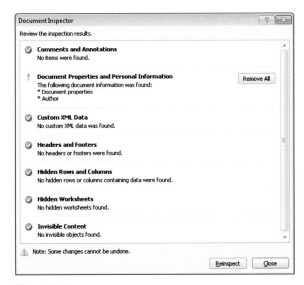

Figure 11-12

3. Click the Remove All button next to Document Properties and Personal Information and then click the Close button.

Later exercises require that document properties and personal information not be blocked, so next you undo that blockage.

4. Choose File⇨Options. The Excel Options dialog box opens. Then choose Trust Center⇨Trust Center Settings.

The Trust Center dialog box opens.

5. Click Privacy Options in the list on the left and then deselect the Remove Personal Information from File Properties on Save check box. See Figure 11-13.

Clear this check box

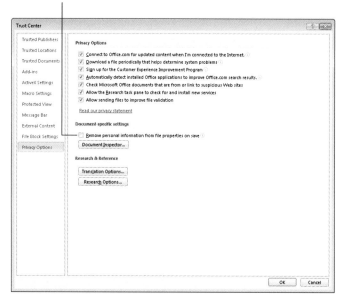

Figure 11-13

6. **Click OK to close the Trust Center and then click OK to close the Excel Options dialog box.**

7. **Save the workbook.**

Leave the workbook open for the next exercise.

Marking a workbook as final

Marking a workbook as final discourages people from editing it; however, doing so isn't a security measure because anyone can easily override it. Instead, marking final is a reminder that the workbook shouldn't be edited casually. You might mark a workbook as final after everyone has approved it, for example. Further changes to it would require another round of approvals, so it shouldn't be done except for an important reason.

In this exercise, you mark a workbook as final and then make additional changes to it, overriding its Final status.

Files needed: Loans Protection.xlsx from the preceding exercise

1. **Choose File⇨Info⇨Protect Workbook⇨Mark as Final (see Figure 11-14); in the confirmation box that appears, click OK.**

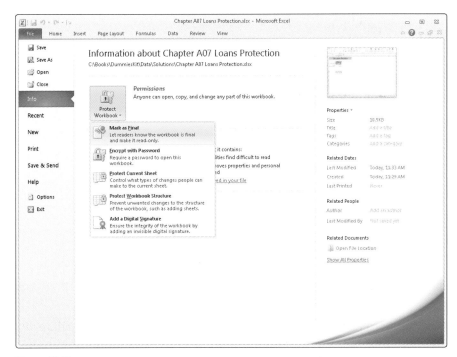

Figure 11-14

A message box appears explaining what's been done. See Figure 11-15. You might not see this box.

Notice in Figure 11-15 the Don't Show This Message Again check box. If you select this check box, you won't see this message box in the future.

Figure 11-15

2. **Click OK to close the dialog box if it appears.**

3. **Click the Home tab. Notice the information bar at the top of the work-sheet, indicating the document has been marked as final. See Figure 11-16. Notice also that the Ribbon has disappeared.**

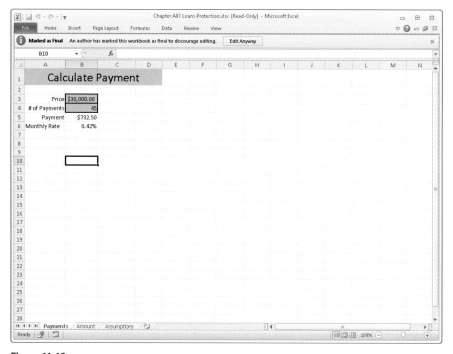

Figure 11-16

4. **Click the Edit Anyway button, and the document returns to regular status.**

Leave the workbook open for the next exercise.

Adding a digital signature

REMEMBER

You can add a digital signature to any document without using a third-party digital signature service. However, the signature doesn't have much authority if it's not verified by an outside source, so most people who rely on digital signatures choose to use a third-party service, which may charge a fee.

LINGO

Digital signatures verify a document's authenticity and certify that it hasn't changed since it was signed. You might add a digital signature to a document to formally approve its contents, such as when you digitally sign a contract.

In this exercise, you digitally sign a document.

Files needed: Loans Protection.xlsx from the preceding exercise

1. **Choose File⇨Info⇨Protect Workbook⇨Add a Digital Signature.** See Figure 11-17.

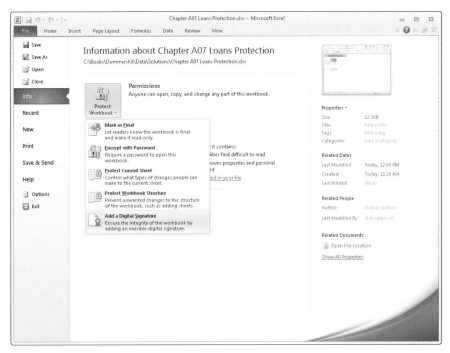

Figure 11-17

A message box appears explaining digital signatures. See Figure 11-18. You might not see this message box.

Figure 11-18

EXTRA INFO

Notice the Don't Show This Message Again check box in Figure 11-18. If you select this check box, this message box doesn't reappear. If you didn't see the message in Figure 11-18, someone may have already done so on your PC. For more information about third-party services, click the Signature Services from the Office Marketplace button.

2. **Click OK to close the message box if it appears; the Sign dialog box opens.**

3. **In the Purpose for Signing This Document text box, type** Approval. See Figure 11-19.

Figure 11-19

4. **In the Signing As box, confirm that your name appears. If it doesn't, click the Change button, choose a different name, and click OK.**

5. **Click the Sign button.**

6. **If a message appears that the certificate you've chosen couldn't be verified, click Yes. See Figure 11-20. Otherwise just continue to Step 7.**

Figure 11-20

7. **Click OK to close the confirmation box that appears, as shown in Figure 11-21.** The workbook is signed digitally.

8. **To make a change to the workbook, click the Home tab to return to the workbook and in the information bar at the top of the workbook, click the Edit Anyway button.** See Figure 11-22.

Figure 11-21

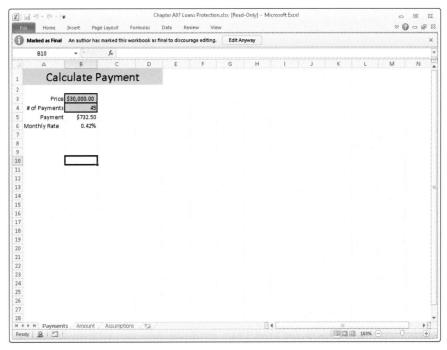

Figure 11-22

9. **Click Yes in the message box that appears, stating that editing the document will remove the signature.** See Figure 11-23.

Figure 11-23

10. **Click Yes; a confirmation appears that the signature has been removed.**

11. **Click OK, and the workbook is once again fully editable, with no digital signatures.**

12. **Save the workbook.**

Leave the workbook open for the next exercise.

Tracking Changes in a Shared Workbook

When multiple people need to edit a workbook, it can be a challenge to manage the various revisions being made, especially with multiple copies circulating, each edited individually. As an alternative to that administrative nightmare, you might prefer to share a workbook on a centrally accessible server. That way everyone can make their changes to a common copy. You can then track the changes that each person makes and merge the changes into a comprehensively reviewed version.

In the following sections, you learn how to share a workbook, how to track changes, how to merge and accept changes, and how to unshare a workbook after the editing process is complete.

Creating a shared workbook

When you share a workbook, you can enable a number of options, including whether to allow multiple users to have simultaneous access, whether to track the changes, and how to deal with conflicting changes. You can also protect the workbook with a password at the same time you share it so that change tracking can't be disabled unless you know the password.

In this exercise, you share a workbook.

Files needed: Loans Protection.xlsx from the preceding exercise

1. **Choose Review⇨Share Workbook to open the Share Workbook dialog box.**
2. **Select the Allow Changes by More Than One User at the Same Time check box.** See Figure 11-24.
3. **Click the Advanced tab and in the Update Changes section, select the Automatically After option.** See Figure 11-25.
4. **Click OK, and a confirmation box appears.**
5. **Click OK to confirm that you want to share the workbook; the workbook is shared.**

Leave the workbook open for the next exercise.

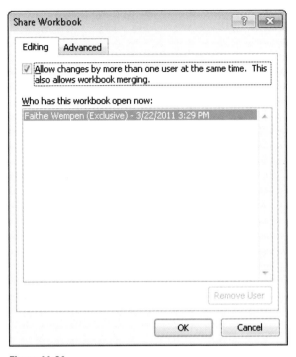

Figure 11-24

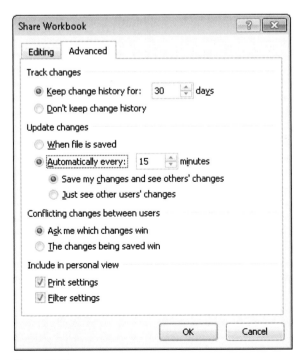

Figure 11-25

Enabling change tracking

Change tracking enables you to see who has made what changes to a shared workbook. For example, tracking marks changes, such as whether rows and columns have been inserted, whether formulas have changed, and whether constant values and text have been altered.

In this exercise, you track some changes to a workbook.

Files needed: Loans Protection.xlsx from the preceding exercise

1. **Choose Review⇨Track Changes⇨Highlight Changes.** See Figure 11-26.

2. **In the Highlight Changes dialog box, make sure that the Track Changes While Editing check box is selected.**

3. **In the When drop-down list, choose All (see Figure 11-27) and then click OK.**

4. **On the Payments tab in cell A1, type** Present Value, **replacing the current entry.** Notice that a triangle appears in the upper-left corner of the cell, indicating a change.

5. **On the Assumptions tab in cell B6, type** 6, **replacing the current entry.**

6. **Point to cell B6 with the mouse.** A comment box opens showing the change that was made. See Figure 11-28.

Figure 11-26

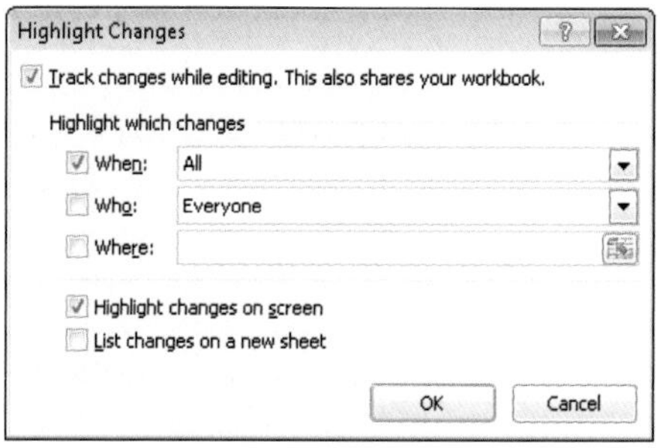

Figure 11-27

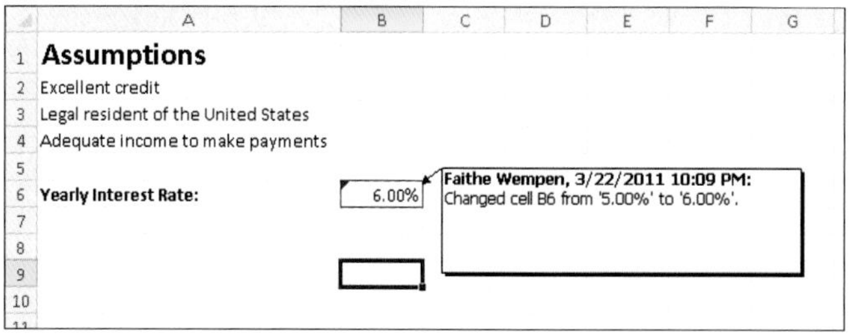

	A	B	C	D	E	F	G
1	**Assumptions**						
2	Excellent credit						
3	Legal resident of the United States						
4	Adequate income to make payments						
5							
6	**Yearly Interest Rate:**	6.00%	Faithe Wempen, 3/22/2011 10:09 PM: Changed cell B6 from '5.00%' to '6.00%'.				
7							
8							
9							
10							
11							

Figure 11-28

7. Save the workbook.

Leave the workbook open for the next exercise.

Accept or reject changes

After everyone makes changes to a shared workbook, you can go through the changes and either accept or reject each one. Excel makes it easy to examine the changes and determine whether each one should stay or go.

In this exercise, you merge the changes in a workbook.

Files needed: Loans Protection.xlsx from the preceding exercise

1. **Choose Review⇨Track Changes⇨ Accept/Reject Changes to open the Select Changes to Accept or Reject dialog box.** See Figure 11-29.

2. **Click OK, and the first change is highlighted.** See Figure 11-30.

Figure 11-29

Dashed border highlights change

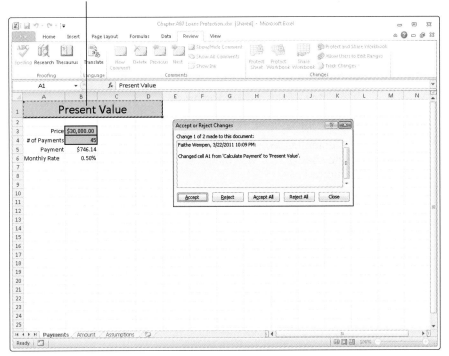

Figure 11-30

3. **Click the Reject button.**

   The text goes back to its previous wording, and the next change appears onscreen (cell B6 on the Assumptions tab). See Figure 11-31.

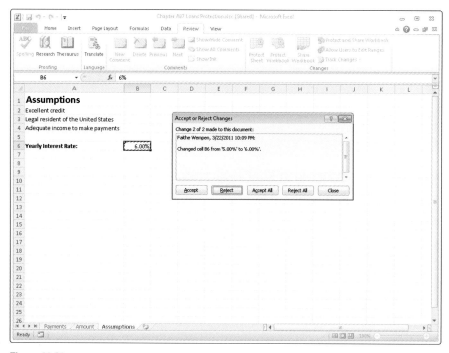

Figure 11-31

4. **Click the Accept button, and a message box appears telling you that there are no more changes to accept or reject.**

5. **Click OK to close the message box and then click the Payments tab. Notice that the change indicator from the rejected change is no longer present.**

6. **Click the Assumptions tab. Notice that the change indicator from the accepted change is still present. Point at cell B6 to review the change that was made.**

7. **Choose Review⇨Track Changes⇨Highlight Changes to open the Highlight Changes dialog box.**

8. **Deselect the Highlight Changes On Screen check box.** See Figure 11-32.

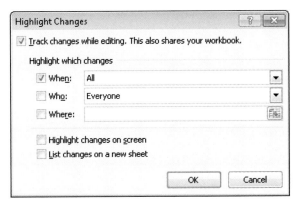

Figure 11-32

9. **Click OK.** The change indicator is removed from cell B6.

10. **Save the workbook.**

Leave the workbook open for the next exercise.

Removing workbook sharing

A shared workbook shows [Shared] in the title bar in Excel to remind you that it's shared.

When you're done sharing the workbook among multiple users, you can remove sharing so the workbook is no longer simultaneously accessible by multiple people.

In this exercise, you stop sharing a workbook.

Files needed: Loans Protection.xlsx from the preceding exercise

1. **Choose Review⇨Share Workbook; the Share Workbook dialog box opens.**

2. **On the Editing tab, deselect the Allow Changes by More Than One User at the Same Time check box.** See Figure 11-33.

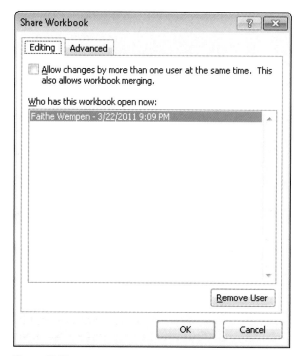

Figure 11-33

3. Click OK, and a message box appears, explaining that the workbook will no longer be shared.

4. Click Yes; the workbook is no longer shared.

5. Save the workbook and close it.

6. Exit Excel.

 Summing Up

Here are the key points you learned about in this lesson:

- ✔ By default all cells are locked on a worksheet, but the worksheet is not protected. Unlock certain cells and then protect the worksheet, and only those unlocked cells will be editable.

- ✔ To unlock a cell, right-click it and choose Format Cells. On the Protection tab, deselect the Locked check box.

- ✔ To protect a worksheet, choose Review⇨Protect Sheet.

- ✔ To protect a whole workbook, choose Review⇨Protect Workbook.

- ✔ To add a password to a workbook, choose File⇨Info⇨Protect Workbook⇨Encrypt with Password.

- ✔ The Document Inspector finds and removes unwanted information from a file, such as properties or headers/footers. Choose File⇨Info⇨Check for Issues⇨Inspect Document.

- ✔ Marking a workbook as final is not a security measure, but it can prevent accidental changes. Choose File⇨Info⇨Protect Workbook⇨Mark as Final.

- ✔ A digital signature can verify a document's authenticity and add official approval to it. Choose File⇨Info⇨Protect Workbook⇨Add a Digital Signature.

- ✔ To share a workbook, choose Review⇨Share Workbook, and select the Allow Changes by More Than One User at the Same Time check box. Doing so makes the workbook simultaneously editable by multiple users.

- ✔ To track changes made, choose Review⇨Track Changes⇨Highlight Changes.

- ✔ To accept or reject changes made to a workbook, choose Review⇨Track Changes⇨Accept/Reject Changes.

Know this tech talk

decrypt: To remove encryption from a workbook.

digital signature: An electronic means of signing a document, to show approval of it or to ensure that it's not changed.

encrypt: To password-protect a workbook so that nobody can open it except those who know the password.

About the CD

- System requirements
- Using the CD
- Troubleshooting
- Customer care

The Dummies eLearning software is included with this book. Just remove the CD and pop it into your Windows computer. This appendix shows you the ins and outs.

System Requirements

The eLearning application is designed to be compatible with the following system requirements. If your system does not meet or exceed these requirements, the eLearning application may not run, or may perform poorly.

Any of these Microsoft operating systems: Windows 7, Windows Vista, Windows XP, Windows 2000, or Windows 2003 Server.

Any of the following Web browsers:

- Microsoft Internet Explorer 6.0 or higher
- Mozilla Firefox 2.x or higher

The following additional hardware/software:

- Adobe Flash Player 8 (or later)
- Shockwave plug-in 8.5 (or later)
- A Pentium III, 500 MHz processor (or better)
- 256 MB of RAM (or more)
- A CD-ROM or DVD-ROM drive

A small amount of hard drive space must be available for tracking data. Typically, less than 1 MB will be used.

If you are reading this in an electronic format, please go to `http://booksupport.wiley.com` for access to the additional content.

Your purchase of this For Dummies eLearning Kit includes access to the course online at the For Dummies eLearning Center. If you have purchased an electronic version of this book, please visit `www.dummies.com/go/getelearningcode` to gain your access code to the online course.

Using the CD

The eLearning application is designed to run directly from the CD. Here's how to start it:

1. **Put the CD in the drive.**
2. **Double-click the My Computer icon to view the contents of the My Computer window.**
3. **Double-click the CD-ROM drive icon to view the contents of the Dummies eLearning CD.**
4. **Double-click the start.bat file to start the Dummies eLearning CBT.**

   Your computer may warn you about active content. Click Yes to continue starting the CD. The CD may create new tabs in your browser. Click the tab to see the content.

The browser offers the option of using the lessons from the CD or from the web site:

- ✔ To use the web version, click that option and follow the instructions. The web version may require a registration code from the book.
- ✔ To use the CD, click that option and follow the instructions. Agree to the EULA and install Flash Player, if prompted. Allow disk space usage by clicking the allow button, if prompted.

Troubleshooting

Depending on your system configuration, you may experience these issues when you attempt to use the application.

The quickskill.html page does not load

It is possible that you have a security setting enabled that is not allowing the needed Flash file to run. Please check to be sure that

- ✔ Pop up blocker is off.
- ✔ ActiveX content is enabled.
- ✔ The correct version of the Shockwave plug-in (8.5 or later) is on the system you are using.
- ✔ Adobe Flash Player 8 is installed.

My existing user name doesn't appear

The course stores your information on the machine where you create your account. If you use a different machine than the one where you created your account, the course will not be able to access your Learner record. Make sure that you are using the course on the same machine where you created your Learner account.

If you are on the machine where you created your account, close the browser window. Depending on the configuration of your machine, the course may load before accessing the user data.

Customer Care

If you have trouble with the CD-ROM, please call Wiley Product Technical Support at 800-762-2974. Outside the United States, call 317-572-3993. You can also contact Wiley Product Technical Support at `http://support.wiley.com`. John Wiley & Sons, Inc. will provide technical support only for installation and other general quality control items. For technical support on the applications themselves, consult the program's vendor or author.

To place additional orders or to request information about other Wiley products, please call 877-762-2974.

Index